C0-AVZ-530

The Rev. Chas. F. Lee.
With kind regards of
Geo. E. Horr Jr.

Dec. 30. 1889.
Charlestown.

Engraved by H.W. Smith

Hosea Ballou.

1,00

HOSEA BALLOU:

A Marvellous Life-Story.

BY

OSCAR F. SAFFORD, D.D.

'T is in the advance of individual minds
That the slow crowd should ground their expectations
Eventually to follow, — as the sea
Waits ages in its bed, till some one wave
Out of the multitude aspires, extends
The empire of the whole, some feet perhaps,
Over the strip of sand which could confine
Its fellows so long time; thenceforth the rest,
Even the meanest, hurry in at once,
And so much is clear gain.

ROBERT BROWNING.

BOSTON:
UNIVERSALIST PUBLISHING HOUSE.
1889.

University Press:
JOHN WILSON AND SON, CAMBRIDGE.

CONTENTS.

ILLUSTRATIONS.

INTRODUCTION.

TWO biographies of Hosea Ballou have already been given to the public; one by Maturin M. Ballou, his youngest son, the other by Thomas Whittemore, a spiritual son. Both have long been out of print. It has not been deemed advisable to republish either of these biographies. That by his son is filially affectionate and appreciative, but was hurriedly prepared, and is wanting in analysis and completeness. Dr. Whittemore's work is a magazine of facts, and is straightforward and plain in style; but it is devoted largely to extraneous matters, and is infeasible for republication by being in four volumes. As the Universalist Church cannot with self-respect suffer its greatest theologian and most picturesque character to remain in increasing obscurity, this new attempt to tell his life-story has been made.

The biographer claims a brief privilege in autobiography.

In my boyhood I heard thoughtful Universalists in the State of Maine frequently speak the name Hosea Ballou with reverent regard. I unconsciously formed a conception of his character as one of the master-spirits in religious warfare. I was yet a lad when I read his "Life" as written by his son. I can scarcely recall the impression the book made. While a very young man I also read Dr. Whittemore's "Life of Ballou." I am bound to confess that the impression made on my mind by this work was, to say the least, exceedingly unpleasant. I had constantly heard Universalism spoken of by its opposers as a religion which made light of sin by teaching that death rather than Christ is the divine agent of redemption. By the reading of Dr. Whittemore's volumes I was led to believe that Mr. Ballou advocated this philosophy. My reading of the work, I confess, was not critical, and my discrimination was not acute. Nevertheless the fact remains, that after reading Dr. Whittemore's volumes, I regarded Mr. Ballou chiefly as an advocate of the theory that death is the immediate savior of all sinners. His philosophy — or the nescience I ascribed to him — appeared to me so contradictory of axiomatic truths, that I could only hope for it speedy and final oblivion.

I remained in this unfortunate state of mind several years.

In 1865, thirteen years after Mr. Ballou's death, I became pastor of the First Universalist Church of Charlestown. Nearly all the older members of the parish had heard Mr. Ballou preach, and I was soon commiserated as not having had that privilege. Certain of these estimable believers remembered with exactness his pithy sayings, his striking illustrations, his fervent words of appeal. I was forced to note that Mr. Ballou had at least the gift of saying things which could not be forgotten. These good people could never tire of their reminiscences of the great preacher. Such copious remembrance of one gone before was then unparalleled in my experience. At the present writing the one kindred experience I can recall is that of certain of my friends in Chicago who had been personally associated with Abraham Lincoln previous to his national renown, and who would with alternate tears and laughter discourse of their old friend at all hours without weariness or willing cessation. I marvelled at this exhibition of the power of Lincoln's personality. Scarcely less, I now discern, was the power of Hosea Ballou's personality over those who had known him in life. These Charlestown parishioners, be it remembered, had known E. H. Chapin and Thomas Starr King as their own pastors. They did not forget the fact; they mentioned it often with pride. But they rarely quoted any saying of either of these cultured masters of expression. The recollections they revived of these men, especially of Chapin, were of rapturous eloquence in unreportable passages. Mr. Ballou they had known only as a neighbor across the Charles River. They had heard him but occasionally, yet it was this preacher who constantly reappeared in their speech whenever the inner fount of their natures was opened; and especially when God's redeeming love was the theme of earnest speech, Mr. Ballou would come to their grateful remembrance.

My curiosity was awakened in regard to this remarkable man.

I recall that in those busy, crowded years I read certain of Mr. Ballou's printed sermons, and found them strong, lucid, graceful, at once simple and profound. I conceded to him unusual skill in the art of sermon-making. I glanced through some of his controversial works, on issues to me by-gone; I was struck with his candor and fertility in resources. As a controversialist I conceded him genius. I at first stumbled in the "Treatise on Atonement," for want of its historical clew; on arriving at a clearer understanding of the horrible nature of the theology, or satanism, it assaulted, the book appeared to me a marvel of common sense and the herald of an epoch.

In 1874 I became pastor of the First Universalist Church in Cambridge, and had Rev. Lucius R. Paige, D.D., as a parishioner and counsellor. He was an enthusiast in his regard for his only teacher in theology. We sometimes discussed Mr. Ballou's affirmation of the no-future-punishment interpretation of the Bible. Dr. Paige stoutly maintained that it neither nullified nor modified any principle in ethics. "Punishment," he said, "will continue till the sinner is by divine love brought to repentance; when it has served its purpose it will be superseded by forgiveness. To me it is biblical and reasonable to believe that this moral change will be a voluntary act of every sinner immediately on his entrance into the realm beyond the resurrection." I combated this with the assertion of the persistency of individuality, memory, and the moral sense as constituents of character. It did not, however, occur to me that the theory, so stated, implied that death is the moral savior.

Before I read Dr. Whittemore's "Life of Ballou" a second time, I had learned to regard its author as a zealous champion of the extreme no-future-punishment theory. Dr. Whittemore had himself in the calm afterthought of his closing days, as quoted by Dr. E. G. Brooks, confessed misgivings as to certain of his ultra positions assumed in the heat of debate. He championed Mr. Ballou's theory in the Restorationist controversy. He was editor of the "Trumpet," in which Mr. Ballou published certain tentative articles on the then inflammatory theme. These articles, some of which were published anonymously, were carefully preserved by the editor, and reappeared in form or coloring in his bulky work. On my second reading of the "Life," I did not believe these unsifted writings fairly representative of Mr. Ballou's central doctrines. It is confessedly not difficult to quote from them negative expressions seemingly indicative of his opinion that sinners need no salvation other than that death itself will bring. This was not — with entire certainty I affirm — at any time Hosea Ballou's belief. Dr. Whittemore saw his spiritual father with his own eyes; Dr. Whittemore had himself, I was compelled to perceive, superficial views of sin and punishment; he virtually idolized death. No one who reads the following pages will doubt my admiration of Dr. Whittemore; yet on this point I regret his zeal. With entire honesty he presented a picture of Mr. Ballou which to me appears twisted out of symmetry. His partisanship led him to regard an incident in Mr. Ballou's career, and an incidental doctrine in his system, as of central and enduring import.

Now, what is the fact as to Mr. Ballou's advocacy of the doctrine of strictly no future punishment? It is significant that he did not believe the doctrine till he was forty-eight years old. What does this prove?

Not that he did not in his later years attach importance to the doctrine. No such claim is made. But it proves beyond denial that he did not, during the early part of his career, hold to the doctrine as essential to his system. He was a believer in future punishment when he wrote his "Notes on the Parables," and his "Treatise on Atonement."[1] He was a believer in future punishment when he formulated the system of theology to which the entire Universalist denomination was converted. The doctrine of no future punishment is in his system subordinate and by no means fundamental. The doctrine, furthermore, as he gave it definitions in careful leading statements, is not held in unconsciousness or disregard of the acknowledged laws of moral science.[2]

By the time I had re-read Dr. Whittemore's work, and added some careful reading between the lines, I had given to Mr. Ballou my unqualified respect. He more and more fascinated me in his human experience. I saw in his early hardships and extreme limitations, contrasted with the achievements of his manhood, a marvellous human story which possessed more than the interest of romance. His simplicity, honesty, transparency, his wit and humor, his genius as a theologian, his oratorical triumphs, his pure home-

[1] In the later editions of the "Treatise," interpolated passages seem to contradict this assertion. The reference is of course to the "Treatise" as at first written.

[2] The statement of Mr. Ballou's position in Chapter XIII. of this volume, "A Discussion and its Sequences," has been by the author submitted to the two men best fitted by knowledge and sympathy to give an opinion as to its correctness, — Rev. Drs. L. R. Paige and A. A. Miner, — and has received their approval as according substantially with their own understanding of Mr. Ballou's doctrine.

life, his mission as a religious reformer, — a reformer in the last degree radical, reforming the very character men ascribed to God, — these aspects of his career, with lapse of time, grew in my estimation.

This bit of autobiography serves its purpose in showing the view-point of this biography.

It is an attempt to picture Mr. Ballou's career in just proportions.

While I doubt not I am myself limited by my own point of view, and by my faculties of perception and sympathy, I claim this advantage over my predecessors: I have, without haste, studied my subject across a well-nigh vanished generation. My scrutiny, I am glad to confess, has found no fraction of Mr. Ballou's career needing concealment; yet I believe I can now see, more clearly than could be seen at the time of his death, what aspects of his life invite the larger record.

With kindly deference to the average reader, I have kept my pages as free as possible from the impediment of references, foot-notes, statistics, and appendices. It was in my design, however, to present a full list of Mr. Ballou's books and pamphlets. My labor at this point has been anticipated by Rev. Richard Eddy, D.D., who in his "Universalism in America" has made as correct a list as possible of Mr. Ballou's works in all their authorized and spurious editions. I believe I best serve the interested reader when I simply refer him for the fruit of no little patient research among public and private libraries, to the name of "Hosea Ballou" in the "Bibliography" of Dr. Eddy's attractive and trustworthy history.

My work has been done with an ever-increasing reverence for the great pioneer preacher of hope, and with an intensifying desire, not altogether selfish, that he may be recognized in his true character, and his memory honored as one of the world's benefactors.

HOSEA BALLOU.

I.

BIRTH; ANCESTRY; EARLY HOME.

HOSEA BALLOU was born in Richmond, New Hampshire, April 30, 1771, the sixth son and eleventh child of Rev. Maturin Ballou, a Baptist clergyman.

A casual reading of this simple record will perhaps suggest for our hero propitious early surroundings. The fact, however, is far different. It was into unusual hardships and exceptional limitations that the new-born child may be said to have been thrust rather than ushered.

But fourteen years previous the first settler had arrived in Richmond. The work of subduing the forest had from that time progressed but slowly. We may wonder, indeed, that Rev. Maturin Ballou, in middle life, with a large family already dependent upon him, should voluntarily become a resident of this almost unbroken wilderness. He was, we conjecture, influenced mainly by two motives. It was natural for him, in the first place, to desire to secure for his children a better worldly prospect than he had himself inherited. This he might hope to do by becoming a landholder in a pioneer settlement. The other motive we find in the attraction of the family tie. Among the first settlers were Anthony and Uriah Harris, brothers of his wife, also two of her sisters and their families, all Baptists, after the pattern of Roger Williams. With such neighbors to offer welcome, it was reasonable for him to hope a forest-home would not be altogether lonely. When Mr. Ballou and his wife Lydia visited their kindred in the wilds they were, we easily conjecture, earnestly invited to cast their lot with the invaders of the wilderness. Still another motive may have had strong influence — perhaps even the strongest — with the Baptist preacher; namely, his desire to establish in the new country a Baptist church. He had, we recall, been a Baptist preacher fifteen years. He was now forty-five; when he was thirty, with a large family looking to him for sustenance, without special education, he had entered on his chosen vocation. He had preached the Baptist doctrine successively at Smithfield, Pawtucket, and Scituate, in Rhode Island. It is superfluous to say he had not found his path of life free from anxieties. We assume that in the prospect opening before him at Richmond to found the second Baptist church in New Hampshire, he saw promise of a continuance of the same life-struggle. For the sake of his children he was with this prospect content.

When Rev. Maturin Ballou moved to Richmond, in 1767, he had eight sons and daughters living; also the sacred memory of one little Amy, a daughter who had died at six, her precious remains mingling with Rhode Island soil. Two additional sons were born in Richmond; the first was biblically named

Stephen; the last, in seeming prophecy of his mission, was named Hosea, signifying in English "Salvation."[1]

Whatever expectation the father may have had of deprivations and trials in the New Hampshire wilds, could hardly have exceeded the reality. His pastorate was gratuitously fulfilled. It is probable that he, like many of the early preachers, had conscientious scruples against receiving any stated compensation whatever for pastoral services. Even if this were not the case, and his people were willing to bear their full share of the cost of the Christian ministry, the circumstances of the people were such that they could scarcely supply more than the salt for their pastor's porridge. He himself, with such assistance only as his neighbors could casually give, must build his own rude house and barn; he must fell his trees, and clear of roots and stones the not over-rich soil; he must himself, with his boys, plant, sow, cultivate, reap, and garner; he must guard against shortage in hay, corn, wheat, rye, potatoes, flax; he must go to the all-surrounding forest for fuel; he must have daily care of horses, oxen, and sheep. Only the slight margin of time left could he give to his profession.

[1] The children of Reverend and Mrs. Maturin Ballou were: 1. Mary, who became the wife of Mr. David Bullock; 2. Benjamin, who became the father of nine children, and was grandfather to Rev. Hosea Ballou, D.D., the first President of Tufts College; 3. Amy, who died at six years of age; 4. Lydia, who married Samuel Moses, and left a large family of children; 5. Maturin, who became a Baptist preacher and died at the age of thirty-five; 6. David, a Universalist preacher for many years; 7. Nathan, at first a Baptist, afterward a Universalist, who left a large family; 8. Sarah, who became the wife of Moses Wheaton; 9. Phœbe, who died a young woman; 10. Stephen, who moved in early life to New York; 11. Hosea.

Within his home was a like stern necessity for unremitting industry. The ordinary daily duties of the housewife could not be easy. Not a garment was worn by any member of the family that did not come from the flax-plot or sheep-flock of the farm; and every garment was the product of the spinning-wheel and loom, and self-taught tailors or dress-makers of the household.

It is to be recalled also that at the time of Hosea's birth the American Colonies were on the eve of the War for Independence. During that sanguinary struggle, lasting till he was twelve years old, the American people were as a whole kept on a strain for mere existence. Such stress, everywhere prevailing, could not fail of deplorable effects in the self-supporting parsonage in Richmond.

And, as we can now plainly see, there was another burden in that home more cruel than all other burdens combined. The father and mother and older children sincerely believed and professed Calvinism; unadulterated Calvinism, we might say, if it were not impossible to adulterate a theology which starts with the idea of a totally depraved God. The baneful heart-depression caused by this theology — the cruelty of the stony answer it gave to the heart-cries for bread — we cannot attempt to describe. It is pitiful to recall Maturin Ballou, who was gentle in heart and mild in manners, and gifted with a natural vein of lightsome humor, in some moment of human cheer narrating a facetious anecdote, then immediately sighing in shamefaced repentance, — the least indulgence of natural mirth appearing to him, under the shadow of his religion, to be sinful. The chief burden and bane of that innocent and right-meaning home was, it is but just to say, its merciless religion. The climate of the hills was severe; trying were the extremes of summer heat and winter cold; the stress of poverty was unrelaxing and painful; yet Calvinism, sincerely believed, was the most galling yoke and the bitterest cup.

We begin to see the surroundings into which Hosea Ballou was born. It may give us a slight sympathetic shiver to be told that while a little fellow he went barefoot in the winter snow. It is a fact, nevertheless, to which he himself without shame testified in his later years; with only pity, indeed, for his father, who endured the deeper pain of helplessness. Another fact remains to be told, which, as pertaining to the little barefoot boy, is saddest of all. When he was two years old his mother died. Poor weary soul, can we wonder? As Hosea grew older, he learned of her excellences by the testimony of his older brothers and sisters. Through life the thought of her was to him tender and sacred. Yet of necessity he carried in his heart all his days an unsatisfied mother-want. His father and sisters, as far as they could, fulfilled to him lovingly and faithfully maternal ministries. He lived in his early years in an atmosphere of holy, sorrowful, self-sacrificing love. Yet who can withhold pity in the recollection of that motherless boy?

His early educational advantages were necessarily slight; to be spoken of, in fact, as a minus quantity. Scarcely any child could in this respect suffer more deprivation than fell to his lot. It seems strange it should be so. Destined to be foremost in a great intellectual contest against the organized scholarship of the schools, strange he should himself have had almost no equipment of early education! If he conquer, it must be as David overcame Goliath, through divine favor, in a method of warfare not learned in the schools. He did not, till he was nineteen years old, attend school one day; and then his self-earned schooling extended through only a few months. There were during his boyhood no schools in Richmond. The strife during the week for hard-earned bread to keep away starvation, and the striving on Sunday for harder bread of Calvinism to save from doom, engrossed the people. He early obtained, it is true, a little knowledge of letters. He learned to read and write, and to master simple mathematical exercises. In after years, yet long before the same fact was told of Abraham Lincoln, he stated to his children that he learned to read on winter evenings in his boyhood by the light of blazing pine knots, — even a tallow candle being a luxury the straitened household could not afford; and writing he learned on birch-bark sheets he had himself taken from the forest trees. The family library consisted of a Bible, a small English dictionary antedating Johnson's, an old almanac, and a dog-eared pamphlet concerning the Tower of Babel. Nor were other books accessible. Newspapers were in that wilderness home unknown. We cannot easily picture a boy living within reach of civilization with educational advantages more meagre. In his youth standard literature was to him entirely an unknown realm. He had virtually no book but the Bible. This, however, he found to be a wonderful library in itself, its literature, history, allegory, poetry, captivating his youthful imagination.

HOSEA BALLOU'S BIRTHPLACE AT RICHMOND, N. H.

We doubt whether, after all, it is now to be regretted that his attention was thus early focused on the English Bible. How else could he so well prepare himself to read the Bible anew exclusively in its own light? Was it an unpromising thing that the shepherd-boy David, shut away from even observation of the prevailing military methods, should be perfecting himself in the use of the simple sling? The time came, we remember, when his patiently-acquired skill was a sanctified means of warfare. So the youthful Hosea, shut from all avenues to history, poetry, and prophecy save through the One Book, was unconsciously preparing himself for the mission to which he was in after years, alike by his genius and circumstances, signally called.

But let us not fail to recognize the fact that there was light as well as shade in his early experience.

He had joy in the passing days of his youth. It was, for one thing, fortunate that he was born with a poet's love of Nature. Richmond is a town among the hills; itself mainly a level plot, Grassy Hill the only height within its borders, but bulwarked by grand elevations in the distance, and diversified on its surface by three small lakes and Ashuelot and Miller's rivers. Nature smiled an early benediction on the young theologian. He was in after years remembered as an erect, muscular lad of vigorous health and ruddy countenance, with dark hair, and blue eyes in which a pleasing light gleamed. It was impossible for even Calvinism to make him in his early years altogether unhappy.

The poverty to which he was born was not of the heart; it was not uncombed nor soapless; it was rather a simple life of providential allotment, bravely and thankfully endured. The boy with bare feet and homespun clothes grew to be a youth of manly qualities and gentle heart. He carried with him, wherever he went, an atmosphere of kindness. The farm animals shared to an unusual degree in his thoughtful care. He had cordial love for his brothers and sisters, and reverent love for his father. There was no guile or envy in his nature; he lived unselfishly, and therefore found content.

The outward hardships of his early experience touched only the externals of his life. Years afterward, when through the transfiguring light of distance he looked back on his youth among the hills, he thought but slightly of the hardships he had endured; he virtually forgot his bare feet in winter, his scanty clothes, his narrow mental vision; he thought more of his innocent country sports, his contests in leaping, wrestling, and pitching the heavy iron crowbar, — sports in which he excelled; he thought lovingly of Ballou Dell, in which stood his native cottage; he still kept his recollection of the hills and vales surrounding; he thought of father and brothers and sisters as making his daily life a beatitude; and he gratefully named this ravishing vision of his early home-life Happy Richmond.

II.

CONVERTED TO CALVINISM.

PERIOD, 1789. AGE, 18.

SO passed, not altogether unhappily, the childhood and youth of Hosea Ballou. At eighteen, an event occurred in his life. He became the subject of a religious revival, and united himself with the Calvinist Baptist Church.

His father had at this time ceased to be the local pastor at Richmond. There had, from some unknown cause, sprung up a contention among the members; a section had withdrawn, and under Elder Artemus Aldrich had started a rival church. A temporary settlement of the trouble had however been effected by both pastors withdrawing, and the two segments of the church uniting under a new minister, Rev. Isaac Kinney.

The church-members, having ceased to snarl at each other, had leisure to unite in a crusade against the unconverted. A revival was the result. Within two years a hundred members were added to the church. It was, as compared with the population, a John-Baptist sweep; scarcely an unconverted soul could have been left.

It may be added here, anticipating a little, that after the revival had passed, the church-members had leisure once more to revive their own quarrel. They inaugurated a vigorous internal bickering. At this time Rev. Maturin Ballou, the resident retired pastor, had a dream. At one of the assemblies in which the belligerents were represented, he told his dream. "I dreamed," he said, "I stood by the oak-tree near my next neighbor's house. While I stood looking at the tree, it withered in my sight, and crumbled to pieces, and became level with the ground." Whoso had ears to hear, knew it was a prophecy that unless the internal quarrel ceased, the church would come to nought. The dream-prophecy was fulfilled. When Hosea came years afterward on a visit to Richmond, he found the Baptist church extinct.

It was while the revival was at its height, and many of his young associates were professing religion, that our hero became touched by the prevailing fright. We infer that the preaching to which he listened was of the kind common in his day. Its message was, "Repent; hell yawns; Satan has already one claw on you!" Such an excitement is dreadful in a community. It is easier to stand against a literal cyclone than resist such a spiritual whirlwind, if one has no shelter of unbelief. Hosea accepted the conviction that he was by nature a child of wrath hastening to destruction; but even in this excitement he did not wholly lose his equipoise. He had such calmness under excitement as might have made him great in fiery battle. He afterward said he was grieved because he could not agonize as others did; he was fearful lest his fear did not reach the regulation standard. However, having made his confession to the church and narrated his experience, he was accepted and immersed by Rev. Mr. Kinney. "I thought it my duty," he afterward modestly said, "to become a professor and join the church, which I did in the sincerity of my heart in the month of January, 1789." He was not one to shrink from immersion in ice-cold water at midwinter.

He had been from his childhood exceptionally upright. His life was always open as the day. Deceit or falsehood was utterly impossible to him. Indeed, not one wrong act or doubtful course can be found characterizing a single member of his father's family. A remarkable statement, yet duly attested. Hence, there was no great visible change in Hosea's life when he became a professing Christian; there was only some addition of gravity in his bearing.

He naturally wished to understand the system of faith he had accepted. He was prompted more carefully to study Calvinism. From his childhood he had been taught its tenets. "I was well acquainted," he said, referring to this period, "with the most common arguments which were used in support of predestination, election, the fall of man, the penal sufferings of Christ for the elect, the justice of reprobation, and many other particulars, such as the moral agency of man, his inability to regenerate himself, and the sovereignty and irresistibility of regenerating grace." He wished to penetrate to the reason of things. This disposition was with him a trait. He had no satisfaction in a doctrine he could not defend.

Before this time he believed, as he was told, that, his mind being unregenerated, he had no ability to reason correctly concerning spiritual things. But now, since his mind and heart had been renewed, he felt a call to explore his profession for its basis in Scripture and sound reason.

What is Calvinism? The system he professed, and, as far as is possible to any soul, believed, is in its distinctive features embraced in Five Points. It is a system of thought in large measure, at this writing, outgrown by the Christian church; it is too barbarous to be courteously recalled. Yet we cannot forget that in Hosea Ballou's youth it was the undisputed theology of his town and virtually of New England.

It is essential to obtain some glimpse of Calvinism, to understand the work of theological reformation to which he afterward dedicated his life. As one must study the slave-trade in connection with Wilberforce, the inhumanities of the European prisons in connection with Howard's mission, the wrongs of negro slavery in connection with the heroes of emancipation, so we must resolutely repress disgust, and try to look old Calvinism in the face, if we would appreciate the work of theological reformation to which our hero was called. These, then, authoritatively stated, are the famous, or infamous, Five Points: —

"I. God hath chosen a certain number of the fallen race of Adam, in Christ, before the foundation of the world, unto eternal glory, according to his immutable purpose, and of his free grace and love, without the least foresight of faith, good works, or any conditions performed by the creature, and the rest of mankind he was pleased to pass by, and ordain to dishonor and wrath for their sins, to the praise of his vindictive justice.

"II. Though the death of Christ be a most perfect sacrifice and satisfaction for sins, of infinite value, and abundantly sufficient to expiate the sins of the whole world, and though on this ground the gospel is to be preached to all mankind indiscriminately, yet it was the will of God that Christ, by the blood of the cross, should efficaciously redeem all those, and those only, who were from eternity elected to salvation and given to him by the Father.

"III. Mankind are totally depraved in consequence of the fall of the first man, who being their public head, his sins involved the corruption of all his posterity; which corruption extends over the whole soul, and renders it unable to turn to God, or to do anything truly good, and exposes it to his righteous displeasure both in this world and that which is to come.

"IV. All whom God hath predestined unto eternal life, he is pleased in his appointed time effectually to call by his word and spirit out of that state of sin and death in which they were by nature, to grace and salvation by Jesus Christ.

"V. Those whom God hath effectually called and sanctified by his spirit shall never finally fall from a state of grace. The believers may fall partially, and would fall totally and finally but for the mercy and faithfulness of God, who keepeth the feet of his saints; also he bestoweth the grace of perseverance, bestowing it by means of reading and hearing the Word, meditations, exhortations, threatenings, promises; but none of these things imply the possibility of a believer falling from a state of justification."

Predestination, Particular Redemption, Total Depravity, Effectual Calling, Final Perseverance,—these are the symbols of distinctive Calvinism. Endless punishment in a fiery inferno, and the Athanasian Trinity are also doctrines essential to the scheme.

What is Calvinism? In the prevailing light of the present day it is complex and aggravated atheism. To deny there is a God, and rest there (if there be rest in such a negation), is simple atheism; to say there is a God, and then affirm him to be an Infinite Satan, with another Personal Satan to assist him in fulfilling his evil plans, — this is complex and aggravated atheism. What can be more essentially atheistic than the characterization Jonathan Edwards obliquely gives to God in words like these: —

"Imagine yourself to be cast into a fiery oven all of a glowing heat, where your pain would be as much greater than that occasioned by incidentally touching a coal of fire as the heat is greater. Imagine that you were to be there for a quarter of an hour, full of fire, as full within and without as a light coal of fire, all the while full of sense. What horror would you feel at the entrance of such a furnace! How long would a quarter of an hour seem to you; twenty-four hours; a thousand years! how would your heart sink if you knew you must bear it forever and ever! Your torment in hell will be immensely greater than the illustration represents!"

And God in the creation — as Calvinism affirms — designed nearly all his children for such a doom, to the praise of his vindictive justice! It was the common thought in Hosea Ballou's early days that not more than one in a thousand of mankind was elected to escape this doom. Well did the Welsh writer Llewallen say: —

"I challenge the whole body and being of moral evil to invent or inspire or whisper anything blacker or more wicked; yea, if sin itself had all the wit, the tongues and pens of all men and angels to all eternity, I defy the whole to say anything of God worse than this. O sin! thou hast spent thyself in the doctrine of John Calvin. . . . I denounce the doctrine as the rancor of devils; a doctrine the preaching of which is babbling and mocking, its prayers blasphemies, and whose praises are the horrible yellings of sin and hell!"

Even such a vigorous characterization of Calvinism is in our day scarcely beyond popular Christian approval. Professed Calvinism is not now what it once was. Edwards, Emmons, Griffin, Park, their compeers and successors, have "modified" the old monster. We have in our day — God save the mark! — an adulterated Calvinism.

Let it not, however, be forgotten that in Hosea Ballou's youth this fatalism, holding in adamant the sinner to his sins from eternity to eternity, was miscalled Christianity, and generally accepted as the indisputable doctrine of the Bible. It was thought to be the divinely vouchsafed explanation of the mystery of the universe.

Pity for Hosea Ballou that in his nineteenth year he was committed to Calvinism! Pity for all who had, or have, real belief in Calvin's scheme for satanizing the universe by making God the arch-Satan! Pity for all such misbelievers! Especially to be compassionated are such misbelievers if they have loving hearts, and feel the woes of others as their own. To be in heart a Christian and believe such a doctrine, is to make life a moral madness. The Father himself must pity such as suffer in their conscience and love through sincere mistrust of him.

But the young Hosea Ballou has, with confidence in his regenerated reason, begun the study of Calvinism. A gleam of historic prophecy is in that fact. He must, it is true, pursue a path of lonely struggle toward the light. He must anon accept battle with the apparent odds against him. A cruel and boastful Goliath is in possession of the land; his shadow darkens all things. It is pleasing to see, however, that our young David has a clear head and a good heart, and unmeasured reserve of native strength. He is "a youth, and ruddy, and of a fair countenance." What can avail him, nevertheless, if his battle be not the Lord's?

III.

DAWN OF A NEW VISION.

PERIOD, 1789. AGE, 18.

THE occasion of young Hosea's special study of Calvinism, mentioned in the chapter preceding, was the appearance in his neighborhood of a new and strange heresy.

In the adjoining town of Warwick lived Rev. Caleb Rich, who had been a Baptist and had subsequently confessed his belief that all mankind would in ultimate eternity become holy and happy. He was now a man in middle life, of estimable character; he had been a soldier in the Revolution; at this period he combined itinerant preaching with farming, and had no little persuasive power in presenting his message of impartial grace. He was the first to turn public attention in Richmond to the doctrine of Universalism. The consternation with which his message was received by the adherents of the popular theology, it is scarcely possible for us now to realize. It was thought to be a fatal heresy. Hosea Ballou wrote in his maturer years: —

"I remember very well how the doctrine of universal salvation affected the common mind when it was first talked of in the vicinity where my youth was spent. The doctrine excited horror, and was denounced as the most dangerous heresy ever propagated: dangerous on account of two certain consequences, — first, the entire prostration of all piety and morality in this world; and second, the certainty of everlasting condemnation in the future. At that time, what is now seldom hinted even in a low voice, namely, 'If I believed so, I would lie, cheat, indulge in deception, wallow in sin of every kind, not hesitating to take the lives of my neighbors, my family, or even my own life,' was loudly vociferated from every lip; and I was perfectly satisfied that such must be the tendency of the doctrine."

Among the persons in Richmond who gave credence to the message of Rev. Caleb Rich were Mr. James Ballou, and his sons James, Jr., and Silas. There was distant relationship between this family and that of Rev. Maturin Ballou, ranging somewhere in the second or third degree of cousinship. These Ballous became local lay champions of the heresy preached by Rev. Caleb Rich. Young Hosea, having perhaps a native tendency to polemics, sometimes engaged these namesakes and townsmen in argument. The discussions were no doubt characterized by intense earnestness, logical acuteness, and bad grammar. The line of the discussion was afterwards recalled by Hosea. He maintained that God has the right to do what he will with his own. They replied, "Of course, then, he has the right to save them." "But," said Hosea, "God has a right to sentence his creatures to endless torment for their sins." "Yet," was the reply, "he has no greater right to make a part miserable than the whole; by what rule would he save one part and condemn the rest?" "All deserve endless damnation for their sins," Hosea asseverated; "and if God takes the elect as brands from the burning, this is no injustice to the non-elect, for it does not increase their suffering." "But is not this partial? If all are alike guilty, why make a distinction? If it be not wrong to save a part of those who are infinitely guilty, why would it be wrong to save all, for the remnant could be no more guilty? If only a part are foreordained to be saved, is not Deity partial?" Hosea was logically compelled to acknowledge that on Calvinistic ground God was not impartial in bestowing his chief favors on fallen man. Said he when reviewing this period: —

"In these conversations I frequently found that my Calvinistic tenets could be managed either to result in universal salvation, or to compel me to acknowledge the partiality of the divine favor. This gave me no small inquietude of mind, as I was always unable to derive satisfaction from sentiments which I could not defend. That which more than anything else contributed to turn my thoughts seriously toward the belief of universal salvation, was the ardent desire with which I found myself exercised that sinners might be brought to repentance and salvation. I found it utterly impossible to bring the feelings of my heart to conform to the doctrine of eternal reprobation; and I was compelled to allow, either that such feelings were sinful, or that my Heavenly Father in giving them to me had imparted an evidence in favor of the salvation of all men, the force of which I found no means to resist."

He now began in earnest the study of the Bible, which study was from that time his chief pursuit for more than sixty years. "The trials I was then undergoing," he afterwards said, "led me to examine the Written Word, to satisfy myself on the great question which had such weight on my mind." This study was in its earlier stages attended with increasing perplexity. He wished at first only to justify and fortify his Calvinism. He sought such aid as his father could give; yet his independent mind thus early could accept no conclusion except it appeared to himself reasonable. "Suppose," he once asked his father, "*I* had the skill and power out of an inanimate substance to make an animate, and should make one, at the same time knowing this creature of mine would suffer everlasting misery; would my act of creating this creature be an act of goodness?" The question troubled his father; it received no answer. His affectionate parent had nevertheless taught him to love all mankind. Was not this, he now asked himself, manifestly wrong? Ought he not to strive to be like God? To be sure of salvation himself must he not (to use a phrase of modern "improved Calvinism") have similarity of feeling with God? He read in the Bible, "Love your enemies;" "bless them which persecute you; bless and curse not." How could he yield obedience to these requirements and be faithful to his creed? Would not "similarity of feeling with God" — namely, hatred of men — be in him wrong, even criminal? He was sorely perplexed. But he shrank from Universalism. The prejudice of his home-education was against egress in that direction. He was cast into a sea of speculation; he intently studied his Bible as his chart, hoping thereby to find a haven.

The next stage in his earnest investigation is best narrated in his own words: —

"In the spring following my union with the Baptist Church, I went with my brother Stephen, next older than myself, who had joined the church a short time after me, to Hartford, in New York, then called Westfield, where we spent the summer.[1] In this town there was a Baptist congregation, enjoying the pastoral labors of Elder Brown, on whose ministry we attended. My brother was apprehensive that my mind was inclined to Universalism, and told me that he had a desire that I should converse with Elder Brown on the subject, by which means he hoped I should become fully convinced that the doctrine was false, and be more settled in the belief of which I had made profession. There was, at my brother's request, a conference appointed for Elder Brown to convince me that I ought to give no heed to the doctrine which labored in my mind. Accordingly we met. The Elder requested me to turn to some passage of Scripture which appeared to me favorable to Universalism, promising to do his endeavors to show me the error of applying it in favor of such a doctrine. I opened to the fifth chapter of Romans. I directed him to the eighteenth verse,[2] and told him I was unable to understand the passage if it agreed with the doctrine of the eternal reprobation of any of the human family. He immediately began, in his way, to speak very loudly, and nothing to the subject. When he would stop, I had only to inform him that what he had offered had no relation to the text I had produced; and, by showing him that the same *all men* who were under condemnation in the first member of the text were under justification in the last, evidently confused his mind, and immediately turned it sour. He was no longer able to converse with a right spirit, and prudence dictated a discontinuance. My brother grew more uneasy, and told me he was sorry I had conversed with Elder Brown; 'for,' said he, 'as he could by no means answer you, and as he mani-

[1] Several summers he had worked away from home, to contribute to the family's support. Two years previous, when seventeen, he had walked forty miles to Guilford, Vermont, where he found employment on a farm; the year previous he had found employment at Putney, Vermont; in each case returning to Richmond for the winter.

[2] "Therefore, as by the offence of one judgment came upon all to condemnation, even so by the righteousness of one the free gift came upon all men unto justification of life."

fested anger, you will think you had the best of the argument, and will feel encouraged to indulge favorable thoughts of Universalism.' "

But a single point lost was not for Hosea the defeat of his cause. He searched the Bible in every part; he kept it at hand while at work in the field, that a leisure moment might be given to its perusal. He was, let us observe, entirely alone in this course of biblical investigation. He had seen no Universalist book; he did not even know there was one in existence. When but ten years old he heard Rev. Caleb Rich preach one sermon, but the preaching made no impression on his mind. It may be he was involved in some of his difficulties by the discussions he had held with his distant kinsmen; but they were not personally present now to maintain their doctrine. His lonely toil on the farm was favorable to deep pondering. Of the course of this investigation he gave afterwards some brief indications. "I continued my researches," he says, "with no small solicitude." "Why," he asked again and again, "has God made me to desire the salvation of all my fellow-men?" That the Scriptures supported this desire by teaching a world-wide charity, became to him, as he studied the sacred pages, more and more apparent. The lessons of Nature, to which he was always peculiarly susceptible, were unmistakably in harmony with universal benevolence. "Can God," he asked, "in all these witnesses — in my own best desires, in Nature, and in the Bible — give false evidence of his own character? Can election and reprobation be true? Is the great majority of mankind irretrievably doomed to endless pain? Was this doom determined in the foreknowledge of God when the world was made? What then must be thought of the character of God?"

Such questions haunted him day and night. They took hold of his life. He was surrounded by those who professed to believe Calvinism, and who appeared to find no difficulty in holding their creed. He appealed to them for help. "Will you," he said, "who are undisturbed in your faith, give me kindly guidance out of my distress?" They scorned Universalism; but not one sound reason could they give him why he should not become a Universalist.

At last an all-diffusive light shone upon him through the pages of Scripture. He could doubt no longer that God is a Father impartial in his love. When a storm subsides and the sun shines again, there will still be floating clouds in the sky: so now there were some minor difficulties in his Bible not cleared away; some problems of faith not brought to solution. But God's impartiality he no longer doubted. This thought became fundamental in his faith. He was confident that all perplexing clouds would be in due time dissipated. He possessed the patience of hope.

He saw he must, in faithfulness to his conviction, accept a place among the people he had despised. Not for a moment did he, after the fact was realized by him, hesitate to avow himself a Universalist. The stake would not have kept him from confessing his dawning vision of truth. Modestly does he tell it all: "Before I returned the next fall my mind was quite settled in the consoling belief that God will finally have mercy on all men."

We have warrant for believing that his homeward journey in the autumn of 1789 must have been pursued with mingled feelings of gladness and sorrow. He could but be glad for the new light that had brightened his inward life, — the light which, shining out of his heart, made all things in the world more beautiful. Yet he could not forget that his change of faith must cause great grief to an affectionate father. His father had himself apparently known no such difficulties in believing Calvinism as his son had encountered; it was therefore scarcely to be expected that he could appreciate the reasons which had wrought the change in his son. Of these things young Hosea must have thought as his summer's work done he turned his face homeward.

He was met on his arrival home, however, by a great and welcome surprise. His brother David, twelve years his senior, now married and living in Richmond, had during the summer avowed himself a Universalist. He had, unknown to Hosea, been for more than a year quietly investigating the problem of faith; he had at last come to a conclusion far removed from the creed in which he had been reared. He had even begun in a humble way to preach impartial grace. The grief of the father over his youngest son's change of belief was probably lessened by the shock not coming singly. His youngest son could not seem to him so much deserving of blame as his mature son David, who was by nature peculiarly calm and meditative. Why this philosopher among his children should peril his soul with such a heresy remained to the father an unexplained mystery.

A little story is told pertaining to these days, which illustrates a certain harmless, playful trait in Hosea's character. "What book are you reading?" asked his father one day. "A Universalist book, father." "I cannot allow a Universalist book in my house," — the words being said not altogether seriously. Hosea carried his volume out of doors, and in sight of the watchful paternal eyes hid it in the woodpile. He saw his father soon after search out the offending volume, and was not unduly hilarious at his father's chagrin on finding his son's Universalist book was the Bible.

The kind-hearted father did not accept his son's new faith; but his love for his youngest child, to whom he had been both father and mother, remained during his life fond and tender. The enraptured young believer fortunately was not required to forsake father and home for the sake of his faith. This would, indeed, have been hard for him, but not to his heroism of faith impossible.

IV.

SELF-MASTERY.

PERIOD, 1780–1781. AGE, 19–20.

YOUNG Hosea cherished as yet no plan of life embracing the Christian ministry as a profession. That he however earnestly desired to commend his new faith to his fellow-men we cannot doubt. Such joy as his could not keep silence.

The ministry as he saw it could not have been alluring to his worldly ambition. His father had been a farmer more than a preacher; his brother David, now beginning to preach, declared his purpose (which was through a long life maintained) not to accept worldly compensation for heralding the news of the great salvation. Hosea thought it possible he might in like manner some day combine Sunday preaching in school-houses, private dwellings, barns, groves, sometimes in a church, with daily employment for his livelihood. "When I engaged in the ministry," he says, "it was not with the most distant expectation that I should support myself by preaching."

Yet he felt that even such a partial ministry as he hoped to fulfil required increased scope in his education. He set himself to books with desperation.

He lived this winter with his brother David, whom he could assist in winter farm-work, and with whom he could also pursue his growing passion for Bible study.

A fortunate opportunity of school attendance was unexpectedly offered. A private school, the first in Richmond, was started by some teacher now unknown; it met in the little unpainted Quaker meeting-house: whatever urchins had parents able to pay their tuition were invited. News indeed to the eager young divinity student! "Here," he said, "I obtained my first instruction in English grammar." Think of it! What wonder that some of his habits of crude speech were hard to overcome, since they were rooted in unconsciousness for almost twenty years! We can easily believe him when he says, "I studied night and day; slept little, ate little." Feverish weeks, in which by swift long leaps he hurried over the deferred tasks of childhood and early youth. Well for him he had vigorous health. Neither days nor nights were long enough for his untiring study. Midnight oil he had none to burn: the whales of the sea made no contributions to that inland wilderness; but we can hope the flickering blaze of pine-knots was succeeded at least by the luxury of a tallow-dip to lighten his late night study.

The weeks of his first school were few, and quickly passed. At the end he had scarcely made a beginning in his new studies. His thirst for knowledge was only intensified.

He now, with some degree of daring, turned his hope toward an academy. We learn of him next as spending one term in the Chesterfield Academy in New Hampshire. To this end he devoted all the slow earnings he had saved. He purposed to make the utmost possible use of his allotted time; he joined classes far in advance of his acquirements, and devoted his nights to the preliminary studies. Such heroic zeal could but awaken helpful sympathy. His teachers, seeing his assiduity, rendered him gratuitous night assistance. The country-boy in homespun found appreciative friends. "I well remember," said he many years afterward, "the kindness and consideration exercised toward me by Professor Logan, the principal of the academy, who seemed resolved that my tuition should be of real benefit to me."

Hosea had before lived among those who but lightly esteemed the advantages of education; he found a different atmosphere among those who placed a high estimate on mental culture. Those flitting weeks at Chesterfield, rendered almost sleepless by his eagerness to turn every possible moment to account, secured to him the elements of book-knowledge. He then for the first time came into association with young men of his own age who had been favored by previous mental training. It worked no harm to him, — for pride or vanity he had none, — to discover himself not their inferior in ability to master the prescribed school problems.

When he left the academy he was granted a certificate of competency to teach a common school. This quickly but dearly-won document was destined to be of substantial value to him in the years immediately succeeding.

Our narrative must not be blocked with panegyric; but the reader will note that this rare young man is thus strenuously preparing himself to preach, with not the most distant expectation that he can ever support himself by preaching. Is he not, without the least thought of it, clothing himself in the invisible mantle of Saint Paul?

During the summer following he worked in Richmond on his brother David's farm. He was about this time duly excommunicated from the Baptist Church, with such courtesy, however, as took all bitterness out of the act. No fault was found with him, but only with his belief. He had always afterward a kindly regard, a "family feeling" he called it, for the Baptist Church.

In fellowship with his genial brother the summer wore happily away. The Bible was Hosea's constant companion; "it was ever in his hands or about his person."

In September he and his brother attended the New England General Convention of Universalists at Oxford, Massachusetts. It was to them both a great privilege. Isolated as they were, they coveted the fellowship of kindred minds. They had heard through Rev. Caleb Rich of Universalism having some foothold on the Atlantic sea-board, and the fame of such names as John Murray, George Richards, Elhanan Winchester, Thomas Barnes, preachers of impartial grace, had reached them in dim reports. To attend a convention of their fellow-believers who had won victories for their faith was, we can well believe, an esteemed privilege. "Here," says Hosea, "I saw John Murray for the first time, and George Richards, and some other public teachers." No record has come to us of the session of the Convention in 1791.

It is not probable any of the recognized preachers gave special attention to the young layman, who came with open heart to hear and see. Yet more important than anything else in the Convention, and all things combined, as pertaining to the future of Universalism, was the silent young man in homespun clothes, in whose absorbent heart was throbbing a new hope.

He returned to his brother's home, and continued his studies in fulfilment of his manifest destiny.

As a Baptist, he had been accustomed to offer prayer and exhortation in lay meetings. In evening meetings of believers of the new faith in his brother's home he had also briefly borne his testimony. The time was now approaching when he must pass the ordeal of his first sermon. The occasion was one in which no little interest naturally centred.

Hosea at nineteen must have been locally popular. He had shown exceptional fleetness in running, skill in wrestling, and brawn in casting the crowbar as a javelin. He was open-hearted, cheery, also discreet and thoughtful. It was to be expected that a goodly company would be present to hear his first sermon.

The meeting was at the house of Deacon Thayer, a man who had been a deacon in the Baptist Church of Richmond, but had become a convert to Universalism under the preaching of Rev. Caleb Rich. It marks the importance of the occasion to find Rev. Caleb Rich, of Warwick, present to hear the first sermon of the young man. David Ballou was also present. There were doubtless besides these other anxious listeners. The text was, 1 Cor. i. 30: "But of him are ye in Christ Jesus, who of God is made unto us wisdom, and righteousness, and sanctification, and redemption." This is the text; the sermon is not extant. No one who heard it could long remember it. It was spoken of with pity. The young preacher rambled in his thoughts, became incoherent, but persevered through the martyrdom of a reasonable sermon-time. The attempted discourse was without manuscript; such was the preaching-custom in that time and locality. The young preacher's perspiration flowed freely, his words quite contrariwise. When he had finished he was shame-stricken. Rev. Mr. Rich and his brother David felt deeply for him, yet did not completely despair in his behalf. When Hosea could look calmly back on this occurrence, and dispassionately narrate it, he said: "According to what I could learn, my brother and Rev. Caleb Rich had doubts whether I had a talent for such labor, but were not without some hope."

It was a gleam of comfort that he did not break down utterly. To be sure, he could not, as the giddy focus of so many eyes, say what he wished to say, or anything akin to it; still he had managed to stumble on and say something, even if not in the least to the purpose. This was a straw for his sinking courage to grasp. It pleased Providence, however, to give the young aspirant a yet deeper humiliation.

"The second time," he says, "I attempted to preach was in the town of Brattleborough, Vermont, where my brother preached in the daytime, and I undertook to speak in the evening, being overpersuaded to do so; but this attempt was a failure, and I was greatly mortified, and thought for a time that

I would not engage in a work for which I was not competent." A small tragedy is here outlined. His previous partial failure had left him in partial discouragement. His kindly brother, however, bade him be of good cheer; he would yet, he was told, be able to bear his message with composure. The sight, too, of the familiar eyes of his curious young acquaintances had before been bewildering to him; but among strangers he might do better. He yielded to fraternal urging. But when he found himself standing again before an audience a tremor ran through his nerves. Into any single pair of those eyes he could have looked steadily, and spoken his mind freely; but the continued gaze of the many eyes dissipated his ideas, clogged his words, relaxed his muscles, and gave him an unwelcome sweat-bath. It is said the best blooded fighting-cock, if once whipped, is always afterward a coward. One flash of recollection of his former defeat may have in this moment modified the courage of our hero. He struggled while he could, and then sank helpless to his seat, thus gaining and giving much relief.

It is not to be wondered at that the young man was now deeply dejected.

Nor is it astonishing such a young man should make such an apparently inauspicious beginning in his public speaking. He is unconsciously aiming at a higher prize than he has yet had courage to covet. In him is the force sublime of kindling life. It is in him to play with audiences as an artist plays a grand organ, bringing from a multitude now the joyful, now the high-aspiring, now "the low, sad music of humanity." Not yet does he dream that he carries such incipient forces within him. How is he to become such a master of assemblies? As all others have done, through self-mastery.

Those of cold nature, not centring in themselves the common thought and feeling, may speak the first time with easy self-poise. Such may be rhetoricians, but not orators; lecturers, not preachers. It was because Hosea Ballou, like Demosthenes, Sheridan, Patrick Henry, had the stuff of the orator in him, that he, like these and many another, was compelled by discipline to learn to control his faculties in the presence of critical eyes, and on his feet organize his thoughts for capturing the common heart. The temporary disheartening of our crude orator need not therefore awaken despair in his behalf.

He tells the sequel of this part of his story: "It was not long before I became encouraged to try again; after which I met with no remarkable failure to produce discouragement."

For some months succeeding he continued to live in Richmond, engaged in farm-labor, but preaching as best he could wherever he found hearers in his native town or in towns surrounding; and little by little, through more ready command of his scriptural knowledge, and his native logical faculties, and his power of expression, he increased his self-mastery.

V.

HIS HORIZON BROADENS; ORDINATION; MARRIAGE.

PERIOD, 1791–1797. AGE, 20–26.

HOSEA BALLOU gave to his vision of truth his first and deepest love, and served it to his last day with heroic consecration.

We advance our narrative nearly three years,—from the time when he began publicly to declare God's love to all men in the winter of 1791, to September in the year 1794.

The New England Convention of Universalists is again in session in Oxford, Massachusetts. Three years ago, it will be remembered, young Hosea Ballou came with his brother David from Richmond, Vermont, to attend the Convention in this same Oxford. It is an indication of the numerical smallness of the Universalist sect at this time, that the Convention, meeting annually in turn among the parishes, comes again so soon to this little town. A reason, however, why this town is preferred may be the fact that among the laymen of Oxford are some persons who have unusual breadth of vision and are anxious to promote a general organization of Universalist preachers and parishes, that the cause at large may be more effectively promoted.

Two important items of business will make this session of the Convention in 1794 memorable.

One is its adoption of the articles of faith and form of church government recommended by the Philadelphia Convention at its session of the previous year, by which all the Universalists of the land, as far as declaration can effect, are brought into harmony of belief and likeness of organization and discipline; the other, and a matter of more direct bearing on our narrative, is the ordination of Hosea Ballou in a service as unique as had been his preparation for ordination vows.

The Convention meets; it proceeds to business by the choice of Rev. Elhanan Winchester president, Rev. Joab Young clerk.

The business of previous Conventions has been largely the expression of mutual sympathy among the brethren. The sect "everywhere spoken against," with a scattered membership, thus gained new courage as it felt the heart-throbs of its common life. But this year there is felt to be business of more practical import to be done. The plan of organization, looking to the unity of all Universalists in America, is fully discussed and heartily adopted. Also a proposition to simplify the system of religion in a catechism for children is held under consideration, and a committee is appointed to devise means whereby the coming generation may be instructed in the Universalist faith. A prophetic spirit is now beginning to stir the common heart of Universalist believers. They feel their faith has come into the world to stay. It quickens their hope to hear reports of unprecedented progress. Thirty-eight new preaching stations have been added to the New England missionary circuit during the year past. The cause moves on.

The meetings for preaching during the Convention are frequent. Many of those assembled will for weeks and months hear no preaching after the Convention dissolves; they can bear, indeed they covet, a generous present supply to be held in memory as a reserve. When Hosea Ballou was here three years since he was, we may recall, a diffident young layman. Now, however, he has attained to readiness and marked effectiveness of speech. It is not in him to keep silent when opportunity offers to bear testimony to his faith. He is still nominally a layman, but among laymen he has exercised his liberty.

Rev. Elhanan Winchester at this Convention meets and hears Hosea Ballou for the first time. "Who," he may have asked, "is this shy but rare young man? What is his history? Is it he who these three years past has been fulfilling such a self-sacrificing ministry in Rhode Island, Massachusetts, and New Hampshire?" Yes, he it is who, with his certificate from the Chesterfield Academy, nearly three years since obtained a position as teacher in Bellingham, Massachusetts, expressly that he might preach on Sunday without price. From Bellingham he went to Foster, Rhode Island, and there also taught on week-days and preached in his own school-house on Sundays. We hear of him also in Scituate, Rhode Island, where his father once preached; in Smithfield, Providence, Pawtucket, in Royalston, Petersham, Brookfield, Sturbridge, Charlton, Hardwick, and here in Oxford has his voice been heard. In Murray's church in Gloucester, Massachusetts, he has preached and met with approval; he has travelled to the Connecticut River west, to Richmond north, and to Hartford and New London south.

And not alone on Sundays has he preached, but on the week-day evenings, after his day of teaching, he has often instructed and stirred the people who have gathered in barns or school-houses or private dwellings to hear him speak of the things of the Kingdom. And he has been meanwhile a strenuous student, with original thoughts budding in him. Such labors have severely taxed even his vigorous constitution. He has felt pain from indigestion, yet has kept at his work; has filled appointments indeed even when compelled to sit while preaching. Young man! what has been your worldly gain? "Mine has not been a hard lot; I have been honored above many others by being permitted to preach in the name of Jesus!" But what has been your worldly gain? "Worldly gain! Only that I have more costly clothing than the homespun with which I began."

Rev. Elhanan Winchester hears this story. It is not told by the young evangelist, but it is in the air and known of all. Several of the new preaching stations this year reported are the result of his Pauline labors. Elhanan Winchester has been himself of kindred spirit. He too was once a Baptist; as early as 1780 he gave up a position of popular regard in his sect that he might proclaim the more hopeful faith that had been born in him. In some ideas of doctrine differing from Murray and Relly, he has been behind neither in self-sacrificing zeal in heralding both in America and England the great hope. He is now well advanced in years. He is held among Universalists in especial honor. The people delight to hear him. He is of large and generous nature, fluent and rapt in speech.

He has heard what has been said of young Hosea Ballou. The story vibrates a sympathetic chord in his own self-forgetful nature.

It falls to Rev. Elhanan Winchester, as President of the Convention, to preach the final sermon. He has invited young Hosea Ballou into the pulpit with him, also Brother Joab Young. He yields himself to the suggestions of the hour, and his utterance becomes fervid. It is a season of awakened hope. The banners of the kingdom are everywhere advancing. Despised the cause may be by those who have set their hearts against it; still it finds devoted friends. The wrath of man is powerless to hinder its progress. What more natural than for the preacher, in the glowing tide of speech, to speak of the victories won for the cross by the modest young man at his side? Not a heart present but is responsive to the preacher. What more natural than for him to ask of the young man, who has heretofore during his ministry been unable to fulfil the special functions of a clergyman for want of ordination, to now stand forth?

"This young man has, brethren, with no help save of God, won his right to ordination. To him we give our trust." The preacher now speaks as one inspired. He takes up the pulpit Bible and says: "Brother Ballou, I press to your heart the written Jehovah!" The congregation is electrified and melted. How harmonious and appropriate is it all! For a moment the venerable preacher holds the Bible to the throbbing young heart; then in kindly, imperative tone of spiritual authority says, "Brother Young, charge him." The charge is voiced by Rev.

Joab Young, who is reputed eloquent of speech, but who could not, even if his temperament were ordinarily cold, fail to speak with a heart at white-heat in an hour inspiring and hopeful as this.

So Hosea Ballou has won the trust of his brethren; he has won his honors, so to speak, in the field. Now, at the close of the Convention, without solicitation or expectation on his part, he finds himself an ordained minister of the gospel. It is not possible for him to betray the generous trust his admiring and loving brethren have so spontaneously reposed in him.

Who can withhold the prophecy that he will make full proof of his ministry in the future years?

Two years pass, and we see the subject of this narrative at another epoch in his life. In the town records of Hardwick the following memorandum is made: "Sept. 11, 1796. Mr. Hosea Ballou, of Hardwick, and Miss Ruth Washburn, of Williamsburg." No one will be in doubt as to the meaning of this. No one whose heart has not withered, but is captivated by the rapture of "love's young dream." It accords with our present purpose to dwell on this epoch in our hero's life only as it illustrates the statement made at the beginning of this chapter. This experience of his life, idyllic, romantic, entrancing as it must have been, was in our mind when we said our hero gave to his vision of truth his first and deepest love, and served it to his last day with entire consecration. This is not saying he was not an ardent lover; it simply means his strongest human love was held in subordination to his deeper life-devotion.

Only a sketch can we gather from the scant testimony of this attractive experience. It appears Rev. Caleb Rich told Hosea Ballou, when he was twenty-six, that he ought to marry and make for himself a home. So altogether absorbed in his love of the gospel had Hosea been, that this very obvious duty seems not before to have occurred to him. "And furthermore," said the clerical match-maker, "I know a young woman in Williamsburg who would make you an excellent wife. She has had good home-training; she is of noble nature; she has been led by her parents to embrace the gospel as we understand it; she has been educated in habits of frugality and industry; withal, she is very attractive and comely in her person. This young paragon of a minister's wife is the daughter of Brother Stephen Washburn, — Ruth Washburn, if you please, — and her single fault is that, being but seventeen years of age, and eight years your junior, she is slightly juvenile for the grave cares you would, in case you should be so fortunate as to win her heart and hand, expect her to assume; but the fault of youth she will in time outgrow." In some such way Rev. Caleb Rich talked to young Hosea Ballou. The plain prose of it is in the record: "Rev. Caleb Rich commended to his attention a young lady of Williamsburg, Massachusetts, Miss Ruth Washburn, who was a few years younger than himself." We report the speech which, as appears to us, Rev. Caleb Rich must in substance have made.

What Hosea said in reply is not by so much as a hint recorded. Perhaps he blushed and said nothing.

The next scene in the drama is Rev. Caleb Rich

making a similar address to the young lady herself. It is very tempting for us again to use our imagination. We refrain. The plain historical prose is this: "She was prepared by the well-meaning elder to receive Mr. Ballou's visits with favor." Well-meaning! Not only in this case did he *mean* well, but he *did* well. The conclusion is foregone. When, years afterward, Mrs. Ballou told this bit of romance to Rev. Thomas Whittemore, she said that as soon as she saw the young man, in company with Elder Rich, approaching her father's house, — a red and tremulous young man he must have been, nevertheless manly and not unhandsome! — she said to herself, or something within her seemed to say, "There comes my future companion." A marriage, and with Rev. Caleb Rich the officiating clergyman, is the inevitable result. In that instance the officiating clergyman well earned his marriage fee; and we wish it could have been larger than the worldly possessions of the bridegroom would at that period justly warrant.

Perhaps some young reader may suspect that such a marriage, entered upon by a method quite unlike that of the story-books, did not prove happy. No greater mistake could be made. A marriage contracted thus, in subordination to the dictates of religion, has the highest possible promise. This proved in fact an ideal marriage. After years have passed, we must look again at this home, now with hope begun. We shall find it based not alone on the stern idea of duty, — from which indeed it never swerved, — but on a conjugal love which had in it the grip of death and the hope of heaven.

But mark this. The love of woman, in the day of his youth, was held quite subordinate to his love for his vision of truth, which imposed on him a cross of daily hardship. Chivalric the hero who says,—

> "I could not love thee, dear, so well,
> Loved I not honor more."

Hosea Ballou was with exceptional ardor devoted to his home; we shall find him an ardent lover at eighty: the notable thing is that he was an ideal husband and father because he loved truth better than houses or lands or wife or children.

After Hosea and his wife had remained at her father's home three months, the young couple moved to a home of their own in Hardwick, where they remained in peaceful content seven years, during which the young theologian made long strides in spiritual attainments.

Before this chapter is closed, a brief account must be given of the effect of Hosea Ballou's preaching during these his most peaceful days. It was becoming apparent even to him that he had unusual power over the people who constituted his congregations. There was now a fathomless joy in his life, and this he in his facile speech diffused. It was, as compared with the accustomed method, "a sea-change, . . . rich and strange," for the common people to hear one talk to them so earnestly, and in their own vernacular, presenting religion as meeting their daily needs, and finding for them in familiar objects and every-day occurrences pictures of hidden realities. Many people came to hear him because made curious by his spreading fame. He had genius in speaking words which necessitated report and iteration. Those who came merely to gratify curiosity were often surprised into captivated adherents. In all the places he visited, his congregations increased. There were always some, it is true, to decry, cavil, and distort; there were some to shudder at the new heresy as a sorcery luring to endless horrors. So it ever has been. Of the Son of Man it was said that he cast out demons by favor of the arch-demon.

Of necessity such opposition made of the young preacher a controversialist. He boldly assailed the challenging Goliath who claimed possession of the land. In those days it was more like a fair and open fight than in the days which succeeded. True, the Goliath of Calvinism was mailed in prejudice and custom; yet it made its claims of Scripture support boldly, and did not, as in a later age, skulk from one covert to another, and nowhere make a stand. The young David had joy in his brave fight. This Calvinistic Goliath, unlike the old Philistine giant, could endure more than one skull-penetrating pebble; with his body weighted with lodged pebbles he could still walk about, making a show of life,— and indeed so continues in the day that now is. But it was a coveted privilege for the young expounder to hurl one after another the explained proof-texts at the giant, together with the plain testimonies of the Bible to God's universal love. In this work the young preacher did not grow hard or bitter. There was such serenity and gladness in his life that he could easily keep patience even with scorners and traducers. He lived the doctrine of human brotherhood he preached. His love of Calvinism is not apparent; it grew less and less every year; but his love of men was strong and sincere. It was born of his responsive love to God. He kindled hope in many a heart in those days of itinerant Christian ministry, by showing how behind every frowning providence God hides a smiling face.

This general characterization of his preaching and its influence is intended to apply to the early years of his ministry, when he travelled long journeys over the steep northern hills, by wagon or sleigh or on horseback, and as a rule preached three times on Sunday, and on almost every evening of the week. Peaceful, happy, busy, prophetic years!

VI.

HARDWICK-DANA, N. H.; BARNARD, VT.

PERIOD, 1797-1804. AGE, 26-33.

HOSEA BALLOU and his young wife at the beginning of their housekeeping remained seven years in one house; yet near the middle of the period their home was, strangely enough, changed from Hardwick to Dana. The explanation is that in 1801 the town of Dana was formed of parts of Hardwick, Greenwich, and Petersham; their home was in the Hardwick section.

During these years Mr. Ballou fully regained his ruddiness and robustness. Referring to this period he says, "My uniform weight for several years was about two hundred pounds." He was six feet in height, and firmly built. He had physical resources for hard work and effective oratory.

During this period his stated compensation was five dollars per Sunday. It indicates the worldly struggle in which the farming population was involved at the beginning of the century, to find that even this seeming pittance could be raised only from a large circuit of preaching stations. Yet he is not a subject for pity. He fared well, if not sumptuously. He kept his own horse and vehicle. He was easily able to maintain whatever "style" was prevalent among his neighbors. There was plenty in his modest home. He lived in grateful content.

During his second year in Hardwick he involuntarily became an author. He was for some unexplained reason moved to address a letter to Rev. Joel Foster, A.M., of New Salem, Massachusetts, inviting him to a friendly discussion of the points at issue between Orthodox and Universalist theology. As the letter was accompanied by the statement that its author had enjoyed but few educational advantages, and earnestly desired the benefit of Mr. Foster's larger experience and well-known scholarship, the request was courteously entertained. An extended discussion was the result. It was admirable audacity in the young man to propose such an investigation. The benefit he received was real. For one thing, he had Orthodox doctrines presented in exact statements. For another, he had the advantage of being politely ridiculed for his verbal inelegancies and inaccuracies. The pen had been until this time an unused instrument in his hands; he could hardly be expected to exhibit the grace of an expert. He had the good sense to be thankful to his critic for even helpful ridicule.

An interesting item of this controversy is that although Mr. Ballou, for the purpose of investigation, had assumed the position that there will be no future punishment, he at the end of the discussion confessed, "I am now satisfied in the idea of a future state of discipline, in which the impenitent will be miserable." There can be no question that at this period such was his belief.

At the close of the discussion Mr. Foster proposed that the letters be published. Mr. Ballou replied,

"As some of my letters contain thoughts which I am unwilling to contend for in public, you will excuse me if I am not willing to publish them." What must we think of a Christian minister who could, nevertheless, publish the discussion, and give his opponent no opportunity at correction or revision? This Rev. Joel Foster, A.M., proceeded to do; entitling the book, "A Literary Correspondence," — an innuendo touching Mr. Ballou's style. It is to our hero's credit that he kept his temper. The book, long since consigned to obscurity, is a curiosity in being a reminder of how Hosea Ballou at first became involuntarily an author. He was born to be an author, and he achieved authorship; he also had authorship thrust upon him.

In the autumn of 1797 he made an extended visit to Boston, during which a famous episode occurred in Rev. John Murray's church. A fact has already been slightly hinted, which will hereafter be more fully set forth; namely, that Mr. Ballou had learned from his study of the Scriptures a different system of religion from that which had from Relly's day prevailed among Universalists. He believed Christ is subordinate to the Father; that he came to do, not to frustrate, the Father's will, — to express God's love to men, not to satisfy his law or palliate his wrath. Some of his ministerial brethren were aggrieved at this departure from their standard of doctrine. Among the most deeply aggrieved was Rev. John Murray, popularly known as the founder of Universalism in America. Mr. Murray held, with Relly of England, that all mankind are saved by their union with Christ. As every man is mystically united to Adam, he said, so every man is likewise mystically united with Christ. "The redemption," said Mr. Murray, "will therefore be, through the substitutionary sufferings of Christ, co-extensive with the fall." When Mr. Murray heard of Mr. Ballou denying original reprobation, and the substitutionary punishment of Christ, he was not pleased. When, therefore, in October, 1797, he wrote to Mr. Ballou at Hardwick, we are not surprised that he should begin his letter: "My dear Brother,—You are sensible, I presume, that some time past you delivered in this town some matters not quite pleasing to me."

This must refer to Mr. Ballou's brief visit in Boston on his way from Cape Ann, before his ordination. We infer that he preached his new views in the presence of the veteran that he might have the benefit of his opinion. Mr. Murray, while not satisfied with the innovation, was yet at this time magnanimous. The letter proceeds from "censures" to "commendations," and soon turns to an invitation to the young preacher to be the author's substitute in his pulpit during his contemplated absence in Philadelphia. The country preacher is offered the enticing remuneration of ten dollars per Sunday, exclusive of his weekly keep; and Mr. Murray, as an added inducement, tells him he may preach evenings in contiguous towns to his heart's content. The plain implication is, however, that the young man from the hill-country is not, in Mr. Murray's absence, to stand in his place and assault his doctrines. We think Mr. Ballou understood this, and that he did not during his ten Sundays in Boston consciously in a single instance violate Christian courtesy.

The scene which occurred on the afternoon of his last Sunday is of little importance save as an exhibition of feminine alertness, and a young preacher's dignified self-control. We accept Dr. Whittemore's account of the matter, in the main, rather than that of Maturin Ballou. The latter says that his father "boldly preached his Unitarian views." We think the son was misinformed. His father could scarcely have done that and observed the courtesy for which he was noted. Some words are quoted as from Hosea Ballou which certainly cannot be his. His producing disturbance by his Unitarian views, and then declaiming that "he had come there to preach no one's convictions but his own," that "he should proclaim the truth as by the help of Heaven he had been enabled to learn it from the Bible, and the truth only," — all this seems inherently improbable. The son in his biography must have been in this instance led into error. The substantial facts were written by Dr. Whittemore, and his account publicly approved by Mr. Ballou;[1] the story bears on its face the evidence of its truth.

The clew is the fact that Mrs. Murray was an "uneasy spirit." It is she and not Mr. Ballou who makes the scene. She has listened to her husband's substitute through all the Sundays on the *qui vive* for some objection. She has seen that the verdant young preacher has strangely captivated the people. Not even her florid and emotional husband was ever heard with more absorbing attention. She was, with due deference to her sex, a woman; she was, furthermore, a solicitous wife; she was, be it kindly

[1] See Trumpet, vol. xx. p. 150.

repeated, an "uneasy spirit." Now, on this last afternoon (we imagine her thinking), this ambitious young preacher is to air his heresy. What else can his text mean? "When all things shall be subdued unto him, then shall the Son also be subject unto him that put all things under him, that God may be all in all." If that refers to Christ (we imagine her saying) it surely implies his subordination to the Father. It must refer to the "son of perdition." Meanwhile the sermon goes on. The text is developed mainly as a testimony to the final triumph of the mediatorial reign of Christ and the redemption of the universe from evil. Rapt the listeners! Something must be done. She sends a Mr. Tirrill to the singing seats with a message for Mr. Jonathan Balch. Mr. Ballou, having offered the final prayer, stands with hymn-book in hand to read the final hymn. Mr. Jonathan Balch from the singing gallery breaks forth: "I wish to give notice that the doctrine which has been preached here this afternoon is not the doctrine which is usually preached in this house." It is to be regretted that the sunlight could not at that moment have opportunely pictured the expression on Mr. Ballou's face. What will he say? If he had said he came there "to preach nobody's convictions but his own," and "should proclaim the truth as by the help of Heaven he had been enabled to learn it from the Bible," he would have cheapened himself by telling what the people knew already. Will he say that he has not consciously forgotten courtesy; that his disagreement with Mr. Murray, as it appeared in his sermon, was but incidental; that he had endeavored in his sermons to respect the opinions of the absent pastor? Truthfully he might have said this; but not a word of this did he say. What he did say, with self-repression and quiet dignity, is, "The audience will please take notice of what our brother has said." Then he proceeded to read the closing hymn.

Poor "uneasy" Mrs. Murray! In a published sermon of her husband on the same text there is no mention of the Son meaning the "son of perdition;" the phrase is interpreted as meaning the human race collectively; and in the aggregate his meaning is not unlike that which Mr. Ballou saw in the passage. The singularity of the occurrence alone makes it memorable. "It was," says Dr. Whittemore, "a matter of Mrs. Murray, and of Mr. Balch as her instrument; the congregation at large were chagrined and wounded by the transaction, and the committee took immediate measures to assure Mr. Ballou of this fact."

These ten Sundays in Boston had prophetic significance. His preaching was such as could not be forgotten. It is proposed to him that if he will come to the city a new society will be at once formed, which will yield him ample support. "I cannot do anything," he says, "to injure Brother Murray, or the beloved society to which he ministers; oblige me by not mentioning the subject again." The whirligig of time, in many an instance, brings unlooked-for things to pass. That Mr. Ballou will some day come to Boston is a prophecy to be based on a strong hope and an enduring purpose.

Now to the hills again! The city with its proffered flatteries has not touched the simple nature of our hero. He resumes his itineracy. We find him journeying from Cape Ann to Vermont, and preaching with more or less regularity in Brookfield, Charlton, Sturbridge, Oxford, and as often as once in four weeks at home in Dana. He has a circuit which it takes two months to complete. As far as is possible, he endeavors to answer all calls made upon him. His sympathy goes quickly to any one who is groping in the terror-filled darkness of the old theology. He knows in himself the pain of such fear. He knows what it is to have heart-hunger for hope. No Macedonian cry can find him unresponsive. In mercy to human nature he is eager to strike the Goliath of Calvinism wherever he may an additional blow. By nature as well as by his experience he is divinely ordained to be a missionary.

In February, 1803, he removed his household to Barnard, Vermont. There was a cluster of promising towns in that picturesque region — Woodstock, Bethel, Bridgewater, Hartland — soliciting the new interpretation of the gospel. Mr. Ballou was urged by the older preachers to sow the seed in this new ground. Regretfully he left Dana, but gladly continued his accustomed tasks in the new communities. To guard against possible difficulty, owing to the legal irregularity of his ordination, he was reordained in Barnard, Sept. 27, 1803, with due regard to all formalities. A sermon was preached by Rev. George Richards; prayer was offered by Rev. Samuel Hilliard; a charge was (for the second time) given by Rev. Joab Young; and the fellowship of the Convention and societies was voiced by Rev. Walter Ferris.

In the same autumn, in 1803, he attended the United States Convention of Universalists in Winchester, New Hampshire, at which the Universalist Confession of Faith was adopted. A committee had the previous year been appointed to present a declaration of principles; and the committee reported through Rev. Walter Ferris a declaration so fortunate in statement that it seemed impossible it could lead to division. It is understood the Confession was written by Rev. Mr. Ferris. It was fully discussed in the Convention. It was opposed by Revs. Noah Murray and Edward Turner, on the ground that no creed-yoke should be put upon believers. It was advocated by Revs. Walter Ferris, Zephaniah Laithe, George Richards, and Hosea Ballou. It was, the minority yielding, finally passed by unanimous vote. It remains to this writing the authoritative creed-symbol of the Universalist Church of America.[1]

In 1804 Mr. Ballou became of his own choice an author. His first book, "Notes on the Parables," is a study of the illustrative stories of the New Testament as interpreted by the Bible itself. It was written during a temporary confinement at home. He had been surprised to learn how generally the para-

[1] PROFESSION OF FAITH. *Art.* I. We believe that the Holy Scriptures of the Old and New Testaments contain a revelation of the character of God, and of the duty, interest, and final destination of mankind.

Art. II. We believe there is one God whose nature is love, revealed in one Lord Jesus Christ by one Holy Spirit of grace, who will finally restore the whole family of mankind to holiness and happiness.

Art. III. We believe that holiness and true happiness are inseparably connected; and that believers ought to be careful to maintain order and practise good works; for these things are good and profitable unto men.

bles were regarded as literal history, and how often they were misapplied to things foreign to the evident intention of the sacred authors. He says in the preface: "After travelling many miles and preaching several sermons in a day, I have found it necessary to explain various parables to some inquiring hearer, when my strength seemed almost exhausted. At such times I have thought a volume such as the reader has in hand might save me much labor, and I have often said, 'If God will give me a few weeks' leisure I will, with his assistance, employ them in writing Notes on the Parables.'" This favor of leisure came in the deprivation of such health as would be adequate for his taxing journeys, but leaving him composed in his study. It is a very valuable book, especially to those perplexed by the figurative language of the parables. Some modern volumes present advantages of knowledge of Eastern life such as was impossible at this time to Hosea Ballou; but no other book better presents the plain common-sense interpretation of the New Testament parables. It has been a book greatly blessed in the enlightenment of darkened minds.

Of another book, the "Treatise," — a book which was an event, the dawn of an era, — we will more fully speak in a chapter following.

The year 1804 was in subsequent years held by Hosea Ballou in solemn retrospect. During its autumn his honored father was borne to his rest. The affection between parent and son was more than ordinarily tender. Hosea was the father's youngest child; he was loved as Jacob loved his youngest son Benjamin; neither is it to be forgotten that the widowed father had tried faithfully, as far as he was able, to fulfil to the motherless boy a mother's ministry. Hosea responded to his parent's peculiar love. It is pleasing again to recall that no divergence of religious views broke the bond which united their hearts.

Through the mists of the years one scene comes to distinct view, upon which we dwell with a pensive gladness. It is in the Richmond church, or in a church near Richmond. Hosea is the preacher. His father is present as a hearer; present also are three of his brothers, two of whom are now in agreement with the young apostle of the world-wide hope. The Baptist father, however, remains steadfast to the church of his early choice; yet he cannot repress paternal pride as he looks upon his son. Hosea has evidently had some anxiety in anticipating this ordeal; these paternal and fraternal eyes are penetrating; he has, contrary to his custom, prepared for the occasion a written discourse. During some minutes after beginning to preach he reads from his manuscript. But in reading his own words he is not an adept; and his feelings are now alive as they were not when in privacy he guided his pen. Always sensitive to his hearers' mood, he feels he is becoming wearisome. Why has he consented to be so tongue-tied? He leaves his manuscript, pushing it quite out of reach, and asserts his customary freedom of utterance. All hesitation in a moment ceases. His speech flows freely, copiously; it sparkles, it burns; it seems the visible pulse of a heart on fire. See the father now! Tears dim his longing eyes and course down his furrowed cheeks. Ah, to be the father of such a boy! Who will say the tremulous beginnings of the great hope may not have been felt by the listening parent? It has been said that Hosea never in his palmiest days spoke with more sublime pathos. Truly this father and son were held together by bonds of love which death could not break.

Only two years before this date Châteaubriand, the eloquent defender of the Bible against French revolutionary scepticism, on hearing of the death of his pious mother, sat down to the writing of his masterpiece, "The Genius of Christianity," as a son's tribute to her revered memory. May we not believe that Hosea Ballou, in writing his "Treatise on Atonement," his next work after his father's death, wrote with a desire that he might embody his vision of truth in such form as his transfigured father would approve?

VII.

"TREATISE ON ATONEMENT."

Period, 1805. Age, 34.

WHAT are we to understand by atonement?

As a creed-doctrine it has a history; a glance at which will show the monstrosities of theory of which good Christians have been capable.

In the early ages of the Church the sophists naturally asked, "Why did Christ die on the cross?" They searched the Scriptures for an answer. They read apostolic testimony that Christ died as a ransom. As a ransom! So much then was settled. But to whom; for whom? Here they had an opportunity to exercise their renowned and peculiar ingenuity. They lived in a barbaric age. They saw banditti capture opulent citizens and hold them for ransom. Beloved, here is the mystery of the cross solved. Who is Satan but the arch-bandit? He captured the children of God in the Garden. He held them for ransom. He was open to barter. Christ offered to die on the cross if Satan would yield his claim on the race. He accepted the offer. So Christ became our ransom. Do we caricature? Not in the least. This was the reputed Orthodox doctrine of atonement in the Church for more than a thousand years. According to this theory men are saved from Satan because Christ "gave the Devil his due."

But in the eleventh century Anselm began to ask, "Where, meanwhile, is God?" He maintained that the Creator and Judge must have been the actual possessor of the race from the first. He proposed as an amendment to the doctrine this; namely, that God in the beginning, to the praise of his vindictive justice, brought the human race into existence for no other purpose than to condemn to endless ruin all save the few elect, and that Christ died to pacify his anger against these few elect. This theory in the interest of Satan was strongly opposed. Why, it was asked, take the ownership of the race from Satan after it has been conceded to him for a thousand years? But Anselm's theory was formally adopted. In fact, the change was slight. One theory said Satan when it meant Satan; the other ascribed satanic attributes to God. The theories were equally satanic. A sect — vile heretics that they were — rebelled against the new theory, declaring that God did not hate the race before Adam lapsed from virtue. Sublapsarians these heretics were called. The doctrine was reaffirmed that God brought his non-elect children into existence for the primal purpose of showing his vindictive majesty. Supralapsarians these more orthodox ones were called. The "Subs" and "Supras" had a long discussion, which was substantially continued under the names Arminianism and Calvinism. Subs and Supras alike held that Jesus died to placate the bad temper of Deity.

Anselm's theory in its two schools prevailed in America at the beginning of our century. The theory is this in brief: God created Adam and placed him in the Garden; Adam fell, instantly involving himself and all his posterity in total guilt and doom; then God the Son, the second person in the Trinity, died on the cross as the infinite atonement to an infinite anger for an infinite sin. Through faith one can (if he be of the elect, interpose the Calvinists) obtain an interest in Christ's expiatory death, which is *the* atonement.

This is the doctrine Hosea Ballou was taught in his youth. It seems now impossible that men ever believed such a so-called theology. Some old sermons we have read seem utterly impossible of sober belief; they seem in the same way satirical as De Quincey in his strange essay, "Murder as a Fine Art." De Quincey, as those who have read his frightful satire will recall, praises a skilful murderer as virile, plucky, and cunning, and assumes it to be wrong to find fault with him on the score of mere commonplace morality. "Through the great gallery of murder, brethren, together let us wander in delighted admiration." How exact this imitation of some of the old sermons! Why expect God to be moral? Earthly kings are scandalous and cruel; none dare call them to account. Why should not the King of kings in like manner be a law unto himself? Whatever God does — whatever Augustine or Anselm or Calvin or Edwards tells us God does — must be right. So God was praised for beating Satan at his own game, and then cruelly demanding of his children that his unrighteousness be called righteous!

It stirs us to recall, even as dead doctrine, these monstrosities of thought. We revive their memory only to show the historical bearings of Hosea Ballou's "Treatise." We must remember that Hosea Ballou had been himself borne along by the current of the common doctrine. With the common drift he accepted it without question. With Relly and Murray, after his conversion to the great hope, he believed in man's universal fall in Adam, and in the consequent need of a Divine pacification; he differed from the Calvinists in believing that the atonement of Christ was effective for the whole human race. For a season he was dazed by this system of terrible doctrines. He asked why the glorious consummation needed to be reached through such a doubtful process. He was also, as he confesses, further perplexed by reading "some deistical writings." He probably refers to Paine's "Age of Reason," a crude but pungent assault on the Bible in its traditional Orthodox interpretation. It was issued in 1796, and at once sent a magnetic shiver of consternation through the whole reputed Orthodox hand-joined circle. What Hosea Ballou learned from this book, or from other deistical writings, was creditable to his candor. "I was led to see," he says, "that it was utterly impossible to maintain Christianity as generally believed by the Christian church."

In his lonely rides over the hills of his northern country we doubt not he pondered his great problem. He was by nature a poet, else he could not have been so true an orator. Nature in panoramic pictures suggests breadth, greatness, harmony, rest. Could he help questioning within himself, Is not one God, the Infinite Good, over all? Did he not foreknow the result of his creation? Is it not all according to his plan? Can there be a rival evil deity? Can Father and Son be co-eternal? Can punishment of the innocent clear the guilty? Can the Bible contradict Nature? A frustrated Creator! a vengeful Judge! a pacified Father! Hard for a free soul to think such disturbing thoughts under the peaceful open sky! A voice within told him that God is better and nearer than the creeds had declared.

At last Hosea Ballou, to his unspeakable joy, reached the solution of his problem. In his "Treatise" he made his solution known.

Atonement, what is it?

Not expiation, but RECONCILIATION. It is satisfaction, in the sense of content, or a want fulfilled. "A being unreconciled to truth and justice needs reconciliation; a dissatisfied being needs satisfaction."

What is atonement? Its precise etymology signifies AT-ONE-MENT, — alienated beings brought to unity.

The unreconciled and dissatisfied beings needing change are men, not the Immutable. "God was in Christ reconciling the world unto himself." The Eternal Father is not a subject of improvement. Infinite Perfection is without shadow of turning.

Why, then, to ask again the old Christian sophist's question, did Christ endure the cross? We have had in church doctrines, as we have seen, a progressive series of answers. The early schoolmen said, "His death is a ransom to Satan, to reconcile the bandit to man's release from inferno." The mediæval schoolmen, under Anselm, said, "He died to placate an incensed God, whose wrath could be pacified only by an offering of his own Son's blood." The New England Theology, or the Edwardsian System (the

New School of Orthodoxy in Hosea Ballou's day, be it understood, is the Old School now), said, "He died to fulfil the demands of the majestic broken law, which must have so much suffering for so much sin, but is indifferent whether the suffering is inflicted on the guilty or the innocent."

It is now declared by this unschooled man of the hills that all these answers are radically wrong; that Christ did not die to pay a ransom to Satan, who has quite enough conceded to him already; that he did not die to placate God, who is amid all the changes of visible creation the Eternal Serenity; that he did not die to answer Shylock demands of a law by which God is withheld from his desire to be merciful, — as if there could be a law other than God's will; but Christ died on the cross as a testimony of GOD'S LOVE, and hence as a moral appeal to MAN. The appeal of Christ to the alienated world is, "Be YE reconciled to God." He was lifted up on the cross, not to draw God nearer to men, but to draw all men to himself, saying, "He who receiveth me, receiveth Him that sent me."

The method of Hosea Ballou in his "Treatise" was necessitated by his circumstances. A man in troubled times erecting a fort bristling with armament in an enemy's country can scarcely have such regard to proportion, symmetry and outlook as one may have in leisurely building a palace on his own land in quiet years. The effective plan of our author was to project his revolutionary thoughts against haughty so-called Orthodoxy where it boasted itself strongest. Weakened there, its whole line would be virtually broken. His inquiries are concerning —

(1) Sin, its nature, cause, effects; (2) Atonement; (3) the Consequences of Atonement to mankind. Like the workmen rebuilding the walls of Jerusalem under Nehemiah, he was compelled to build with a trowel in one hand and a sword in the other, — and to the sword he gave his right hand.

The system of doctrines of which this interpretation of at-one-ment is a constituent, is, in brief summary, this: God is the Sole Sovereign of the universe, Omnipotent, Omniscient, All-Good. What he planned in the beginning will be fulfilled. He was not disappointed, nor in the strict sense angry, when men became sinners; he foreknew that, in the exercise of the power of choice between good and evil with which he endowed man sin would result. But he controls all evil, and will cause it to serve his own ultimate purpose of good. While men are in sin they suffer, because they are out of harmony with his image in themselves. Hosea Ballou's own words are, "As long as men sin they will be miserable, be that time longer or shorter; as soon as they cease from sin they will begin to experience divine enjoyment." Christ came to the world, as out of the Father's bosom, to bear witness to the truth of God's love and providence and Fatherhood. Because the right is not only the best thing but the strongest, God through Christ will subdue all enemies. The at-one-ment with the Father will be finally complete, when through repentance of evil and choice of good the last prodigal returns, receiving the ring, a symbol of endless love, and the kiss of pardon.

The "Treatise on Atonement" should, like every book, be read with due regard to the time in which it was written. The author was a pioneer, *blazing* as he traversed the forest. He had no human guide or companion. All unknown to him was the incipient struggle against Trinitarianism in Boston; his "Treatise" antedated the Unitarian sect in America ten years. If there had been some endeavor among the Universalists of the Middle States to base their doctrines in the nature of things, the news had not reached him. To compare his book with some which have followed, especially with Horace Bushnell's great work, "Vicarious Sacrifice," which advocates essentially the same view of at-one-ment, would be like comparing an Atlantic-traversing steamship with the vessel in which Columbus first crossed from the Old World to the New. Fulton's first steamboat, Morse's first telegraph, Howe's first sewing-machine, Edison's first electric light, have prophetic and poetic interest no subsequent improvements supersede. Read in the remembrance of the shadowed days in which it was written, the "Treatise on Atonement" is luminous as a prophecy of the coming epoch.

Nor is the interest of this book merely historic. He who on opening it and coming soon to some bungling in the phrasing puts the book away as the presumptuous essay of a sciolist, suffers loss for his haste. It is to be regretted, to be sure, for the sake of the fastidious, that the book is not classic in expression. But can we doubt that it has served its purpose better for being in homespun, untailored garb? There is toughness of fibre in the book, and great persuasive power. Little need is there, if read candidly, of mistaking what the author intends to say. It is, in main part, homely talk on great themes; its marked merit is in bringing abstractions to the clear apprehension of the unlettered reader. "Our Creator," he says, "made us reasonable beings; all the truth necessary for our belief is not only reasonable, but reducible to our understandings." His illustrations are drawn from familiar objects and every-day life. His method is strikingly similar to that of Abraham Lincoln, in whose homely talk, says Lowell, "the American people heard themselves thinking aloud." As the argument in the "Treatise" proceeds, the style naturally assumes purity and dignity. The tide of inspiration which possessed the author enables him finally to indite passages which will suffer little by being compared even with Abraham Lincoln's unique address at Gettysburg. What a book to be read and pondered, and re-read and shrewdly discussed, by New England country firesides at the beginning of the nineteenth century! And it is now more the fault of Universalists than of the book, if it is in their homes dust-covered in these closing years of the same century.

Attacking so-called orthodoxy at almost every point, our author is sometimes content to refute doctrines by simply giving them a clear statement, and bringing them to the touch of reality. In the passage following he takes home to experience one of the stock-doctrines of the popular creed: —

"I am born into this world of sorrow and trouble; the first vibration of sense is want; I endeavor to supply my needs, and to maintain my existence, which my Maker has bestowed upon me; but as soon as I come to years of understanding, I am told of an *infinite debt* which stands against me, which I owed thousands of years before I was born;

and that my Maker is so angry with me, and has been ever since the debt was due, that he has prepared a furnace of endless flames to torment me in, according to the due requirements of justice!"

To this his answer by parody is: —

"My father gives me a farm, and puts me in possession of it; I am pleased, and prize it very highly. In consequence of my possession, I paint to myself many pleasing prospects. But to my mortification a person comes and presents me with a mortgage of my farm for five times its value, the mortgage running so as to hold the possessor obliged to clear it. I will leave the reader to say whether my father was kind or unkind."

He shows by simple statement the absurdity of the "governmental theory," in its affirmation that the second person in the Trinity paid the debt due from the sinner: —

"The sinner owed a debt to divine justice which he was unable to discharge; the Divine Being cannot, consistently with his honor, dispense with the pay, but says, 'I must have what is my due;' but as the debtor has not ability to pay the smallest fraction, Divine Wisdom lays a deep-concerted, mysterious plan for the debt to be discharged. And how was it? Why, for God to pay it himself!"

Effectively and simply he answers another monstrosity of the "scheme": —

"It is argued with much assurance that God has a just right to do with his creatures as he pleases, because he has it in his power so to do; and that he never does anything because it is right, but what he does is right because he does it. If this statement is just, moral holiness consists in the power of action, and not in the disposition that designs the action. If so, we are driven to say that unholiness, or sin, is the want of power to perform an evil action, and holiness consists in having the power to do it. One man designs to murder another for his money; he makes the attempt and fails. His sin consists in not having power to execute his designs, but in his designs there is no evil. On the other hand, he makes the attempt, and succeeds; here is no evil at all, because he had the power to do it. On this principle, everything that can be done is moral holiness, and everything that cannot be done is sin, or moral evil."

In his justification of the ways of God to man as a Judge, he by a question takes the reader to the root of the problem: —

"Which reflects the more honor on the divine character, to contend it was necessary for him to create millions of rational creatures to hate him, and every divine communication he makes to them, to all eternity, to live in endless rebellion against him, and endure inconceivable torments as long as God exists; or to suppose him able and willing to make all his rational creatures love and adore him, yield obedience to his divine law, and exist in union and happiness with himself?"

Our author answers the query as to his understanding of the ethical application of his doctrine in words which will still bear emphasis: —

"God, in infinite wisdom, has constituted all moral beings so that their duty is their happiness, and strict obedience fulness of joy. Why, then, my brethren, shall we starve? Why live poor? Why should we be so parsimonious of those heavenly stores that never can be exhausted? 'Blessed are they who hunger and thirst after righteousness, for they shall be filled.' 'Ask, and ye shall receive; seek, and ye shall find; knock, and it shall be opened unto you.' God forbids none; 'the Spirit and the Bride say, Come; and let him that heareth say, Come; and whosoever will, let him take the water of life freely.' Remember, the salvation which God wills is salvation from SIN. Then, as much as you desire salvation, you will wish to avoid sin and wickedness. There are none who say they do not want salvation; but how few there are who say they want it by their own conduct! No man understandingly wants salvation any further than he wants more holiness. The Universalist, who is really so, prizes his duty as his heaven, his peace, his most sublime enjoyment."

When describing the true at-one-ment in experience,—the knowledge of the goodness of God leading the sinner to repentance,—he becomes a poet of Nature under guidance of Scripture:—

"The earth, in time of drought, ceases to be fruitful; the streams and springs thereof are dried up; the fields put off their robes of green, and the gardens afford no fragrant delights! But when the heavens give the wonted blessings in gentle showers, how suddenly is the face of Nature changed! The purling rill murmurs through the mead, pastures and fields teem with vegetation, and gardens blush with enamelled beauties. So the soul, unwatered with the rain of righteousness, and destitute of the waters of eternal life, is like the barren fig-tree that yields no wholesome fruit. But behold the transition! the moment ATONING GRACE is effective in the mind, the parched ground becomes a pool, and the thirsty land streams of water. The soul is like the earth that drinketh in the rain that cometh oft upon it, and bringeth forth herbs meet for them by whom it is dressed; and, like a garden well watered and cultivated, yielding all manner of precious fruits."

The marshalling of scriptural imagery in the final passage of the book, describing the universal at-one-ment perfected, possesses an eloquence kindred to that of the Seer on Patmos:—

"The fulness of times will come, and the times of the restitution of all things will be accomplished. Then shall truth be victorious, and all error flee to eternal night. Then shall universal songs of honor be sung to the praise of him who liveth forever and ever. All death, sorrow, and crying shall be done away; pains and disorders shall be no more felt, temptations no more trouble the lovers of God, nor sin poison the human heart. The blessed hand of the Once Crucified shall wipe tears from off all faces. O transporting thought! Then shall the blessed Savior see of the travail of his soul and be satisfied, when through his mediation universal nature shall be brought in perfect union with truth and holiness, and the Spirit of God fill all rational beings. Then shall the law of the spirit of life in Christ Jesus, which maketh free from the law of sin, become the governing principle of the whole man once made subject to vanity; once enthralled in darkness, sin, and misery, but then delivered from the bondage of corruption, and restored to perfect reconciliation to God, in the heavenly Adam. Then shall the great object of the Savior's mission be accomplished. Then shall the question be asked, O death, where is thy sting? But death shall not be, to give the answer. And, O grave, where is thy victory? But the boaster shall be silent. The Son shall deliver up the kingdom to God the Father, the eternal radiance shall smile, and God shall be all in all."

What is atonement?

The expiatory scheme is withered fruit of a dying tree; among thinkers abreast of the age, a dead issue; to be classed with calashes, whale-oil lamps, and the grewsome "Alonzo and Melissa" and "Clarissa Harlowe," over which our great-great-grandmothers shed hot tears. It is inharmonious with the Bible, Nature, and the inalienable sense of right in the human soul.

The at-one-ment, the RECONCILIATION, as set forth in the "Treatise," is the revelation of God interpreted by the plain nature of things. The principles of this doctrine are already interwoven with the best representative Christian thought of the age. The Universalist Church, when it instantly and instinctively adopted the doctrine of its great pioneer, set its face toward the dawn.

VIII.

BARNARD, VT.; MISSIONARY JOURNEYS; HYMN-MAKING.

PERIOD, 1803–1809. AGE, 32–38.

SIX years Hosea Ballou preached to the Universalist societies in the vicinage of Barnard, Vermont. Busy years, full of content, swiftly passed!

Alike through the crisp oxygenated air of the bright winter days, and deepening drifts of Vermont winter storms, and through the dreamy air of summer, and during the wondrous transformations of the vernal season alike at its beginning and close, he "rode over the hills and through the valleys and by the winding streams," to his weekly appointments. Ever afterward he treasured the memory of these years of intrepid itineracy in Vermont.

We find him still faithful to his mission as a seed-sower.

The sequences of a sermon he preached in Rutland, in June, 1805, are illustrative of the spirit which in those days prevailed. He was invited by some leading citizens of the town to preach in the parish meeting-house, which they had been able to obtain for his services. The pastor of the parish was a Presbyterian, Rev. Samuel Haynes by name; an educated colored preacher, of marked local popularity. He was fluent, and given to pulpit effects. When Mr. Ballou appeared, he invited Mr. Haynes to accompany him into the pulpit. Mr. Haynes at first declined, but yielded after a little urging, remarking, "I may have a word to say after the sermon." Mr. Ballou preached from the text: "Herein is love, not that we loved God, but that he loved us, and gave his Son to be the propitiation for our sins. Beloved, if God so loved us, we ought also to love one another" (1 John iv. 10, 11). Mr. Ballou (a contrary impression was received by some from hearsay, however) was a man noted for his courtesy. He now purposely avoided such topics as might offend those "of the contrary part." In the main his sermon was a plea for mutual forbearance and Christian unity. At its close Mr. Haynes, by Mr. Ballou's invitation, made some remarks. He proceeded, with great excitement, to declare that the preacher had just preached the Old Serpent's doctrine. Mr. Haynes fulminated and perorated his prepared screed. Some in the audience were grieved; some thought such impudence an exhibition of genius. It was not a reply to anything Mr. Ballou had said or hinted; it was a reply to what Mr. Haynes may have imagined Mr. Ballou would say. It must be confessed the situation was trying to Mr. Ballou. In beholding him remain calm and offering no word of rejoinder, we see him at his best. That "flash of eloquent silence" has dignity like that of an old Roman drawing his toga about him. Yet it was kindly. He assumed that the over-zealous preacher would on reflection feel a becoming shame. He closed the meeting as if nothing had happened. What was his surprise, therefore, when some months afterward Mr. Haynes's screed, entitled "The First Lie Refuted," appeared in print as a sermon. Then Mr. Ballou, in a published letter, spoke his mind. "The design of this epistle," he says in the opening paragraph, "is to inform you and the public how I viewed your conduct at the time you delivered your sermon, to which I reply; and what I think of said sermon and its general complexion." The epistle is illustrative of how a man of calm temper feels, for instance, when stung by a gad-fly. Not in a sentence, however, does he forget courtesy or dignity. Mr. Haynes hastened to promise the public a reply; but it never appeared. Here the discussion ended.

Yet for years afterward Mr. Haynes's "Sermon" was circulated among reputed orthodox people as an acute and effective assault on Universalism. Some people have wondered why Hosea Ballou was a controversialist!

By appointment of the General Convention Mr. Ballou visited Western New York in the summer of 1806, to assist in organizing the "Western Association of Universalists." There had been an "Eastern Association" organized in Maine; a "Central" in Massachusetts; now it was fitting the Convention should have its eye on what was then the far West. He was accompanied on this visit by Revs. William Farwell, Joshua Flagg, and Paul Dean. The Convention in those days was fortunate in being able to send to its important work its most influential preachers. Mr. Ballou's reputation at this time was popular power; wisely was it utilized to missionary ends.

How the coming of the appointed brethren to their field of labor was regarded by the scattered resident

Universalists, is suggested in the words of Rev. Nathaniel Stacy, written in his "Memoir." Mr. Stacy, gentle and apostolic in spirit, was at this time doing pioneer missionary work in Utica. "My heart," he says, "was so full of the anticipation of meeting my brethren again, after having alone and at so great a distance, and for a whole season experienced the unmerciful buffetings of the storms and tempests of sectarian wrath, that the approaching meetings caused me to weep for joy." From the same "Memoir" we take (with some condensation) a graphic account of the meetings which were held: —

"As the season approached that would call our ministering brethren from the East to preach with us, and counsel and assist us in organizing an Association, my heart beat high in anticipation of peculiar felicity. I could hardly wait its arrival. All preparations in our power were made for the coming event, to render it as satisfactory as possible to the visiting committee and profitable to the glorious cause, by securing as large a congregation as we could induce to attend. Information of the meeting was widely extended through all the country, with earnest invitations both to friends and opposers, and as ample provision was made for their entertainment as circumstances would permit. The place for meeting was appointed in Columbus, Chenango County, not because more friends of the cause were there, but because it was the most central location we could obtain where we could find accommodations. No Universalist society was at that time thought of there, but there were a few families in the immediate vicinity who were ready to do all they could, and whose liberality was ample. The country was thinly settled; no meeting-house had been erected. But a building had just been built designed for a tavern, with an extensive ball-room; this the owners generously offered and we gratefully accepted as the most eligible place that could be found. And here was organized the first Association of Universalists in the State, — the third organization of the kind effected in America. Four discourses were delivered on the occasion: one by Mr. Flagg, one by Mr. Dean, and two by Mr. Ballou. A numerous congregation for the time and place was in attendance; and in the afternoon of the first day, and both parts of the second, we were compelled to repair to the adjacent forest for our religious exercises, the chamber not being sufficient to hold a tenth part of the congregation. The weather was fine for the season, and we found ourselves comfortably accommodated, with the verdant and waving foliage of a dense forest to screen us from the scorching rays of a summer sun, and the trunks and fragments of fallen trees, mostly, for our seats; and here we listened with intense interest and fervent gratification to the preaching, which, it appeared to me, was almost sufficiently piercing to penetrate the dark vault of the tomb, and powerful enough to raise the dead to life."

A year afterward, in 1807, Mr. Ballou again visited Western New York by appointment of the General Convention. Not alone at the Association he had helped to organize did he manifest his desire to serve the cause; but having spoken his quickening words of counsel to the brethren there assembled, he went about his accustomed missionary work in the growing towns of that section. His preaching at Utica was especially memorable, because heard by a boy whose heart was prepared soil, which received the word, and brought forth fruit an hundred-fold. Rev. Stephen R. Smith, one of the pioneer preachers of Universalism in New York State, was in mature years strikingly like Hosea Ballou in essential traits of character. In simplicity of spirit, rugged honesty, strength of religious conviction, power over the common heart; in eloquence of extemporaneous address, in the content, gratitude, and dignity with which a humble homespun way of life was accepted for his unpopular faith's sake, Mr. Smith was like Mr. Ballou. It is vastly interesting to read the words of Mr. Smith, descriptive of his first hearing of Mr. Ballou. It was during his second visit to Western New York. Says Mr. Smith: —

"By what means the intelligence that Mr. Hosea Ballou would preach on the following Sunday, in a place some fifteen miles distant, could have been conveyed to a very young man, who did not then know a single Universalist in the world, is not remembered. He went, however, and heard a discourse in the morning from Zechariah vi. 13, and for the first time in his life felt that he had listened to a sermon that involved neither an absurdity nor a contradiction. The congregation was not large, and occupied a school-house in the present city of Utica, then a meagre and muddy village. A larger congregation was anticipated for the afternoon, and arrangements were made for the services in the open air, under some trees, on the bank of the Mohawk River. There in due time a large auditory assembled, and listened to one of Mr. Ballou's best discourses, from Deuteronomy xxxiii. part of 16th with 17th verse. It was a glorious day, early in June; the silence of Sunday was around us; the bright blue heavens above us, partly veiled by the branches of a few scattering oaks; the clear, quiet river at our side; the ruddy and healthy preacher in all the vigor of manhood before us, and pleading the cause of God and humanity with a group of most attentive hearers. Such a scene is not to be forgotten; and, altogether, it was one in every respect calculated to make the most favorable as well as lasting impressions. And such certainly were its effects on the mind of the writer. For while it left him without any pretension to the knowledge or belief of Universalism as a system of religious truth, it entirely satisfied him that it was consistent with itself and with all that we see and know of the Deity and his moral government. It is scarcely to be doubted that similar impressions were made on many persons in that congregation."

How excellent this description, and how pleasing to see, in the mirror of a kindred spirit, our young David, now matured into "a ruddy and healthy preacher."

Mr. Ballou (we must add with some tinge of regret) received another commission of the General Convention, first in 1806, renewed in 1807, of which he, while doing his best, made a not over-creditable fulfilment. With Revs. Sebastian Streeter, Edward Turner, and Abner Kneeland, he was appointed "to prepare a hymn-book for the use of the Universalist societies." No doubt there was need of a new hymn-book. The Universalists naturally could not heartily sing the prevalent Orthodox hymns of perdition; their only existing hymn-book, which had been issued by Mr. Murray's society in Boston, was objectionable on account of embodying in many of its hymns the rejected ideas of the Trinity and vicarious punishment. A new hymn-book was surely in order. But the members of this committee gave an interpretation to their powers which the Convention, if clothed in its right mind, could hardly have intended. They assumed it their duty to themselves write all the hymns of the new book! The volume contains four hundred and seventeen so-called hymns; and, sad to recall, Mr. Ballou wrote one hundred and ninety-eight, almost one half the whole. It is of little consequence that of the remaining, Mr. Kneeland wrote one hundred and thirty-eight, Mr. Streeter forty-eight, Mr. Silas

Ballou (a distant relative of Hosea) twenty-three, Mr. Turner ten. It is such a hymn-book as was, under the circumstances, to be expected. Mr. Kneeland's hymns are "weak and insipid," without either reason or rhyme. It is scarcely strange that he afterward rejected Christianity, since he had expressed his estimate of it in such hymnology. Mr. Ballou's hymns, however, do, as a rule, have at least some reason. They even attempt, in phrases often badly cramped by the count for metre, to reason out a logical argument. As sermons, they are fleshless bones; as sacred songs, flat failures. A real hymn, a lyric of the soul, we are wont to think, is one of the highest and rarest productions of human genius. It sings itself in some rapt heart; thence it is instinctively adopted by the common heart. "Rock of Ages," "While thee I seek," "Nearer, my God, to thee," are hymns. No real hymn is machine-made, or merely hand-made.

It is not, perhaps, so much a matter of regret that Mr. Ballou wrote these wretched rhymes, as it is that he seemed ever afterward to enjoy his endeavors to make words jingle. He in late life confessed he had never studied the rules of poetry, not even for an hour. It is to be regretted that he did not, for an hour at least, study rules of prosody. What a revelation it would have been to him to read the accepted great masters of versification! He would thereby have been taught to distinguish in his own productions gold from dross, and to consign the dross to oblivion. For we must acknowledge there is gold to be found in this unsmelted yet not quite unmetred ore. Three hymns, at least, are not misplaced in any collection however choice. Here is a lyric of faith:—

> "In God's eternity
> There shall a day arise,
> When all the race of man shall be
> With Jesus in the skies.
>
> "As night before the rays
> Of morning flees away,
> Sin shall retire before the blaze
> Of God's eternal day.
>
> "As music fills the grove
> When stormy clouds are past,
> Sweet anthems of redeeming love
> Shall all employ at last.
>
> "Redeemed from death and sin,
> Shall Adam's numerous race
> A ceaseless song of praise begin,
> And shout redeeming grace."

We can easily believe this hymn sung itself to the author before he offered it for singing. The hymn written for opening an Annual Convention, beginning,

> "Dear Lord, behold thy servants here,
> From various parts together meet,
> To tell their labors through the year,
> And lay the harvest at thy feet,"

is worthy of yearly repetition in the Annual Convention. The hymn beginning,

> "From worship now thy church dismiss,—
> But not without thy blessing, Lord;
> Oh, grant a taste of heavenly bliss,
> And seal instruction from thy Word,"

after having been sung in the closing moments of a Sunday service, could not easily leave the heart of a believer. If Mr. Ballou had published these hymns only, in which the sentiment is so rhythmic as to compel completeness and grace of expression, he would have won such fame as a sacred lyrist as his voluminous hymn-making did not achieve.

The hymn-book was, of course, by the deluded societies which adopted it, soon found out and discarded. Yet the willingness of Mr. Ballou even to attempt, with some assistance, to write an entirely original hymn-book (like the after-dinner proposition of the drink-dazed statesman to himself pay the public debt) indicates an exceedingly lavish zeal.

We close this free-hand criticism by asking the reader, if he ever should see a thin, neglected volume entitled "Ballou's Poetry," not to think of the author less highly than he ought to think. The making of the verses was his amusement when he was too tired for work; it was done sometimes merely to give "variety" to his newspaper. He is to be regarded with forbearance also, because he did not himself gather up his verses and publish them as a book. It was done for him, and badly done; verses not his, although quite as lame, were palmed off under his unprotesting name. In the collection of limping, jerky lines, however, are some of human interest, as we may hereafter recall.

Let us concede that rhyming was Mr. Ballou's foible. If we have no foible of our own, we may freely cast our gibe at him.

At the end of his six years of earnest work (in which his hymn-writing may be reckoned as earnest endeavor) he removed his home to Portsmouth, the chief city in his native New Hampshire. His removal from Barnard was the occasion of deep and general regret among the people cherishing the larger hope; but they were led to see that their pastor should not withhold himself from the wider field.

His going from Barnard was a corresponding satisfaction to those in that community who believed his mission was to blight souls. One good deacon, of the Calvinist persuasion, was especially delighted to hear that Mr. Ballou was to leave the place; the more so, perhaps, because he had an intelligent daughter-in-law who was inclined to regard him with favor. The good deacon, on receiving the news, as he was sitting down to dinner, was inclined to be facetious. "Mr. Ballou to leave town?" he asked. "I am very sorry; for I suppose we may expect to have the Devil himself here next!" "Why, father," said the apt daughter-in-law, "do you think Mr. Ballou the only man who can keep the Devil out of Barnard?"

Maledictions and benedictions in this world are sometimes strangely blended.

IX.

PORTSMOUTH, N. H.

PERIOD, 1809–1815. AGE, 38–44.

THE world — the kindly world, which has remained "good," which neither misbelief nor misdoing has perverted — beamed in friendliness on Hosea Ballou when he arrived in Portsmouth.

Children had been born to him; his domestic life was a garden of delights, his home-content was without flaw. He was nearing his maturity. Gristle had hardened to bone; he had become firm and fibrous; he had not discovered the bounds of his physical vigor. He bore no scars, but many laurels, from his former conflicts.

And Portsmouth at this time was an ambitious and attractive village. The town is located on the south bank of the Piscataqua River, at the head of an extensive harbor. Its marked distinction was then, as it has been since, its neighborhood to the United States Navy-yard, situated on an island in the river. The narrow, straggling streets were adorned with graceful shade-trees; even at that day the village was beginning to be ornamented with fine buildings. The future city had high hope; it assumed a right to the first choice in all things. That the Universalists of Portsmouth should believe their growing village the appropriate field for our hero, proves them possessed

HOSEA BALLOU

AT THE AGE OF 50

of discernment and enterprise. They pledged to him "eight hundred a year and the contribution money." And this to our hero was a vision of worldly glory to almost dazzle his eyes. A proffer of the kingdoms of the world and the glory of them could scarcely be to him more alluring.

And for this vision of visible splendor he had not been even invited to fall down and worship Satan. For the popular Satan of his day, indeed, he professed even less than respect. For the ubiquitous firemonger and salamander, the beast-reptile, with cloven feet, enscrolled tail, and three-tined fork for handling live fuel, — for this Satan, most important deity of the Calvinists, — sub-deity, *abb-gott* (ex-god), we might call him, if he had not so evidently obtained the mastery of his Creator, — for this Satan Mr. Ballou had no propitiatory offerings. He quietly but constantly proclaimed defiance. He called him unreasonable, unbiblical, impossible, ridiculous. Before that Satan, at least, he was not likely to fall in worship.

The providential lines had allotted to Mr. Ballou a pleasant place, but he was not looking for a bed of roses. No dropping the knapsack yet for comfortable bivouac; no sheathing the sword. He had enlisted as a minute-man for the whole war. He stood on guard for the truth, and had no aversion to an aggressive campaign. He found Calvinism a miasma that pervaded the sea-breezes. In the village it blighted love, hope, mirth, and health. It was not then coy, nor of a retiring disposition; it had learned none of its modern modesty. It was a pestilence that wasted at noonday and gave terror by night. We cannot under such provocation expect our zealous soldier of the cross to suffer the sword of the Spirit to become rusty in its scabbard. He had no personal quarrels to wage, and never had; but in the good fight of faith he was an instant and persistent soldier. He could not be otherwise; yet he maintained the high courtesy of a true Christian. He was respectful and deferential toward his clerical neighbors with whom he came in contact. He was a personal exponent of the gospel of good-will and fraternity.

The history of his Portsmouth settlement is largely a story of discussions. He was destined to participate in a varied, and at some points a bitter warfare during his entire stay in the city by the sea.

His ministry, let us first observe, however, was in its method greatly changed. He had before devoted himself to pioneer work. As an itinerant, he had repeated his sermons throughout his circuit, and revised them as he rode to his appointments, improving them on repetition, becoming a helpful critic of himself. Now, two sermons each Sunday to the same people was the order. He used no manuscript in preaching; he had no "barrel." Each new sermon must be evolved fresh from his brain. But the emergency did not daunt him. He soon became the popular preacher of the thriving village, and his church the focus of eager Sunday crowds. Converts to the religion of hope were numerous, and his parish for a season prospered.

His initiatory discussion at Portsmouth was, in one point of view, a foreign contest. During his first year there came to him a pamphlet of sixty-nine pages, from Rev. Isaac Robinson, of Stoddard, New

Hampshire, entitled "A Candid Reply to a Doctrinal Controversy between the Hopkinsian and the Universalist." It was the continuance of a controversy begun while Mr. Ballou was at Barnard. He had been drawn into it as assistant of Rev. Ebenezer Paine, a Universalist, and by force of his superior aptitude for debate he had become a principal. Rev. Mr. Robinson, the Hopkinsian, a believer of "modified Calvinism," was liberally educated, of discriminating mind, and estimable character; for fifty years he was a pastor in the town of Stoddard. The "Candid Reply" was a renewed challenge to Mr. Ballou. Of course he could not decline an answer. A merely personal assault sometimes found him a non-resistant; he could then turn the other cheek. But when his vision of Truth was assaulted, he resisted evil with good; he turned to the assailant, not the other cheek only, but a full-face view of Truth. He was soon before the public in a lengthy pamphlet entitled "A Candid Review." As a specimen of sagacity in discerning the weak statements and self-contradictions of an opponent, this pamphlet is interesting. "Do Universalists verily believe," asked Mr. Robinson, "that a good earthly father would treat any of his children as they know and acknowledge God has treated some of his offspring?" "Observe," said Mr. Ballou in reply, "it is the *good* earthly parent he will not allow to be a fit emblem of our Father in heaven!" Mr. Robinson avowed belief that God "from all eternity designed that certain of his children should never taste the sweets of his nature." "My blood feels as if freezing," exclaims Mr. Ballou. "Oh, my God, in whose hands my breath is, pardon the folly of thy benighted children!" In its main issues the "Candid Review" is now fortunately out of range of popular interest; but it was for its day an effective polemical work. Mr. Robinson was content to leave the field; he vouchsafed no more "candid replies."

Soon Mr. Ballou found himself face to face with another assailant; in this instance a neighbor. Rev. Joseph Buckminster was the pastor of the first Congregationalist Church of Portsmouth. A graduate of Yale College, twenty years Mr. Ballou's senior, a conscientious Calvinist, he was, from commendable motives, moved to attempt the rescue of his heretical neighbor. Under date Dec. 28, 1809, he writes to Mr. Ballou a lengthy private letter, urging him to flee from his dangerous position. He does not revile, nor censure, nor impeach his neighbor's sincerity; he writes under shadow of the "Great Day." He says:

> "I cannot bear the thought of your being able, when the scheme of Universalism shall all vanish like the baseless fabric of a vision, and all hopes built upon it will be like the spider's web, to say I never warned you of this issue, nor admonished you of your danger."

Here was a *Christian* believer in inferno! Mr. Ballou says in the first letter of his series in reply: —

> "In your truly affecting entreaty, inviting me to direct my mind to the day of judgment, when I am called to give an account of my stewardship, you ask what my situation must be if the system I advocate should, in the final evidence, prove false. I have seriously thought on this question, and this is my conclusion: My Judge will know that I am in this instance honest and sincere; he will know how I wrestled against his Word in order to avoid believing that he would save all men; and he will know that my

deception was in understanding his Word as a simple, honest man would understand a plain testimony void of scholastic dress. In this case, I am willing to throw myself on the mercy of the Judge. . . . On the other hand, dear sir, I have made a calculation: suppose I adhere to your testimony that the doctrine I believe is not true, and abandon it as heresy, and preach it down to the utmost of my ability; and then the doctrine at last — when you and I stand before the Judge who knows the hearts of all men — shall prove true (of which I have not the least shadow of doubt), with what a blush must I give in my account! My Judge, who has suffered everything for me, asks, 'Why did you deny me, and preach the dishonorable doctrine that I did not purpose to redeem all men in eternity?' Abashed beyond description, I must answer: 'A man I conceived was my friend, who preached that God never intended to save all men, told me the doctrine I preached was not true.' How would my soul thrill with grief when a look such as was cast on Peter when he had denied his Lord accompanies the question, 'And who told you, in the first place, it was true?' "

The series of private letters became in due time an appeal to the public. That Mr. Ballou maintained his cause with his accustomed courtesy and ability, the above extracts will suggest. Mr. Buckminster deserves for his good-hearted endeavor the tribute of grateful respect. His example, in appearing to have some grains of honest belief in his creed, as attested by his human pity, is not unworthy the emulation of the clergymen of a later day, who nominally profess to believe the same creed, but hide its sulphuric flame under a bushel. How can they hope to escape in the "Great Day"?

No truce yet for our soldier of the cross; no day yet for scabbarding his sword of the Spirit.

Rev. Joseph Walton was pastor of the Third Congregationalist Church of Portsmouth. He was also Mr. Ballou's senior by many years. He was for some reason a volunteer attendant at two funeral services conducted by Mr. Ballou. He heard him speak of death "as originally designed by the Almighty for the good of mankind." He protested in a very earnest letter. Mr. Ballou's reply was not needlessly delayed. He had looked into Rev. Mr. Walton's creed, to find it contained the words, "God foreordained whatsoever comes to pass." Since it was evident Mr. Walton believed God originally designed death, would he please show good cause for not believing he designed it for good? Why must we think evil of him? Mr. Walton had quoted in his letter from 1 John iii., and added: "If you will read the whole chapter, and seriously consider it, and pray to God to open your understanding, that you may understand the Scriptures, you would not misapply and pervert them, as I fear you do." Mr. Ballou said: —

"Are you sufficiently acquainted with my preaching and writing to warrant the propriety of the suggestion that I am in the habit of misapplying and perverting the Holy Writings? Are you sufficiently acquainted with my retired studies and religious exercises to warrant the suggestion that I get along without acknowledging the wisdom of God? . . . Judge not another who must stand or fall to his own Master. . . . Friendly advice to be constant in fervent supplication would be received by me as a mark of a Christian. . . . Are you willing to have me go into your desk with you, in presence of your church and congregation, and there read the whole of the above-named chapter, and then in humble and solemn prayer to Almighty God through Christ Jesus implore a true and just understanding of his truth written in this portion of his Word, and close my performance with a candid dissertation on the chapter? Grant me liberty to do this in your hearing; after which I will not object to being informed of any misapplication or perversion you may think you discover. By what law is a man condemned without first having his defence heard?"

The subject was pursued in a series of letters, which was given to the public by aid of printer's types. Mr. Ballou's closing letter, of Feb. 1, 1811, was a model of keen analysis and effective home-thrusts.

Even here is no rest.

One Rev. George Forrester, a teacher of the sciences in Portsmouth, a recently-arrived foreigner, a pedant, saw it was the fashion to strike at Mr. Ballou, and thought he saw his opportunity to gain personal fame to answer the hunger of his conceit. He would show his brother Calvinists how to snap the head off such a heretic. He came before the public in a pamphlet entitled "Strictures on 'The Treatise on Atonement,' and 'Notes on the Parables.'" He assumed a stilted style of severity, ridicule, and contempt. His arguments were but poor reproductions of familiar Calvinistic formulas. Mr. Ballou would have been like some men if he had taken no notice of his conceited reviewer. His foeman in this case was scarcely worthy his steel. "A braying ass does not cause the stars to fall." But Mr. Ballou was too courteous not to treat even a swollen pedagogue with respect. He replied in a series of letters entitled "An Attempt with a Soft Answer to turn away Wrath." He answers the stock objections to his books with gentleness and completeness, and makes an earnest plea for Christian forbearance and charity. He says: —

"Come, dear brother, let us reason together. 'Have we not all one Father, hath not one God created us?' It surely appears to me you have not treated me as a brother; you have not written as if you realized that we have one Father and Creator. I do not complain on my personal account; but it is a matter of no little grief that one who professes the religion of the Savior should dishonor that profession by such angry animadversions as appear in your 'Strictures.'"

He takes his opponent through a course of reasoning and expounding which might have been of benefit to him had he not been already filled with east wind. Sometimes, however, pearls are wisely cast before swine, because other than swine-eyes will see them. It was a general opinion in the community that Mr. Forrester had injured his cause, and that Mr. Ballou, by his manifest candor, had gained respect for the cause he maintained.

In these contests, it is to be observed, Mr. Ballou was not the assailant. Who will say he was not justified in turning the full force of his vision of Truth on each one of these who had given him an uninvited blow? And in all these contests, be it further observed, he was, by example and precept, giving counsel and courage not alone to believers in his own parish, but to many along the lines of the progressive army.

There were, however, some agreeable aspects of his life during his Portsmouth pastorate.

In January, 1811, a Ministerial Association was formed in Gloucester, composed of the Universalist clergymen of the New England seaboard cities. Revs. Edward Turner, of Salem, Thomas Jones, of Gloucester, and Abner Kneeland, of Charlestown, were Mr.

Ballou's associates in these friendly gatherings. He had great happiness in these fraternal meetings. The censorious popular church offered him but little grace of fellowship; to share his toils and cares with his own brethren, and become enlivened under the touch of mutual sympathy, kept the untainted, unperverted good world in his view.

It is noteworthy that Rev. Edward Mitchell, of the First Church of Boston, was not a member of this Ministerial Association. This is suggestive of an important fact. Mr. Mitchell was at this time, excepting the now feeble John Murray, the only clergyman in New England who preached Universalism on the basis of the Calvinistic "scheme." Remarkable fact! When, six years before, the "Treatise on Atonement" was published, all Universalists were Trinitarian Calvinists; now the denomination had become almost unanimous in its acceptance of the New Theology. The pastor of the First Church, standing alone and aloof from his brethren, is a significant indication of the change which had been wrought in the denomination through Mr. Ballou's influence.

The "Gospel Visitant," a quarterly of sixty-four pages, was published in Salem, June, 1811, as the organ of the Ministerial Association. This was the first stated Universalist publication. That it was especially Mr. Ballou's project cannot be doubted, when we recall that he was the only Universalist clergyman of that day who had enthusiastic faith in printer's types. The contributions of Mr. Ballou's now practised pen to the "Visitant" were numerous and valuable. In the first number we find a letter from him to Rev. Asa Kent, a Methodist minister of

Portsmouth. In the second number we find a careful review of a sermon preached by Rev. Samuel Worcester, of Salem. In the "Visitant" for March, 1812, is an article from Mr. Ballou worthy of distinct attention. It is an exposition of 1 Peter, iii. 18-20, in which he makes affirmation of his belief in limited future punishment. He subsequently modified his opinion, as will be shown; at this time he believed there would be punishment of the impenitent in the future world till they should be brought to repentance; and this period he did not regard as necessarily very brief. He made manifest in the article to which we refer, his opinion that "the spirits in prison, to whom Christ preached, were the disobedient ones who lived on earth in the days of Noah." From Noah's day to Christ's day, according to his view, these rebellious spirits had been in misery, because left in ignorance of God's forgiving love.

But some aspects of his Portsmouth ministry, in its later days, were not so agreeable. With his neighboring ministers he continued in good fellowship; with his own parish he did not continue in unbroken concord. He learned by experience what bitterness can animate the hearts of alienated brethren.

It will be observed that his ministry in Portsmouth covered the period of the second war with England. The appeal to arms brought stagnation of the common industries and a great increase of partisan excitement. There was in the city intense opposition to the war-policy. The Federalists, as the opposition party was named, were more numerous among the wealthy citizens. Their influence was felt outside the city; it was regarded as a serious hindrance to the national cause. And many of these anti-war Federalists were Mr. Ballou's most capable financial supporters. They were themselves very outspoken and domineering in their opinions; their speech at times almost touched overt treason; but they expected of their minister, unless he agreed with them, to say no word in the pulpit on politics. But Mr. Ballou was to the bone a patriot. His Universalism and his faith in American Democracy in many points coincided. He retained also a little of the popular grudge against England, dating from the Revolution. On Fast Day, Aug. 20, 1812, he expressed his convictions in regard to the national crisis. He preached a decided and vigorous war sermon. He was temperate, but uncompromising. No patriot, he said, would side with his country's enemy in the terrible trial of war. Now there was commotion! That he should dare to so express his opinion! The rancor into which some of his leading people on that day fell, was to Mr. Ballou a surprise. Some who differed from him in political matters nobly remained his supporters; others withdrew and began an active opposition. Their partisan politics had nullified their religion. The parish was in a tumult; many of the best people were in discouragement. What will Mr. Ballou do? Many a minister in a similar situation has run away. Many an one has declaimed his grievances and posed as a martyr, and lived on his financial credit in the hope of some favorable issue. Mr. Ballou did none of these things. He showed the texture of his manhood by quietly maintaining his position, and accepting without complaint the partial support the disturbed parish could offer him, and by teaching a private school making both ends of his family cash-account meet. He did not during this strain neglect his pulpit, nor the sick and unfortunate needing a pastor's friendly counsel; and his pen became accustomed to late hours. But by the added burden of wearing daily teaching he earned his right to speak a telling word for his country. We know not whether his justification of the war was right; but this we know, his following his conviction, and speaking for his country in her stress, was right, and grandly right. He now, across the chasm of the years, offers his hand in fellowship to all independent, patriotic, heroic spirits. Whoever can by faith clasp that proffered hand must feel ennobled by its pressure. It pulsates with better than royal blood.

Things, naturally, could not always remain in this condition. In 1815 the Salem pulpit had been vacant more than a year; in the spring of 1814 Rev. Edward Turner had removed to Charlestown. Mr. Ballou, at a venture, was called to the Salem pastorate. He submitted his case to the Portsmouth parish. He required, as a condition of remaining in his pastorate, a fair support for his family. There was needless deliberation over the matter. Salem, having some assurance of hope, became urgent. The name "Salem" signifies "peace," — a good omen to a peace-seeking man. One day the Salem invitation was accepted. Then Portsmouth was aroused! The acceptance must be recalled! The Portsmouth parish now pledged "nine hundred dollars and the collection money." Too late!

Midsummer, 1815, Mr. Ballou removed to the city of weird witchcraft fame.

X.

SALEM.

PERIOD, 1815–1818. AGE, 44–47.

SALEM, among American cities, must be conceded a character distinctively its own. Peculiar fascinations are in its atmosphere. Traditions of its hard-faced Pilgrim founders, of a period antedating the settlement of Boston; ghostly yet captivating legends of its witchcraft delirium in the closing years of the seventeenth century; numerous mementos of the latter part of the eighteenth century, when Salem dreamed its manifest destiny was to become the commercial metropolis of New England, — mementos of a blighted hope, which give the pathetic suggestion of a wonderful city of Might-Have-Been; idiosyncratic architecture in the angular two-big-one-little storied houses with depressed pyramid roofs, built by the opulent East India merchants, — these things still give to the old town a character and an atmosphere not found elsewhere in America.

Nathaniel Hawthorne, more fully than any other, has interpreted his weird native city of Salem. A strange humor prompted him to speak of its "flat unvaried surface, chiefly covered with wooden houses, few or none of which pretend to architectural beauty;" of "its irregularity, which is neither picturesque nor quaint, but only tame;" of its "long and lazy street, lounging wearisomely through the whole extent of the peninsula." Such being in his eyes the visible features of his native town, he declared he felt for it no more sentimental attachment than he could feel toward a disarranged checker-board. His mother-city might indeed be wanting in figure and fashion; but ought her son therefore to compare her to a washer-woman in her suds? Poor, solitary Hawthorne! It is not strange Salem did not love her taunting son. Nevertheless, the author of "The Scarlet Letter" and "The House of the Seven Gables" had open eyes to see and graphic words to picture the Salem of the past. The former city, the city within the city, was not, under the enchantment of distance, wanting to him in picturesqueness or quaintness, and it was far from being tame. If he could only have seen with as kindly eyes the Salem of his day, he might have found it also attractive. He was artistically far-sighted; he could not rightly focus his æsthetic vision on the Salem in which he lived.

Hawthorne, we remember, born in 1804, was passing through his shy, sensitive adolescence during the two years and four months Hosea Ballou lived in Salem. We do not know that he ever saw the popular Universalist preacher, or indeed could have seen the real man, had his eyes been turned on him, more than he could see the real Salem. Hawthorne was in spirit a dreary sort of literary Calvinist. Generations of his ancestors, the "Hathornes," were believers in Calvin's gloomy fatalism; Nathaniel was prompted by the artistic instinct to add the becoming consonant to his name, and drop the unlovely theories of Calvinism from his faith. He disliked Calvinism as unbeautiful;

for the same reason he disliked the Quaker fashion in dress. He early became an optimistic latitudinarian; yet inherited melancholy was in him a constitutional tendency. He says of his ancestors, whose spirits he imagined still lingered in the atmosphere of Salem, "Let them scorn me as they will, strong traits of their nature have intertwined themselves with mine." America's greatest imaginative writer was thus not able entirely to escape from the heavy spiritual atmosphere into which he was born. Gloom pervaded his vision and limited his genius.

If he had given a pen-picture of Hosea Ballou, would it have been a correct picture? It would, without doubt, have been an accurate likeness of the man Hawthorne saw; but the picture would have been, as judged from our own standing-point, essentially untrue. With mild disdain he would have seen a man intensely in earnest in his religion. He would have had no good-speed for him in his assaults on the diabolism underlying the Pilgrim austerity and the witchcraft fanaticism; yet Hawthorne himself had cynical scorn of the entire old delusion. He was too fastidious, too much of a *dilettante*, to look with favor on a man natural in speech, and fluent, idiomatic, and popular, but not bookish, and far from classic. Not even in Mr. Ballou's country-pronounciation could he have found amusement; nothing would have seemed to him quaint in commonplace Salem. It marks the partialism of Hawthorne's vision, to recall that the Universalist Church of Salem, with its earnest, thoughtful, working people, cherishing a world-wide hope, had not even literary attraction for him. Had the heavy-hearted artist, with his peerless candor, been more broadly human, he would have seen in this heresy one of the most characteristic and prophetic movements of his generation.

Our esteem for Mr. Ballou is not lessened when we perceive how largely, as the biblical preacher of hope, he was incomprehensible to the shadowed man of letters.

Mr. Ballou's ministry in Salem was fulfilled during the business depression resulting from the war. The time was not favorable to religious interest; yet his preaching attracted widespread attention, and was tonical for the whole population. He withheld from the service of his cause no reserve of time or strength.

We shall find controversy still a necessary and important feature of his work.

He had not been long in Salem when a pamphlet against Universalism, written by Rev. John Kelly, of Hampstead, New Hampshire, appeared as a claimant for public attention. It was entitled "Solemn and Important Reasons against Becoming a Universalist." Quickly came Mr. Ballou into the field, with a reply entitled "The Divine Benevolence." This brought from Mr. Kelly a pamphlet which he designated as "Additional Reasons against Universalism; or, Divine Benevolence Vindicated in the Distribution of Future and Everlasting Rewards and Punishments." In a very short time Mr. Ballou was again in the field with a pamphlet designated by the title "Divine Benevolence further Vindicated." The effect of this discussion was a marked increase of believers in the Universalist faith. The discussion awakened an interest throughout New England. Mr. Ballou's championship of his cause was regarded by both friends and opponents as able and effective.

During his second year in Salem one of his neighbors, Rev. Brown Emerson, made a public attack on Universalism. He was met promptly by a pamphlet from Mr. Ballou. Mr. Emerson immediately subsided. He saw he could not help his cause in the public estimation by the controversy he had invited. He appeared to have but little solicitude for Mr. Ballou's safety in the "Great Day." He made an easy retreat, claiming no laurels. Discretion, with him, was better than valor.

The discussion, however, eclipsing all others of that period in present interest, is the one he held with Abner Kneeland on the Authenticity of Divine Revelation.

Mr. Kneeland subsequently became a noted sceptic. We will delay, and outline his varied career. He was ordained a Universalist preacher in Langdon, New Hampshire, in 1805; Mr. Ballou preached the ordination sermon and gave the symbolic right hand of fellowship. He was associated with Mr. Ballou in a missionary tour to western New York, and also in the preparation of the famous original hymn-book. He was not a successful missionary, and as a hymn-writer he was a more complete failure than Mr. Ballou. Of his one hundred and thirty-eight hymns, not one was sufficiently exceptional to the prevailing insipidity to warrant its preservation under the law of the survival of the fittest. He had, nevertheless, some attractive personal traits. He was singularly free from envy, and could be an enthusiastic friend. He was installed pastor of the Universalist Church in Charlestown,

Massachusetts, Sept. 5, 1811; Mr. Ballou came from Portsmouth to preach the sermon. He remained in Charlestown three years. In his correspondence with his parish relative to his retirement, he stated that his wife was in the millinery business in Salem, and needed his assistance; he was inclined, unless his people objected, to withdraw from the ministry and become the business assistant of his wife. The parish was willing he should go or stay, but not willing he should stay unless he gave a larger share of his time to his ministry, and less to Salem, than he had for some months chosen to give. With good-nature he took up his residence in Salem. Whatever he was as a sceptic, as a Christian he was not heroic. While a professed believer, he preferred to be a milliner's assistant rather than a preacher of the gospel. He had a natural tendency toward materialistic views. While in Salem he became newly troubled with sceptical queries. He proposed to Mr. Ballou to discuss with him in a series of letters the credibility of the Bible. He proposed to assume the position of unbelief, and state his objections to Christian faith in as strong a manner as possible, while Mr. Ballou was to champion his own biblical faith. The correspondence was carried on during the greater portion of Mr. Ballou's ministry in Salem. At its conclusion Mr. Kneeland acknowledged himself convinced of the error of his assumed position, and of the truth of the biblical record.

We break the straight line of our narrative to continue our sketch of Mr. Kneeland's checkered career to its close.

In 1816, his wife's business having failed, he removed to Whitestown, New York, where he preached a portion of the time, and was remembered as a calm, gentlemanly preacher of dry metaphysical discourses. Thence he went to Philadelphia, as pastor of the First Universalist Society in that city; thence he removed to New York City. He was now becoming reputed as having sceptical tendencies. The Kennebec Association in Maine, on the basis of reports it had heard in regard to his preaching, by an extraordinary action withdrew from him its fellowship. The Southern Universalist Association, of which he was a member, met in May, 1829, at Hartford, Connecticut. He appeared with the singular request that he be allowed to "suspend himself" until he could induce confidence that he was what he professed to be, "a real believer and defender of the Christian religion." The request, mainly through the influence of Mr. Ballou, was granted. In September following, however, Mr. Kneeland, in a paper entitled the "Free Inquirer," announced to the public that he "no longer believed in the existence of God, or in man's conscious existence in a future state." Mr. Ballou sent him a question-challenge, "What evidences necessary to prove God's existence can be added to those already furnished?" He deigned no reply. He came to Boston and gathered an audience of professed Freethinkers in the old Federal Street Theatre. He also commenced the publication of the "Investigator," which still continues a free lance against all faith. We have heard eye-witnesses describe those Federal Street Theatre meetings. Mr. Kneeland would read portions of the Old Testament, not designed for public reading in a non-Jewish assembly; he would dramatically cast the

Bible across the hall as a book not fit to be kept in decent company. In 1838 he was, for words published in his newspaper, indicted for obscenity and blasphemy; he was convicted, and sentenced to sixty days' imprisonment in the common jail. This arbitrary treatment helped his cause; his name, with many, became associated with the right of free thought. There is no warrant for denial, however, of the fact that he in his speech transgressed civility and decency. While he was in jail, Mr. Ballou visited him and gave him such cheer as was possible under the circumstances. He was a friend in his need. On his release he resumed his teaching, if teaching it may be called; but his prestige even among the vulgar was gone. He fell into penury, and in March, 1839, left Boston for Iowa, and soon after reaching that region died of bilious fever. Mr. Ballou persisted in thinking him more worthy of pity than of blame. He had a naturally unbalanced mind. At the time he was decrying all superstition and credulity, he was himself under lead of common fortune-tellers. We may freely concede to him sincerity; we may freely pity him as one who fell into self-torturing mistakes; we will further believe the unveiling of his spirit has brought his honest mistakes to their full correction.

From this long, this scout-report, in the march of our narrative, we return to summarize the discussion in Salem.

It is interesting to observe that Mr. Kneeland's assumption of the sceptical position for the sake of argument, was preliminary to his actual acceptance of sceptical opinions. He naturally remembered his own arguments longer than he remembered their refutation. It is to be hoped, for his own self-respect, that in undergoing his actual conversion to scepticism he argued against his former self with more effect than he in this correspondence reasoned against his neighbor. It is not improbable that if Mr. Ballou had been at hand when his opinions were once more in an unsettled state, he would have been again led back to the renewal of his early convictions.

Some extracts from Mr. Ballou will show his method of argument. He says: —

"You will duly consider that in disproving the religion of Jesus Christ, you disprove all religion. The choice is between the gospel and no religion at all. Let us have the worst of it. Show, from undoubted authority, that there never was such a man as Jesus; or show that he was a wicked impostor, and deservedly lost his life. Show, moreover, that there never were such men as the apostles of Jesus; or that they were likewise impostors, and properly suffered death for their wicked impiety. Give the particulars of Saul's madly forsaking the honorable connection in which he stood, for the sake of practising a fraud which gained him an immense income of suffering. But you say the apostles were not bad men. Very well. Yet how could good men tell so many things they knew not true, and suffer and even die in attestation of what they knew to be false? You cannot suppose honest men can bear testimony to falsehood under pretence of doing good, as this would destroy all testimony at once. Even your own could not be relied on, if you admitted this detestable principle."

It is a suggestive fact that Mr. Kneeland, in rejecting Christianity, rejected all religion. He maintained blank theoretical atheism.

Strongly does Mr. Ballou state the central historical

argument for the credibility of the New Testament record: —

"The proofs of which the gospel is susceptible, are in all respects equal to what they would have been in any other way within the reach of human conception. This is going to a great length, I confess; yet I am strongly inclined to this opinion. . . . No set of men ever lived in this world who could either have planned such a scheme as the gospel, or have invented such a chain of evidences for its support. If the single miracle of the resurrection be considered, the fact on which all the other facts of the gospel rest, it is confidently believed that no human invention could have conceived a system so well calculated to secure a knowledge and belief of the fact to all future generations, as that which was adopted by the divine economy. Had the whole of the Jewish nation, with their Gentile neighbors, together with the Roman authorities, all confessed Christianity, being fully convinced of the resurrection of Jesus, and had they inscribed all the miracles of the New Testament on monuments which should defy the hand of time to bring them to decay, it requires but a moment's reflection to see that all this would have vastly increased the difficulty now to prove that it was not all contrived by man's invention. Let us consider the unbelief of the Jews; the violent opposition of the ancient priesthood; its coalition with the Roman government against the gospel; the great jealousy which the acknowledged miracles had excited; the vigilance with which he was watched by his religious enemies; the careful scrutiny to discover fraud if possible in his miracles; and then add to these considerations tnat the miracles of Jesus were publicly performed, and of such a nature as to admit of the easiest possible detection if they had not been real; and finally, to disarm unbelief at once, consider that the ministry of the gospel was set up by the apostles on the bold declaration that God had raised the crucified Jesus from the dead, — a declaration which, if it had not been true, could have been easily refuted and rendered the derision of all people."

Rarely, if ever, has the historical argument for the central facts of Christianity been more clearly or justly stated. This is but a specimen of his statements which show him thoroughly familiar with the historical grounds of Christian faith. His thoroughness, exactness, and eloquence alike surprise us. When he comes to the testimony of human nature to Christianity he is buoyantly confident: —

"It is a soul-rejoicing fact, that of the precious things brought to light by the Sun of Righteousness, the hope of immortality is the most precious jewel. This makes everything valuable. Hence we may lay up our treasures where neither moth nor rust can corrupt, nor thieves break through and steal. Here will God's bright favor never grow dim, nor will our love and gratitude ever decay. Do you see that celestial form leaning on her anchor unmoved, while the raging waves of a restless sea dash against her feet? Do you observe her aspect firm, and her eyes turned toward heaven? It is Hope. And would you wish to cast her down, and dash her on the rocks of unyielding doubt? Go to the chamber of sickness, where life's waning embers can no longer warm the dying heart; there hear from cold and quivering lips this hope expressed, 'I long to be with Christ; I long to be at rest.' Would you blast this amaranthine flower of faith and joy? would you plant in its stead the nightshade of despair?"

Mr. Kneeland confessed himself unable to refute Mr. Ballou's arguments. He says: —

"Notwithstanding when I found that I could not help doubting, I have tried to reconcile myself to my doubts, and have sincerely and honestly tried to make myself believe that I was perfectly reconciled either way; yet the moment I begin to think about the certainty of immortality and eternal life, I am all on fire; I hardly know how to contain myself."

Before Mr. Ballou wrote the final epistle of the series, Mr. Kneeland had decided to re-enter the Christian ministry. This fact will show the bearing of his fraternal closing words: —

"To conclude; as you, my brother, have labored together with your fellow-servant to look into and examine these things which belong to the kingdom of righteousness, and as we have been favored with mutual satisfaction in these researches, may it please the Great Head of the Church still to hold us in his hand, still to engage us in his blessed cause, and render our mutual labors promotive of his grace among men. And however distant from each other it may best suit the Captain of our Salvation to place us, may it be his pleasure to continue our fellowship in the bonds of the gospel."

Mr. Ballou's steadfast affection for Mr. Kneeland after he had, by lapse of faith, become widely separated from him in opinion and purpose, his free proffer of sympathy and help to his forlorn old friend in prison, show us an aspect of our hero's nature we cannot too strongly admire. He was not a friend simply for a summer day.

During the last year of Mr. Ballou in Salem, it became apparent that he was destined to a ministry in Boston. Certain influential Universalists in that city had set about building a commodious church on School Street; the index-finger of all concurrent events pointed to Mr. Ballou as the coming metropolitan pastor. After Mr. Murray's death, Sept. 3, 1815, there was no one to dispute with Mr. Ballou the first place in the esteem and confidence of the Universalist Church. More even than Mr. Murray he was the doctrinal founder of the denomination. In the nature of things the strongest man would be called to the place of largest influence.

His ministry in Salem left a deep and lasting impression. Fifty years afterward there were those in that city who spoke with kindling eyes and trembling voices of the joy which came to them in their youth through his awakening and melting words.

XI.

SCHOOL STREET CHURCH.

PERIOD, 1818–1819. AGE, 47.

ON the first Sunday in January, 1818, Mr. Ballou began his ministry in Boston. Various circumstances conspired to make this an epochal event in the history of Universalism.

Forty-four years prior, John Murray was stoned while preaching in the old French Church, which stood on the site afterward occupied by the School Street Church. With the quick wit for which he was noted, Mr. Murray took in his hand the stone which had lodged in his pulpit, and said, "We confess the argument is solid and weighty, but it is neither scriptural nor convincing." Mr. Murray was loyal to his own vision, and fought a good fight; in honored old age, after years of feebleness, he was in 1815 summoned to his long home. In 1811 Rev. Edward Mitchell was settled as his colleague. Like Mr. Murray, he was a Rellyan, believing all mankind unconditionally share the expiatory sacrifice of the Savior; he was very intolerant of the Unitarian view. His ministry was for some reason not satisfactory, and at the end of a year it quietly ended. Rev. Paul Dean was his successor; and after Mr. Murray's death he was the sole pastor of the First Church for nine years. Some things in regard to Mr. Dean it is disagreeable to recall, yet essential to an understanding of the circumstances under which Mr. Ballou began his ministry in Boston. The pastor of the First Church was in many ways an estimable man. His preaching at this period was æsthetically pleasing, and offended as little as possible any one's prejudice. He trimmed close to the wind, and was willing to spread for whiffling breezes. Was he a Rellyan or a Unitarian at this period? He was neither decidedly. Such a passive ministry was at this formative period ill-timed. Orthodoxy was confident and arrogant. Mr. Dean's soft assaults were not worthy even its notice. He was snowballing a granite fort; those inside were scarcely interested to look over the parapet. It is to be feared also that Mr. Dean was a victim of his own jealousy. He expressed no word of approval when he saw the new church on School Street in process of erection. It is well attested that he endeavored to obstruct Mr. Ballou's coming to Boston. "The inevitable rivalry which will result," he said, "will be harmful to the First Church." Mr. Ballou replied: "If Providence should lead me to Boston, I will suffer nothing to be done to the injury of the First Church." Mr. Dean was still ill at ease. His trial was really not a slight one. He had once accompanied Mr. Ballou on a missionary tour, and knew his power of popular appeal. Mr. Ballou in a Boston pulpit would, he knew, be the point of attraction for all the Universalists of the city. Mr. Dean had been victorious in some trials of patience; but he could not now, if he tried his best, be a cheerful Tantalus. When the new church was dedicated, on the 16th of October, 1817, Mr. Dean sat in the pulpit, but resolutely declined to take any part in the services. He pleaded ill health, and no doubt his plea should be allowed. Mr. Ballou was not present, being absent in the country on a preaching tour. Mr. Dean's attitude toward the new church and the new neighbor was certainly not cordial.

Another fact is perhaps of more import. The new Universalism, as embodied in the "Treatise," had at this time secured no hearing in Boston. Mr. Murray, it is well known, had been decided and at times petulant against the new theology. His policy of exclusion was heartily espoused by Mr. Mitchell and was tacitly continued by Mr. Dean. What had the Universalists of Boston heard from their own pulpit? A scheme of doctrines embracing an Adamic fall, an angry Deity, a prepared inferno, a personal Satan, a deferred dramatic judgment-day, and universal redemption through the expiatory death of the second person in the Trinity. One can now see at a glance that such a system of Universalism is heavily mortgaged to Satanism. This was the only Universalism that had been preached in Boston. It is true Mr. Ballou, twenty years before, had preached ten Sundays in Mr. Murray's pulpit; but it was under circumstances precluding the free expression of his peculiar personal convictions; and it is doubtful if he had then entirely formulated his own system. So it was that, while the "Treatise" Universalism found instant acceptance by the denomination elsewhere, Boston remained the Gibraltar of Rellyism.

There were intelligent Universalists in Boston who were not satisfied with this state of things. They determined to break the policy of inertia which had so long prevailed. With the spirit of reformers they brought the author of the "Treatise" to the New England metropolis.

Another matter needs to be understood as having an important bearing on Mr. Ballou's advent in Boston. In 1812 there appeared in Belsham's "Life of Lindsey," a Unitarian preacher of London, letters from several clergymen of Boston, which revealed the fact that there were a number of prominent Congregationalist ministers in secret protest against the Athanasian doctrine of the Trinity. Three years afterward, at the close of the war with England, this "Life of Lindsey" fell into the hands of the editor of the "Panoplist," a Boston Congregationalist newspaper, and a division of the Congregationalist sect was an immediate effect. Several Congregationalist churches, discovering that they had Unitarian pastors, promptly voted themselves Unitarian. The controversy between the two divisions of Congregationalism was hot and bitter. It is to be particularly noted that during the first three years of the Unitarian discussion in Boston the Universalists stood with the Trinitarians. The Unitarians and Universalists were thus hindered from coming to an early understanding of their need of each other. When Mr. Ballou arrived in Boston the Unitarians had lost their first zeal, and were anxious to prove themselves "Orthodox" on all points save the Trinity. It was during this reactionary period of Unitarianism that Mr. Ballou saw in it so much to condemn. That these two bodies, with so many interests in common, were thus started on opposite roads is a matter for regret. That Mr. Ballou should find Calvinism behind Unitarian intrenchments is now one of the curiosities of history.

Such were the circumstances attending Mr. Ballou's arrival in Boston. There was no cordial welcome for him seemingly, anywhere, save among his own people. There was a bit of jealousy at the First Church, a bit of haughtiness among the Unitarians; there was profound unconcern among the dominant so-called orthodox.

But to Boston Mr. Ballou has at last come. Some "common people" are prepared to hear him gladly. We may be sure of one thing, — the spell of the timid policy will be quickly broken; there will now be plain speaking and fair fighting. The new Universalism will be brought boldly to the front.

He was installed Dec. 25, 1817. It is suggestive of a conciliatory spirit in Mr. Ballou that by his request Mr. Dean preached the sermon and proffered the fellowship of the churches in the installation services. The installing prayer and charge were given by Rev. Edward Turner.

The commotion produced by Mr. Ballou's first Sunday's preaching yet lives as a tradition. He was in the full maturity of his powers. Wherever the magical finger of Fame points, human eyes must follow; and Fame had made some overtures toward this man from the hills. It is true, Boston blue blood received no quickening from him; yet it cannot be questioned that he touched the best life of Boston. His vigorous health, his dignified and striking person, his strong and flexible voice, — powerful in emphasis, melting in appeal, — his mild blue eyes, which sparkled in moments of humor and flashed as with heat-lightning in moods of moral indignation; his self-command in the pulpit and freedom from manuscript; his simple yet irresistible reasoning; his pictorial illustrations; his entire self-absorption in his themes, — these things were noted as his recommendations by the people on the first Sunday of his ministry in Boston.

From that day the popular Sunday tide was turned toward his church. His sayings were repeated; his adroit witticisms were kept on their errands for weeks among the people; his reasonableness and fearlessness were generally conceded by those who had once heard him in the pulpit.

In order to accommodate the throngs which desired to hear him, he usually preached three times each Sunday. The seats of the church would be filled in the forenoon; the aisles would be filled in the afternoon; in the evening, the doors, stairs, windows, and pulpit-steps would be crowded to the last inch of room. These immense congregations were completely under the preacher's control. Smiles and tears, joy at the discovery of some new aspect of the gospel, sympathy for mankind in the light of the Divine Fatherhood, gratitude for a faith answering to the soul's deep need, — these sentiments, like clouds in still water, were pictured in the face of the congregation when under the rapt preacher's sway.

The evening sermon of his first Sunday has fortunately been preserved. Mr. Henry Bowen, a young printer, with a heart to serve his faith and an eye for business, prevailed on Mr. Ballou to write it out for publication; and this, by the way, was the beginning of an enterprise which was the agency afterward of conveying many of Mr. Ballou's sermons to the larger public. The text of this first published discourse must itself have been an astonishment to those who had a suspicion that Universalism could be believed only by refusing to note certain passages in the Bible. "And to you, who are troubled, rest with us, when the Lord Jesus shall be revealed from heaven with his mighty angels, in flaming fire taking vengeance on them that know not God, and that obey not the gospel of our Lord Jesus Christ, who shall be punished with everlasting destruction from the presence of the Lord, and from the glory of his power" (2 Thess. i. 7–9). "When," asked the preacher, "is the event here described to come to pass?" He turned to Matthew xvi. 27, and read: "The Son of Man shall come in the glory of his Father with his angels; then shall he reward every man according to his works." "Clearly, this is the coming to which the text refers. When was it to occur? The Savior does not leave it to conjecture: 'Verily I say unto you, there be some standing here, which shall not taste death till they see the Son of Man coming in his kingdom'" (Matt. xvi. 28). Other Scriptural proofs were adduced to prove that the revelation of the Lord Jesus from heaven, with his mighty angels, to take vengeance on unbelievers, was an event of the past. "What is to be avenged? Unbelief. Why will vengeance be taken on unbelievers? That they may be taught to know God, whom to know is life eternal. It is the vengeance of love. It is a flaming fire from heaven; but the Lord Jesus and his mighty angels are in it, therefore it is heavenly. Fire is purifying. Vengeance, in God, means purifying punishment, according to the Psalmist's teaching: 'Thou wast a God that forgavest them, though thou tookest vengeance of their inventions.'" On this line the merciful meaning of the text was

THE OLD SCHOOL-STREET CHURCH.

made to appear. The vengeance of God must be harmonious with the character of God. The preacher's moral appeal against the prevailing interpretation is characteristic. We give a passage: —

"The kind of divine vengeance we have been usually taught to contemplate, is consistent with nothing but the worst and wickedest of human passions. One would be led to believe, on seeing the tragical scene of horror generally represented as the fulfilment of the text, that some powerful angel from the imaginary regions of darkness was let loose on mankind! Who would suppose it to be that humble, meek, kind son of Mary, of whom we have an account in the New Testament? Will Jesus, who opened the eyes of the blind, who opened the ears of the deaf, who caused the lame man to leap as an hart, the tongue of the dumb to sing, who raised the dead, cast out devils, and cured all manner of diseases among the people of a wicked age and nation, ever appear in our world as a destroyer of human beings? Will that blessed, that adorable Son of God, whose name is music in heaven and consolation to every believer, who gave himself a ransom for all mankind, and prayed for his murderers on the cross, who taketh away the sin of the world, ever come with hostile intentions against the redeemed, and fulfil all the vain imaginations of superstition by scattering firebrands of vindictive wrath and eternal death among the offspring of his Father?"

The effect of such preaching was electric. Nothing like this had the Universalists of Boston previously heard. Their preachers had dealt in the stock Orthodox phrases. They were accustomed to hear of the literal ignoble anger and vengeance of the Infinite Father, and of his pacification by the Son. Here was fundamental denial of the whole scheme.

There was immediate quickening of the Universalist

pulse in the city. Hope was revived and courage strengthened. Those who, profiting by such words of instruction, were received into the household of faith, counted it joy to give themselves to a cause so inspiring.

Meanwhile Mr. Dean, at the First Church, was grieved and hurt. He was instinctively a gentleman, and was not without noble impulses, but he was human. He has been severely blamed by many who would probably in his place have been far more fretted. That he did not, for instance, possess such a spirit of self-abnegation as Nathaniel Stacy, who was eager to yield his own established missionary circuit in the Mohawk Valley to Mr. Ballou, and find a new one for himself, if thereby he could bring the stirring preacher to New York,—that Mr. Dean was instead thoughtful especially of himself and the First Church, is, to say the least, so like human nature, as the most of us know by very particular acquaintance, that we would cover the shortcoming or failure with the mantle of charity. The matter would find no mention in these pages save for its relation to some important subsequent happenings.

Mr. Ballou's Boston ministry, as we have seen, was begun with a vigor to match the first Napoleon's. He summoned all his forces to the front, and made no provision for retreat. School Street Church at once became the representative battle-ground, not only for the Universalists of Boston, but of all New England. It focussed the Universalist cause.

"Sixteen Universalist societies, twelve Universalist preachers,"—such was the meagre numerical record of the cause in Massachusetts when Mr. Ballou came to Boston. He lived to see the number increased to more than a hundred preachers, and a larger number of societies.

He was in School Street Church a tower of strength for the Universalist cause, and a leader and defender of the people.

XII.

A VIGILANT WATCHMAN.

PERIOD, 1818–1852. AGE, 47–81.

THE symbol is not strained in the least when Hosea Ballou in School Street Church is called a tower of strength for the Universalist cause.

We have read in some book of ancient warfare, of the Martello Tower, a high, circular stone building, with a single catapult or cannon on the summit, mounted on a traversing platform, to be quickly turned in any direction. Mr. Ballou in the School Street pulpit was like a watchman on a Martello Tower. When he mounted guard, a new security was felt by the Universalists of Boston. His words of reassurance were more tonical than the Boston Bay breezes on an August afternoon. The people had confidence in his vigilance and in the integrity of his judgment. Universalists became aggressively in earnest; they no longer felt themselves casting unheeded snowballs at an intrenched enemy. They knew the eagle-eyed watchman on the tower would keep a faithful lookout for all assailants.

And soon assaults came.

Rev. Timothy Merritt was one of the Methodist preachers in Boston. He was the first volunteer against the new disturber of Orthodox complacency. He issued a pamphlet entitled "Strictures on Mr.

Ballou's Sermon delivered at the Second Universalist Meeting-house in Boston on the Evening of the First Sabbath in January, 1818." We concede to Mr. Merritt credit for zeal, and appreciate his desperate endeavor to be witty. But his lame argument — lame even then with old age — we can scarcely regard as worthy of reproduction. He maintained that the Scriptures prophesy a literal end of the material world as preliminary to a day of judgment; and he based his proposition mainly on passages the revisers have since cleared of all appearance of such meaning as was then ascribed to them. Mr. Ballou was soon face to face with the new assailant. We assume he preached a sermon or two on the theme; the sermon was his cannon on a traversing platform, to be fired in any direction where there was need. He also made a sortie with a pamphlet entitled "A Brief Reply to the Strictures." It was an opportunity to explain to such as would use their eyes the meaning of the scriptural phrases "judgment," "that day," and "end of the world." The work was done with civility and faithfulness. Mr. Merritt was not satisfied; he was soon again before the public with a pamphlet entitled "A Vindication of the Common Opinion relative to the Last Judgment and the End of the World, — in Answer to Mr. Ballou's Reply." It seems he hoped now to end the controversy; but while there was little in his pamphlet to require answer, his opponent was not one voluntarily to retire from a discussion while it could be made a means of enlightenment to honest inquirers. Mr. Ballou followed quickly with a "Brief Reply;" the brevity admitting of an exhaustive treatment extending through forty closely-printed octavo pages. As a specimen of Mr. Ballou's reasoning against the doctrine of endless punishment, we extract as follows:

"If such a tremendous punishment is to be inflicted on some to prevent others from sinning in this world, why should the whole affair be kept out of sight? The King of Babylon once had a furnace in which to burn those who would not worship the image which he had set up; and he had it where the people could see it. This was remarkably effectual, for we have no account of more than three who were not terrified into submission. If there be in reality such dreadful torments in another state for crimes committed in this world, it seems reasonable to conclude that they are kept out of sight of mortals lest they should have the effect on them to prevent their committing those sins for which it is just to punish them in this unmerciful manner. If this be the scheme, it is not agreeable to it to persuade people to do well. . . . As we cannot find the necessity of this doctrine of punishing people in another state to prevent wickedness here, we will endeavor to look for its necessity in the state where it is supposed to exist: and as our preachers are constantly calling our attention to this awful subject, we will approach it now in good earnest. Well, then, suppose the time is come. This material world is burned up. Eternity commences. The righteous are received into heaven, and the wicked are sent to hell. What are those poor miserable wretches in hell to be tormented unmercifully and eternally for? Answer: as a warning to others, and for the security of the divine government. Here the absurdity of the whole scheme stares us in the face. What! must the blessed in heaven be terrified with the torments of hell to keep them from committing sin? Must the righteous husband see his sinful companion, with whom he lived in this world in love and peace, in the torments of hell forever in order to keep him from becoming a sinner in immortal glory? Must the righteous wife see her sinful husband, with whom she lived in this world in harmony and love, and raised a family of children, some for heaven and some for hell, in this horrible torment, in order to prevent her from apostatizing from glory? Will it be necessary in heaven for parents to see their own offspring in the burning lake, in order to make them love God? And must children there, in immortal bliss, see their parents in hell, in order to inspire them with the true spirit of devotion to the God of mercy? Will all this unspeakable horror be necessary to heighten the hallelujahs which surround the throne of God and the Lamb? Is this the message proclaimed by the angels to the shepherds, — 'Fear not, for behold I bring you good tidings of great joy, which shall be unto all people'?"

Mr. Ballou maintained that the power of the gospel is not in such fears, conjured by the imagination, but in the attractions of the Father, and the moral efficacy of love. "The goodness of God leadeth to repentance." As a confession of his positive regenerating faith, these words, with which he closes the controversy with Mr. Merritt, are worthy earnest attention: —

"Before the majesty of Love the writer of these sheets prostrates himself, and to it yields himself a willing captive. Yes, and he avails himself of this opportunity of testifying to the public, and particularly to his opponent, that this Love is all his confidence. He knows no law, no gospel, no savior, no justice, no holiness, no truth, no life eternal, no solid peace, no substantial enjoyment, but this same Love. If the doctrine of universal, unchangeable mercy cannot be supported by Love, it falls to the ground; but if Love Divine lies at the bottom of this doctrine, the more it is examined, the more it is opposed, the more it is persecuted, the more it will manifest its immovable foundation."

Here the discussion closed. During its progress the Universalist cause and not the Methodist gained converts. This was not what Rev. Timothy Merritt desired. He retired to silence with his withered laurels.

Our Martello-tower watchman is not long, however, in discovering another assailant worthy a sermon and a pamphlet. He never disdains a challenge of Calvinism, the Goliath of his youth. Calvinism in 1818, we must remember, was, if wounded, yet alive; it scarcely dreamed the hurts it had received were fatal. Mr. Ballou thought it not amiss to sling another pebble or two into its exposed forehead.

Dr. Nathaniel Emmons, of Franklin, Massachusetts, published a book of sermons; one of the sermons was on the text referring to Pharaoh (Ex. ix. 16): "In very deed, for this cause have I raised thee up." According to Dr. Emmons, God raised up Pharaoh on purpose endlessly to torment him, and God is to be justified in the act. This was made as plain by the tender-hearted doctor as De Quincey makes it plain that murder is one of the fine arts. The beautiful doctrine of reprobation was valiantly defended by Dr. Emmons, who, it is suggestive to remember, was one of the new-school Calvinists of his day. Let us observe how fairly and justly Mr. Ballou describes the dear old doctrine: —

"Why did Pharaoh oppress the children of Israel? Answer: for the promotion of his own worldly glory. Would he have been thus cruel if he had not believed that he should promote his own interest by it? No. Why does God exercise his unmerciful vengeance on his creatures? Hear the Doctor's answer: 'God made Pharaoh for himself, as well as for the day of evil; and he would not have made him for the day of evil, had it not been necessary in order to declare his own glory. God has the same end to answer by bringing all the non-elect into existence. He intends they shall be the means of displaying his own glory, both in time and in eternity.' Now, let the mind be free from all prejudice and superstition, and let it answer the following question: Which would you choose to be, Pharaoh's bondman, or God's non-elect in hell? There is no doubt the Doctor would choose to be Pharaoh's bondman. And if so, it is a fact, whether he will own it or not, that he has a better opinion of Pharaoh than he has of God!"

Another passage from Mr. Ballou's pamphlet describing a different phase of the dying Satanism, so long miscalled Christianity, is worthy attention: —

"We may now notice what the Doctor says concerning the blessed in heaven. The following are his words: 'It is absolutely necessary to approve of the doctrine of reprobation in order to be saved. None can be admitted to heaven who are not prepared to join in the employments as well as the enjoyments of the heavenly world; and we know that one part of the business of the blessed is to celebrate the doctrine of reprobation. While the decree of reprobation is eternally executing on the vessels of wrath, the smoke of their torments will be eternally ascending in the view of the vessels of mercy, who, instead of taking the part of those miserable objects, will say, Amen! Alleluia! Praise ye the Lord.' This he calls a 'touchstone,' by which we must stand or fall. All who have not a heart which perfectly accords with this eternal reprobation 'must be excluded from the abodes of the blessed, and sink speechless into the bottomless pit of despair.' With these sweet words the reverend Doctor closes his sermon, — a sermon which will serve as a monument of human weakness and beggarly superstition when its author, as we confidently hope, will rest in the arms of that merciful God whom he has so misrepresented. The preacher makes our cordial willingness that our fellow-creatures should be eternally reprobated to endless torments an indispensable condition of salvation. All men who are not willing their dearest connections in life should be endlessly miserable, must be made so themselves! This sentiment is too absurd to need any argument to refute it. Did our blessed Savior preach in this way? Did he who gave himself a ransom for all men, who prayed for his enemies, and who teaches us to pray for our enemies, ever inform us that we must be eternally miserable if we are not willing others should be so? O Jesus, to whom shall we go? Thou hast the words of everlasting life."

A Universalist seminary now stands on the old Emmons estate at Franklin. The theology Dr. Emmons bequeathed to posterity has suffered a similar transformation. We will hope with Mr. Ballou that the Divine Mercy has, in the world where he now is, pardoned the "human weakness and beggarly superstition" of the doctrines he taught while on earth.

Who next, and where?

Of all the challenges and bouts, the defensive strategies and sharp thrusts, with "the sword of the Spirit, which is the Word of God," we cannot give full account. Of the inquirers answered, the opponents met in conflict, the supercilious critics punctured with keen-edged wit, we cannot attempt even an inventory. We confess our inability to understand how physical human nature could endure such a strain as Mr. Ballou put upon himself during those early years of his Boston ministry. Three sermons in the crowded church on Sunday; occasional journeys into the country, to give the encouragement of his presence and inspiring words to scattered believers; frequent lectures nearer home on week-day evenings; a faithful ministry as pastor to the sick and bereaved,—this was work to exhaust a man's strength. Yet he had strength and zeal for large additional labors. We shall hereafter speak of his editorial cares. Here we observe that he was rarely without a controversy on his hands. At scarcely any time during his mature years, indeed, do we find him not engaged in an exacting doctrinal discussion. Twenty-six "Lecture Sermons," preached on alternate Sunday evenings during a year, and generally prepared in answer to inquiries for clear thought and consistent doctrine, were published separately; when completed they made a volume of sermons which became famous. The life Mr. Ballou lived in these days is wonderful for its fulness. He was a cheerful man, else he could not have been such an intense and untiring worker.

One discussion in which he was engaged during his first year in Boston we shall carefully study in a chapter by itself. We refer to his controversy with Rev. Edward Turner on future punishment. The effect of this discussion on Mr. Ballou's own faith must also be described.

It is to be regretted, but under the circumstances it was inevitable, that Mr. Ballou should come into collision with the Unitarians. When a Unitarian newspaper, "The Kaleidoscope," was started in the professed interest of "rational and liberal Christianity, as distinguished from Roman Catholicism, Calvinism, Hopkinsianism, *Universalism*, and Deism," Mr. Ballou did not feel complimented to have his cause so classified. It occurred to him to say as much. When the editor of "The Kaleidoscope" pressed him to avow his position on future punishment, saying, "If not inconsistent with your views and feelings, we respectfully request you to inform us and the public on this point," he parried the proffer with some stinging home-thrusts. "'If not inconsistent with *my* views and feelings!' as if any but Unitarians could hold opinions in private not to be confessed in public!" When the Unitarian, Dr. Ware, in reply to a charge of Dr. Leod that the Unitarians were tending to Universalism, declared, "The doctrine of a tremendous retribution, inconceivable, indescribable, awaiting the wicked in a future world, is a part of our creed and of our preaching," Mr. Ballou was moved to observe that "after all the heart-chilling and soul-appalling horrors actually described by Calvinistic preachers, the Unitarians declare their dissent because the future punishment in which they believe exceeds the power of conception and defies all description!" He did not therefore, he says, court Unitarian fellowship for Universalists; quite the contrary. "Universalists," he said, "can never consent to show fellowship with hypocrisy."

Yet Hosea Ballou was a Unitarian.

When Sylvester Graham came to Boston in 1837, preaching the superiority of a vegetable diet, he was mobbed in Amory Hall. One would naturally expect to find butchers the persecuting rabble. It was, however, a "bakers' rising." If Mr. Graham had simply recommended patronage of bakers instead of butchers, he might have been the recipient of loaves in abundance; but he recommended coarse, home-made bread, and he was rewarded by the generous bakers with decayed eggs and brickbats. A little difference is sometimes equivalent to much.

Hosea Ballou was a Unitarian. He had, by his unaided teaching, brought his entire denomination to the Unitarian standard. One would think this should entitle him, when he came to Boston, to Unitarian favor. Because, however, he was something more than a Unitarian of those days, he was held in contempt.

Time nevertheless has brought correction. Bakers now make and sell "Graham bread," and Unitarians as a body confess the Universalist hope.

That Martello-tower watchman is still profoundly remembered in the city of the Mathers. His thirty-five years of ministry in Boston justified its early promise. "To the hero the hour is great when he mounts guard." Mr. Ballou made the hour epochal when he came to Boston in championship of the cause he held dearer than his life.

XIII.

A DISCUSSION AND ITS SEQUENCES.

PERIOD, 1817–1818. AGE, 46–47.

WHEN in 1817, before he had left Salem, Hosea Ballou sent a fraternal challenge to Rev. Edward Turner, of Charlestown, to discuss with him the question "whether the doctrine of future punishment is taught in the Scriptures," we surmise he little imagined the inter-denominational strife which would be thereby initiated. It is not the first instance that a fire, the fuel being susceptible, has been kindled from a spark.

Rev. Jacob Wood, of Haverhill, was the immediate instigator of the discussion. It has been intimated that as a go-between he, without exact facts to warrant, told each respectively that the other was very desirous of the controversy. Mr. Wood afterward figured prominently in the Restorationist secession.

Mr. Ballou had a natural fondness for debate; but why, when he had at least one other discussion on his hands, he should propose this new one, is an unsolved puzzle. "The human mind," he said in his friendly summons, "never becomes acquainted with its own resources until opposition and difficulties call them into action." We have heard a somewhat similar observation in a young men's debating society; but why two mature men, greatly burdened with cares, should wish to engage in such a method of self-culture is not clear.

"At first thought," he further continues, "it might seem that the two who are to conduct the discussion should be of opposite sentiments on the subject argued." A very natural first thought! Men do not often argue, with self-satisfaction at least, unless their arguments accord with their convictions. Attorneys, it is true, sometimes pretend to opinions; this is expected in the legal profession, but religious questions are not, as a rule, discussed save on a basis of sincerity. "On more mature consideration, however," he adds, "a thought suggests itself, — that the inquiry will be more likely to be kept free from injudicious zeal if the parties are of the same opinion, than if they were of opposite sentiments." No doubt; if there be no real disagreement, there can be little temptation for the disputants to present other than the good and pleasant sight of brethren dwelling together in unity.

These brethren, be it understood, were at this time fellow-believers in the doctrine of limited future punishment. Nearly twenty years before, Mr. Ballou, in his discussion with Rev. Joel Foster, had temporarily assumed unbelief in any future punishment, but at the close of the discussion confessed faith "in a future state of discipline in which the impenitent will be miserable." Some years afterward he discarded the doctrine of "penal sufferings," which we interpret as meaning penalties arbitrarily inflicted, the fulfilment of which God will accept in the stead of obedience. He believed that punishment is corrective; that when it has wrought its object of correction it will cease. Obedience, not suffering, he said, God exacts from his children. On this theory he could believe in future punishment only as the result of actual sinning in the future world. Yet he regarded certain passages of Scripture, notably Peter's obscure statement in regard to Christ preaching to spirits in prison, as teaching that there will be future sinning and suffering. While there may have been, therefore, incipient tendencies in his thought toward his subsequent diverse views, he was, as he confessed, now in substantial agreement with his brother Turner, and with Universalist clergymen in general, in believing that punishment of sin will extend into the spiritual realm. It certainly shows him not deeply prejudiced one way or the other, that he could make this proffer to Mr. Turner (we quote his exact words): "You have the privilege of choosing the side of the question that you would prefer to vindicate, and move as directly to the merits of the argument as you think proper, and leave the other to be vindicated by me."

The discussion which ensued — Mr. Turner accepting the challenge and choosing to "vindicate future punishment" — is extant in the "Gospel Visitant." It is unique reading; but as a discussion of the complex question involved, we must be allowed to think it crude and inadequate. Mr. Turner is chary, diffuse, in many of his sentences obscure; and Mr. Ballou is in the first part exceedingly unlike himself. It is said of Abraham Lincoln, that when as a lawyer he had before a jury a case not in accordance with his sense of justice, he was limp as a water-soaked reed. It is not to Mr. Ballou's discredit that in this respect he exhibits some likeness to Mr. Lincoln.

Nevertheless, these letters are important, in Mr. Ballou's life-story, as a turning-point in his faith. "While attending to this correspondence," he wrote to Thomas Whittemore in 1829, "I became entirely satisfied that the Scriptures begin and end the history of sin in flesh and blood, and that beyond this mortal existence the Bible teaches no other sentient state than that which is called by the blessed name of life and immortality."

Scanning these fourteen epistles, we find in the verbiage some threads of argument. Mr. Turner proposes this for a test-question: "Does death necessarily produce such a moral change in the mind of the sinner as to make him at once a willing, obedient, happy subject of the moral kingdom?" Mr. Ballou, in reply, is not willing to accept the question in a form conceding such power to death; affirming that "at the dissolution of the natural corruptible body the Savior of sinners, who has conquered death and him who had the power of death, may do what death could not effect, and clothe the subject of his grace in his right mind, as he did the man among the tombs." Here this thread is dropped. Mr. Turner takes up another, affirming that as one may suffer for sins committed a year before, there may be by the same law of memory painful consequences of sin carried forward into the future life. Mr. Ballou replies: "That the powers of man can remain for a year without temptation, without being led into sin, and without being liable to be led into sin, and yet suffer for sins committed before this period, surely needs some evidence." Mr. Turner responds with the statement that the brethren of Joseph painfully remembered their sin of years before, and their regret was apparently not occasioned by sins afterward committed; Paul also had painful regret for his crime of persecution long after his experience of repentance, conversion, and divine forgiveness. Mr. Ballou affirms in reply that regret is not identical with guilt or punishment; also that the immortal state is such a complete deliverance from the limits of mortality that we are not justified in adhering very closely to the earthly analogy.

So the thread is sent back and forth, as in a shuttle on a loom, and the fabric of controversy is woven.

Mr. Turner is at length constrained to say: "That I have never had much claim to the character of a close investigator, and still less to that of a deep controvertist, are circumstances with which you are perfectly familiar." He is apologizing for the open secret that he is conducting his argument with worrisome feebleness. Mr. Ballou rejoins in these overgenerous words: "To me it is entirely inconceivable how an argument could be better managed than the one you have adduced to prove that the guilt and condemnation of sin not only may be but actually are protracted beyond the existence of the sin itself." We misjudge if we think him satirical. His esteem for his opponent's ability was unfeigned. He believed his argument had been skilfully conducted. He thought the argument, however, insufficient to support the doctrine of future punishment.

Mr. Turner, as a new thread, refers to the passage in 1 Peter iii. 18–20, where Christ is spoken of as once suffering for sins, the just for the unjust, that he might bring us to God, and went also and preached unto the spirits in prison, which were sometime disobedient.[1] Mr. Ballou is at once touched and aroused. He has in a previous issue of the "Gospel Visitant" expounded this intricate passage. He has maintained its obvious import to be that the people who were on earth in the days of Noah were in a prisoned condition in the invisible world at the time of the crucifixion of Christ, and that Jesus then went to preach to them the emancipating gospel. This is, of course, to assume the existence of sin and punishment in the spiritual state. He now sets resolutely about a review of his former exposition. He conceives the meaning may be that Christ in the power of his resurrection preached to imprisoned Gentile souls, — souls imprisoned in sin, prejudice, and ignorance. He finds prophecies of Christ's work in the earth as an opener of prison doors that the oppressed may go free. He becomes, without pretence, convinced that he has found the right clew to the perplexing passage. He is soon entirely certain of the correctness of his new rendering. His exposition is lengthy, full, yet concise; he is, as respects debating power, himself again; disagree as one may with his point of view, no one who candidly reads can deny that he has accomplished a remarkable work of exegesis in behalf of his cause.

[1] The passage reads: "For Christ also hath once suffered for sins, the just for the unjust, that he might bring us to God, being put to death in the flesh, but quickened by the spirit; by which also he went and preached unto the spirits in prison; which sometime were disobedient, when once the long-suffering of God waited in the days of Noah, while the ark was a preparing, wherein few, that is, eight souls, were saved by water."

This virtually ended the controversy. Mr. Turner made some objections; his tone assumed a quality of slight petulance. Mr. Ballou easily disposed of the objections offered; it is evident he now argued without assumption and in self-enjoyment. The correspondence abruptly closed with the cessation of the publication of the "Gospel Visitant." That the controversial laurels, whatever the merits of the cause, are to be conceded to Mr. Ballou, must be the voice of acclaim.

This summarizes the controversy so important in its sequences.

We indulge a query: What would have been the probable result if Mr. Turner had chosen to defend the no-future-punishment doctrine? "A man," says Sterne, "picks up an opinion as he picks up an apple; it becomes his own; if he is a man of spirit he would lose his life rather than give it up." Under stress of defence one easily exaggerates. "The cricket had been singing five minutes," said Dickens; "contradict me, and I 'll say ten." We have seen how Abner Kneeland, by assuming the position of a sceptic, was apparently helped into scepticism. We recall that Hosea Ballou in his youth, by assuming in his conversation with Elder Brown to be a Universalist, was helped into Universalism. It was only, we observe, on this question of future punishment that Mr. Ballou ever assumed, save incidentally and briefly, a position other than his own. It is of course no evidence that his conclusion is wrong, to see that he was led to its adoption under subtle laws governing human nature. It was a foregone conclusion in such a discussion, that, however the sides were chosen, Edward Turner would be vanquished. It is an interesting query how far, as respects denominational tendencies, Edward Turner held the decision of destiny in his hands when it was left to him to choose which side of the issue he would maintain.

We do not purpose to review at any length the old inter-denominational controversy. We have not space to give to this dead issue. The general discussion which followed is to be characterized, however, as not altogether free from "injudicious zeal," to repeat Mr. Ballou's phrase; it was often even partisan and violent. Paul Dean showed himself at his worst in this doctrinal warfare. Under his lead the discussion in 1831 resulted in actual schism; eight clergymen initiated the unfortunate, in fact almost still-born, Restorationist sect. But it is our privilege and duty to say that throughout this sharp controversy, as far as we learn of it in its published records, Mr. Ballou maintained a degree of personal dignity and judicial equanimity to which we must accord cordial admiration. On this point of doctrine we do not profess implicit agreement with him; but in our disagreement we would do him justice. Universalists are, and have been since the decline of Rellyism, in substantial unity in the acceptance of the "Ballou theology" as a system of doctrines; freedom of disagreement on the question of future discipline has never been more earnestly claimed than it was by Mr. Ballou cordially conceded.

What were Hosea Ballou's distinctive ideas on future punishment?

For many years, as we have seen, he assented to the doctrine. At first he held to the "penal code," that is, the arbitrary exaction of suffering as the substitute for obedience. Afterward he believed that sinful acts carry in themselves judgment and punishment; hence that punishment in the future world will depend on actual sinning in that world. He finally arrived at the opinion that there can be no sinning in the future life; hence that there will be no punishment. The movement of his thought, whether progressive or not, was orderly.

His doctrine has been grossly perverted, because some have failed to make distinctions which seem to us as visible as a church by daylight.

It has been asserted that he believed death to be in an absolute sense a moral savior. His saying that the biblical history of sin is confined to "flesh and blood," has been interpreted as a confession of faith that sin is in flesh and blood, and does not touch the soul. He plainly means by the phrase, however, only the earthly time-section of our lives. In 1833 Dr. Channing said the interpretation of his doctrine is: "Moral evil is to be buried in the grave." Mr. Ballou was not a little indignant that he was so interpreted. "It has the appearance," he said, "of a canting throw at what he is not disposed to treat with his usual candor." Again, Dr. Channing said Ballou-Universalists ascribe the "power to death of changing and purifying the mind." Mr. Ballou did not mean to be misunderstood in his reply: "He certainly never heard any of us state such views, nor has he ever read any such statement in any of our writings." It came to be a fashion with some to speak of his doctrine as "death-and-glory," implying that death is synonymous with glory. He at one time patiently explained that the phrase could no more describe his doctrine than any doctrine of blessed immortality. His doctrine was censoriously caricatured as "salvation by mud" and "salvation by rot." He withheld reply. Those who charged Christ with casting out demons by the prince of demons were far gone in perversity; having eyes they would not see. The keynote of Mr. Ballou's thought on this point — from which he, save inadvertently, neither flatted nor sharped to the last — is his refusal even to discuss whether death produces a saving moral change in the character of the sinner. "Never," he said to Dr. Channing, "did we ascribe the power of cleansing from sin to anything but that which the Scriptures mean by 'the blood of the Lamb.'"

Yet he undoubtedly ascribed an important agency to death. He said with Paul, "to die is gain." In his view death is cessation of bodily ills and the drawing away of the veil from the spiritual realm. As amusement seekers are impatient for the curtain to be drawn away from the theatre stage, that the scenic life may begin, so death may be longed for as "happy release" from the darkness of mortality and the unveiling of the glories of immortality. To say that death, according to this theory, is identical with the experience of the holiness and happiness of heaven, is as inaccurate as to say that the theatre play consists entirely in the withdrawing of the curtain. The withdrawing of the veil cast over all nations, that the hidden realities may be known, is of measureless importance; but it is not itself to be confounded with the moral power of the spiritual realities then revealed.

He believed the wages of sin is death; sin is moral

death in itself; its destiny is literally to die. He believed the good only is to live. From the bath of death the soul rises, washed of its sins, but possessed of all the good it has achieved. The present punishment of sin, instant in all sinful deeds, he held to be the practical and biblical doctrine of judgment.

He believed that the soul on arriving at immortality, with earthly and sinful desires all gone, will immediately behold such heavenly illumination as will cause a glad forgetfulness of the things behind, and a pressing forward toward the things before. This result of glorious salvation, however, he believed would be effected by no arbitrary means or interference with the individuality or free choice of the soul, but by the moral power of the Father's all-conquering love.

Such are outlines of Mr. Ballou's theory as regards future punishment. In his many discussions of the topic there are certain crude phrases which may bear a contrary construction on some points; but this, after a careful reading of all his writings which bear on the theme, seems to us fairly to outline his thought. "No man," he says, "can love heaven, or desire to be in it, any further than he loves righteousness." We interpret him as meaning to teach the same ethical theory as Tennyson: —

"The wages of sin is death; if the wages of Virtue be dust,
Would she have heart to endure for the life of the worm and the fly?
She desires no isles of the blest, no quiet seats of the just,
To rest in a golden grove, or to bask in a summer sky;
Give her the wages of going on, and not to die."

Important are Mr. Ballou's own words as interpreting his understanding of the ethical nature of his doctrine: —

"The Universalist who believes that this mortal state, in flesh and blood, is the only state of sin and misery, stands on the same principle as does his brother who believes there may be a future state of discipline, which will eventuate in bringing all sinners to a state of holiness and happiness. Neither difference respecting the time when the creature is to be made happy, nor the particular means by which this event is to be brought about, makes the least difference in principle. Two brothers, sons of the same father, may perfectly agree in their sentiments respecting their parent. They both believe he will not fail to give them all the instruction they need, that his discipline over them is designed for their benefit; and yet they may entertain different views respecting time and means. One may think that they are to be kept at school till they are eighteen, the other may be of the mind that they are to be continued under tutors and governors a year longer; yet both believe that their father knows best, and will order their concerns according to his own wisdom and goodness. He who believes that all sufferings end with this mortal state, and he who believes that they end at the expiration of any other period, differ only as it respects time, not as it respects principle; for both believe that all discipline is for the good of the punished."

XIV.

IN LABORS MANY.

A MARVEL of Hosea Ballou's life is its small indebtedness for idle words and vacant hours.

From 1818 onward, for more than thirty-four years, his figure was increasingly familiar on certain of the Boston streets. Tall, erect, gracefully cloaked, wearing a broad-brimmed silk hat, his eyes fixed on the ground, an air of abstraction about him, a look of intense thought in his face, and his lips moving in articulation of inaudible words, — he was pointed out to the unfamiliar beholder as he passed; and when once thus seen he was not soon forgotten. Some who met him, especially thoughtful boys, regarded him with an almost superstitious awe; he seemed conversing with invisible companions. A greeting by a neighbor or parishioner, however, or the sight of a child (children felt no shyness in his presence) would bring him to consciousness of the passing moment; a smile of recognition and the light of friendliness would come quickly into his face.

Such preoccupation was incident to the ardent mental state in which he lived.

He preached three discourses on Sunday (three being the rule) without manuscript, but not without abundant preparation. Such specimens of these sermons as have been preserved exhibit painstaking in every part. In strong grip of the main thoughts; in regard for proportion; in ease, simplicity, and fulness of expression; in illustrations which illustrate; in such mastery of the central theme as enables the preacher at moments to treat it with a playful yet dignified familiarity, — in such qualities as these, which enter into the effective popular sermon, his discourses are far above the ordinary. No student will doubt that every one of these discourses must have been the result of severe brain-work. He was gifted by Nature with rare facility in speech; but he did not abuse his gift. As often as he spoke he took good care to have something worth the saying. His heart was equally alive with his brain. Not one of these sermons but is impact with emotion. Had his life-aim been simply achievement of dialectic skill in artistic sermon-making, his success would have been evidence of an exceptional industry.

To his work as a preacher he early added the cares of editorship. He had always something of Luther's sagacious faith in printer's types as missionaries. From his coming to Boston he had aided Mr. Henry Bowen in the weekly publication of one of his sermons. This had been, owing to Mr. Ballou's popularity, of pecuniary profit to both publisher and author. After this order of things had been continued more than a year, Mr. Bowen conceived the project of turning a small struggling quarto sheet he was publishing, entitled the "Weekly Magazine and Ladies' Miscellany," into a Universalist newspaper. In pursuance of this project, on July 3, 1819, the first number of the "Universalist Magazine" appeared, "devoted to doctrine, religion, and morality," and "edited by the

Rev. Hosea Ballou." This was the first Universalist newspaper published in America; it could have had no predecessor in the world. Its only precursor as a stated Universalist publication was the "Gospel Visitant," which from June, 1811, during two years, was issued once in three months in Salem, then was suspended for five years; was revived in April, 1817, and continued till July, 1818, and was then finally suspended for want of remunerative patronage. Thirty-seven years after the first "Magazine" was issued, Rev. Thomas Whittemore, then the editor of the "Trumpet," which was a successor of the "Magazine," had the diminutive sheet before him. With his practical turn for facts, he measured the little four-page sheet, to find it "just twelve inches by nine and a half." He gave his reader various side-reminders of the newspaporial progress made in his day. For a less price than was asked for the "Magazine," his readers could have the privilege of reading the "Trumpet." The editorship of such a small journal as the "Magazine," however, before journalism had become a profession, was attended with anxiety, and was fulfilled only by persistent painstaking. In the editor's initial article he said: "If any are oppressed with sorrow that right views on the subject of religion would heal, they are invited to make known their sorrows through the medium of this sheet." What a family affair a religious newspaper was in those days! He also in his first editorial invited "members of different sects of Christians to present in this sheet their views, clothed in their most simple light and shining in their purest lustre." This sentence is the only "fine-writing" we discover in the editorial department of this first newspaper; it is curious it should itself be an invitation to aspiring fine-writers, who have since been an Egyptian plague to editors. But even on such a hospitable basis it was not easy to fill the little sheet with original matter. In our day the editorial problem is what to omit; then it was how to fill the meagre space. The editor's pen was of course in large requisition. The editor endeavored heroically to make a readable paper. There can be no question about his success. It reveals his own interpretation of his editorship, to find him confessing years afterward, in regard to his poor rhymes, that he wrote them to give variety to his newspaper. He must surely be accorded the credit of making a very valiant endeavor in his editing. We accord to Horace Greeley lasting renown as the founder of the "New York Tribune." The memory of Hosea Ballou has a somewhat similar claim on his successors, as the founder of the "Universalist Magazine." The "Magazine" became the "Trumpet;" the "Trumpet" became the "Universalist;" the "Universalist" became the existing "Christian Leader."

He remained sole editor of the "Magazine" two years. The paper was then for a year under impersonal editorship; at this period the Restorationist controversy became conspicuous in its columns. During this controversy we may be sure Mr. Ballou did not remain a silent spectator. In 1822 Mr. Ballou became again the chief editor, with Rev. Hosea 2d and Rev. Thomas Whittemore as assistants. From this time till his death Mr. Ballou was either editor, assistant editor, or contributor to the "Magazine" or its successor the "Trumpet." When Thomas Whittemore entered the newspaper field, it was in the nature of things that he should soon be accorded the chieftainship.

In July, 1830, the first number of the "Universalist Expositor" appeared, published in Boston by Marsh, Capen, & Lyon, 362 Washington St., and edited by Hosea Ballou and Hosea Ballou 2d. This publication, issued once in two months, was designed as the repository of labored essays and systematic disquisitions on doctrines, critical exegesis, and reviews of books of special interest to Universalists. It was intended to foster the spirit of inquiry and research among the Universalist clergymen and educated laymen, by bringing them into mutual intellectual acquaintance. Two years the publication was continued under the firm which originally issued it; then, the patronage not being deemed sufficient, it was suspended. On the following January, 1833, it was revived under the supervision of H. Ballou 2d, T. Whittemore, G. W. Bazin, and Wait & Dow. Mr. Ballou remained a contributor. This magazine is the predecessor of the "Universalist Quarterly." Mr. Ballou did not fail to do his full share of this more elaborate editorial work. His younger namesake, Hosea 2d, — Dr. Ballou, as he was in due time distinguished, — was, it must be conceded, without a peer among his brethren for scholarly attainments; his contributions to the "Expositor," and afterward to the "Quarterly" (of which he was editor), are not surpassed in Universalist literature, scarcely in any religious literature, for critical insight, grace of style, and spiritual wisdom. Yet the senior Ballou's more scholarly writings, as preserved to us in these volumes, are not unworthy the company in which we find them. Ruggedness, directness, common-sense, freedom, are their literary characteristics. He especially exhibits mastery, we may say even genius, as a biblical expositor. His culture did not, like that of his younger namesake, enable him freely to roam in various literatures and philosophies; but it was full, exact, luminous in the English text of the Scriptures. His articles — we recall particularly his "Criteria of True and False Preaching," his "Doctrine of Endless Punishment the Cause of Persecution," his "Orthodoxy Inimical to the Scriptures," his "Scripture Doctrine of Punishment" — exhibit a wonderful ability in implicitly following the lead of his adopted principle. In this respect we question whether Jonathan Edwards was his superior. He was as logical a believer in God's fatherhood as Edwards was in God's malignity. Ballou's peculiar genius as a theologian is seen in his evolution of underlying biblical principles.

Not yet do we by any means compass the measure of his labors. His preaching in his own pulpit and his editorial writing may well have taxed his power of endurance. But he was in addition the spontaneously-recognized, therefore divinely-commissioned bishop of the general Universalist Church. His commission was in his natural dower and his achieved graces. His paternal regard for the local churches, his unmatched awakening power in speech, invited innumerable labors of love. To an extent which causes us to wonder, he fulfilled the duties of his democratic and Christian bishopric. In his earlier days the novelty of Universalist ordinations, installations, and church dedications made such services attractive to the multitude. It was for years regarded an important incidental reward of Universalist endeavor in many a struggling parish, that Mr. Ballou would be willingly present to assist in dedicating the new church or consecrating the new minister. In an incomplete list we count thirty-one ordination sermons, thirty-four installation sermons, preached by him, and thirty-one services of church dedication in which he fulfilled leading assignments.

He also continued his preaching tours in the country-towns. Leaving an acceptable clergyman to preach to his people in Boston, he would answer the requests which came to him from a distance, and go forth as a missionary of a world-wide gospel. In such labor he exerted an influence beyond our power of measurement. At home, his average sermon was thirty-five minutes in length; in the country-places, alike on Sundays and week-day evenings, he preached, to answer the urgent demand, from one hour to two hours. His convincing force in argument, his persuasive power in appeal, were effective in the conversion of multitudes to his standard. It is a question whether any preacher before him in America was instrumental in a larger number of conversions by the agency of speech than he effected in his zealous and mighty ministry.

In the winter of 1821–22 he made an extended visit to the cities of New York and Philadelphia. In the latter city he preached the famous "Eleven Sermons," which, after being stenographically reported, were published as a book. The last sermon of this series, "A Feast of Knowledge," he preached in the room of the Washington Benevolent Society, known as the Grand

Saloon; his congregations on the preceding evenings having uncomfortably crowded the church. His congregation on this occasion numbered fully seven thousand people. It testifies to his ample physical reserve, that during his long sermon he was easily heard in the remote corners of the immense hall. For more than an hour he held the vast throng in a high state of rapture. This visit to the southward seaboard cities was in after years many times repeated. Several published volumes of sermons is one of the results. He was at different times urgently invited to remove permanently to New York. Inducement of pecuniary gain was held out to him. He could not, however, be persuaded to leave Boston. He compromised with the solicitous New York brethren by promising to make them a "professional visit" as often as was in his power.

We must also recall that during all these busy years he was in constant attendance on the annual Conventions, both State and General. This sometimes required a chaise-journey of weeks. For many years a Convention was regarded as sadly incomplete if he was not present to preach one of the sermons,—the sermon of the occasion, whoever might be the other preachers. And not more did his brethren esteem the privilege of seeing his notable presence, and hearing his wise and cheery words, than he esteemed the privilege of greeting those of like precious faith, and counselling them as to the interests of the common cause.

He was, by natural fitness, undoubted integrity, fidelity to his convictions, kindling zeal, the peerless bishop; and he magnified his bishopric more in its duties than in its honors. "We doubt," says Rev.

Otis A. Skinner, "whether in all the history of the Church, another instance can be found in which a minister has had so high rank in his sect, and manifested less desire to rule."

His son Maturin computes that his printed words, not including his newspaper contributions, if gathered, would make a series of one hundred volumes, each of four hundred duodecimo pages. He also estimates that during his ministry he preached, including his week-day evening discourses, not less than ten thousand sermons. These estimates must be approximately correct.

And meanwhile, we recall, he was not forgetful of his work in the specific parish relation. Of his ordinary pastoral attentions to persons in health we have only meagre reports. His employments were too absorbing to admit of a large degree of this social work. But as a pastor where the need was real, as a messenger of sympathy and helpfulness to those in sickness or bereavement, the reports are numerous. He always brought some beams of the dayspring from on high to those he visited under the shadow of death. He knew how to adapt his gospel to the actual need. There were times when he knew deeds would preach more of the Savior's gospel than any possible rhetoric. Dr. Whittemore gives an illustrative instance. Mr. Ballou was sent for to visit a sick man whose wife was a Baptist. She, seeing her husband in danger, sent for her minister, who came and prayed that the sufferer might be saved from the second death. The prayer did not avail for his comfort. He asked to see Mr. Ballou. The wife resisted; but the request for Mr. Ballou was repeated so urgently that she at last consented that he should be called. In a few hours he was by the side of the sick man; the wife at once left the room. He looked about and saw signs of destitution. He sat down and said: "Well, my friend, you are quite sick, and I am sorry to see you so low. Sometimes the sick suffer by not permitting themselves to make their wants known." The feeble man was constrained to say that the trouble in his mind was partly occasioned by an indebtedness of seventeen dollars to their landlord. "Well," said Mr. Ballou, "he will probably not harm you; do you not feel the need of any little matters of food that might strengthen you and do you good?" Mr. Ballou took a ten-dollar bill from his purse. "I thought you would need something," he said; "I have heard of your case from others. Take this, and let your wife purchase for you such nourishing delicacies as you need. Don't pay your rent with it; it is not enough for that, and the money is for your own private use; the rent we will talk about another time. Now, brother," continued Mr. Ballou, "we trust your case is not hopeless; you are indeed very sick, but possibly you may recover, with the blessing of God and the help of good nursing. Cast all your care upon the Lord. He is our Shepherd; he will not permit us to suffer more than is for our good; and though we walk through the valley of the shadow of death, we should fear no evil, for he is with us, his rod and his staff will comfort us." The sick man, quickened by a new hope, confessed that while he had not been wilfully perverse, he had been too unmindful of the blessings God had given him. "I have a dear son absent at sea," he said; "pray for us and for him, that he may return; then all will be well." Mr. Ballou offered prayer, commending the sick man, then his wife, and the absent son, to the kind care of God. The sufferer's "Amen" was expressed in audible sobbing, bringing relief to his pent heart. "I am unwilling to leave you alone," said Mr. Ballou, when about to retire. The sufferer intimated that his wife would return as soon as she heard him go downstairs; and thus he left. The sequel is not unnatural. The wife, on the recovery of her husband, had such a change come over her spirit, that she became a member of Mr. Ballou's church, and held him in fervent respect as long as she lived. And by her this story, so illustrative of the nature of Mr. Ballou's pastoral care, was given publicity.

So do we find him "redeeming the time." His genius as a theologian, his great success as a preacher, resulted from exceptional painstaking in private study. If he had worried or fretted under his burden he would have fallen midway in life. As it was, indeed, he for a period when near the age of fifty found himself overstrained and dispirited; for hours, during this period, he would sit despondent, and surrender himself to gloomy forebodings. But this lapse of his splendid physical powers was only temporary. With some lightening of his labors, and rest, and sensible medical treatment, and especially help at home, he recovered his buoyant health. He had the rare fortune of entire mental as well as physical adaptation to his high life-calling. His heart was in his work: —

"And the heart
Giveth grace to every art."

His toil was his recreation. No martyr ever more completely devoted his life to his cause than did Mr. Ballou. He made his sacrifice, not in one supreme moment, but day by day, hour by hour. He could proffer no greater gift to his cause than his life: this he gave without reserve, and found his reward in his free gift.

XV.

IN TRIALS.

PERIOD, 1790–1852; OR, DURING HIS MINISTRY.

IF Hosea Ballou's career had been cast in a different age, and the trial of his faith brought to a mortal crisis, would he have endured the test? If he had, for instance, lived in the period of which Eusebius of Cæsarea gives account, when it was the fashion to test Christian faith in a battle with wild beasts, or in the period of which Fox gives account, when a live Christian was often honored with the *san-benito* and *auto-da-fé*, would he have won a crown of life by being faithful unto death?

His lot was cast in a period when Christians were becoming sceptical of torture as a means of Christian persuasion. He was not, therefore, proffered a martyr's visible crown. He was privileged to give his life to his faith, hour by hour, day by day, year by year; but not as a single gift, in mortal martyrdom.

If the supreme trial had come to him, however, we believe it would not have found him unprepared. There was in him the stuff of which martyrs are made. He was always sane; no wildness or fanaticism characterized his zeal. He was not one needlessly to covet martyrdom. He had no desire to personally experience burning fagots, pronged wheels, a Procrustean bed, or a dark dungeon. He would, we are sure, have tried his best to have a question in dispute decided by more judicious methods. Yet in intensity and completeness of conviction, as regards the central points of faith, he was peer of the heroic believers of any age. If his request for fair judgment, therefore, had been disregarded, — as by the old inquisitors it would have been, — if it had been left him to choose whether he would profess faith in a future burning for the children of God, or have knowledge of how a blistering flame feels in the flesh, we believe it would have been easy for him to achieve a martyr's crown.

It is at least a fact that in every trial which actually came to him he was found faithful. In not a single instance did he show want of nerve, or fall short of complete mastery of the occasion. His dangers, indeed, were not hazards of his life: he was tried rather in his courage, patience, and good-will.

It is a question whether any man before him in America was so much a target for bigotry. We say this after carefully considering what has been said in regard to Thomas Paine, not overlooking how obnoxious the author of the "Age of Reason" was to the so-called orthodox churches. But Paine was coarse and crude; he was neither aggressive nor persistent in his negations. Popular Orthodoxy could afford to ignore him. It was not so as regards Mr. Ballou. He was active, positive, and persistent against established Calvinism. His gospel of winning love made irresistible headway in displacing the popular fear. He caused widespread disturbance among the sedate believers in the prevailing Satanism. They could not ignore him if they would. It was not easy or consistent for them even to tolerate him. They no doubt honestly thought him engaged in decoying souls to the fiery lake they had been religiously taught to fear. Why should they, from their view-point, not give him a foretaste of his own doom? What, indeed, was Torquemada's fault, save that he tried to be perfect as the Orthodox God is perfect? Why should mortal man be more just than God?

How did it happen, then, that Mr. Ballou escaped actual torture at the stake? Surely the logic of the popular creed of his day made slow burning for misbelief a comparative mercy. How, then, did he escape martyrdom? It must be that even before his day professors of the mediæval Satanism had begun to be better than their creed.

Yet he did not escape the trials of persistent detraction, scornful opposition, and merciless defamation. How he bore himself in these trials, with what ability, dignity, patience, good-nature, and equanimity, we will show in some examples.

In 1799 the General Convention of Universalists met at Woodstock, Vermont. At that time the name of this body was more imposing than the body itself. There were but three preachers present, — Revs. William Farwell, Walter Ferris, and Hosea Ballou. The people, however, came in multitudes to hear these heralds of hope. The resident Universalists had applied for the use of the county court-house. As it was customary for the civil authorities to grant such requests, permission was not withheld in this case. But there arose an unexpected obstacle. The sheriff of the county, Rice by name, did not wish the court-house polluted by Universalism. He declared it must not, should not be. He was a man of local importance; in his own esteem he was a great man. He determined to be bold in the cause of his Lord. As the door of the building had been opened, and it was not in his power to close it, he determined to guard it from desecration, if need be, with his life. He declared no one, save by his permission, should enter that door. He stood on the stoop with a drawn sword in his hand. Fearful to behold! The time of the appointed meeting arrived. The procession of ministers, Hosea Ballou — although youngest — at the head, approached. There stood the valiant, bold-faced sheriff, flourishing his broad-bladed weapon. What was to be done? Was it prudent to hazard bloodshed? There was a brief consultation — a council of war, so to speak — among the perilled ministers. The decision was in favor of a forward movement. The procession marched. When the door was reached, Mr. Ballou, with the easy, courtly dignity with which his presence was at times instinct, said to the sheriff, in the language of Scripture, "Peter, put up thy sword into his place." Whether the sheriff was startled at being called "Peter" (as the irate fishwoman was subdued when Dr. Samuel Johnson said, "Madam, you are a *phenomenon*"); or whether there was something not to his liking in the resolute eye of the preacher who so strangely called him by a name other than his own, or whether he concluded it not to be strategic to hazard a battle at that time and place, are points not made clear in the authenticated tradition. But the unquestioned and central fact in the tradition is that the sheriff instantly surrendered. He wilted, became starchless, looked demure as a lamb.

Nathaniel Stacy, who was present, an open-eyed boy, records that the bold sheriff retreated to his home hanging his head. No further molestation was offered. The people, we may be sure, were captivated by a man who could, like Ethan Allen at Ticonderoga, make a verbal request equivalent to an irresistible assault. The hero of this story, it is needless to say, is not the sheriff.

A similar exhibition of personal courage we find in Mr. Ballou's experience in Atkinson, New Hampshire. During his ministry in Portsmouth he preached one Sunday in Atkinson, and some then heard his testimony with faith. In 1819 the town at its annual meeting voted that its meeting-house should be occupied impartially by the different denominations of Christians. A committee was appointed justly to apportion the Sundays to each. The Universalists preferred their claim, and it was allowed. On the first Sunday assigned to them, the last of May in that year, they invited Mr. Ballou to preach. He accepted the invitation. Then a breeze of religious indignation arose. Universalists allowed in a church made holy by Congregationalist possession! When even a Baptist preacher in New Hampshire, about that time, had preached one Sunday in a school-house, the autocratic Congregationalists would not enter the school-house afterward until they had publicly cleansed it with smoke. If they were thus scornful toward Baptists, we may infer what must be their feelings toward Universalists. The breeze of indignation increased to a gale. A committee of the Congregationalist Society, on the 25th of May, five days before the appointed Universalist meeting, addressed a letter to Mr. Ballou at Boston, in which their case is very emphatically stated. He is warned not to come to Atkinson. The Congregationalists have had possession of the church nearly fifty years. They propose to maintain their right to continued possession. They have met and voted "that it is the duty of this society to meet as usual at the meeting-house for public worship on the Sabbath; that whatever person or persons shall disturb or molest this society in its public worship on the Sabbath, shall be considered and dealt with as disturbers of the peace and of the public worship of God." What will Mr. Ballou think of the prospect? Here is an opportunity to test the comfort of a New Hampshire jail as a peace-breaker and disturber of public worship! The letter of the committee kindly concludes by saying, "Should any unpleasant consequences result to you or your friends here from your leaving your people in Boston and coming here to preach in this meeting-house, you will have the candor to acknowledge you were apprized of the existing difficulties previous to your coming." The problem was still further complicated by the dying of the venerable Congregationalist clergyman of Atkinson, Rev. Stephen Peabody; his funeral was held in the church on the Thursday previous to the Sunday on which Mr. Ballou was to preach. Mr. Ballou, on receiving the letter, resolved to go to Atkinson at once, and judge of his duty by a direct knowledge of all the circumstances. By his advice the statement was made to the senior deacon of the pastorless Congregationalist Society that the Universalists would waive their right to the meeting-house on the next Sunday, on condition that they should have the use of the academy building, of which the aforesaid deacon had control. The reply was defiant: "We are as willing you should occupy the meeting-house on the next Sunday as on any Sunday in the year; we do not mean you shall occupy it at all." It was no longer a question of courtesy: a right must be maintained! The gale in the town had now become a tornado. Mr. Ballou decided to preach in the church. A citizen favoring his claim held the key to the building, and would not surrender it to the opposite party. On Saturday afternoon the meeting-house was broken into by the Orthodox braves, and the doors and windows flung wide open. A watch was accordingly set in the church by the Universalist party on Saturday night. Early on Sunday morning a company approached to capture the church, but finding it guarded, retired. On Sunday, at the usual time of worship, the church on being opened was immediately thronged. Mr. Ballou entered the pulpit, and proceeded, in beginning his services, to read from the Scriptures. Meanwhile the Congregationalists had organized, and under lead of Rev. Isaac Brown, the oldest minister of the Congregationalist Association, came in and marched to the front. Mr. Brown ascended the pulpit-stairs, and stood at the pulpit-door in waiting till Mr. Ballou had finished reading the Scriptures. Then he asked, as if not quite believing his eyes, "Do you expect to render divine service here to-day?" Mr. Ballou, without hinting that his acts spoke of themselves, mildly replied, "I do, sir." "By what authority?" asked Mr. Brown. Mr. Ballou had the orator's faculty of being emphatic without being loud, and dignified without loss of courtesy. There was emphatic yet courteous dignity in his reply: "I have my authority, sir, from the selectmen of Atkinson." This blusterless remark had an astonishing effect. It meant that the heretic was for once under the protection of civil law. In America, that protection is not slight. An assault of the preacher would be an assault on the selectmen: to assault the selectmen would be to aim a blow at the State. There was a hurried consultation among the Congregationalist braves; then they quietly withdrew, to hold their services in the academy. Mr. Ballou preached without molestation morning, afternoon, and evening. The threat was made, however, that he would be arrested early Monday morning. Mr. Ballou remained in Atkinson during nearly the whole of Monday, that the officers might have no needless trouble in securing their prisoner; but the officers did not appear. Having gained two points, — secured the Universalists of Atkinson in their legal church claim, which was not afterward withheld, and demonstrated his entire willingness to be a fellow-prisoner with Bunyan, Silas, and Paul, — he returned to his home in Boston. He had exhibited an intrepidity which had commanded the respect of even his opponents.

Dean Stanley narrates a mediæval legend which, he affirms, has some foundation in fact; the story being that a pope was once arrested for heresy and condemned to be burned, but for his legal execution it was necessary he should, as pope, sign his own death-warrant. He kindly consented to do so, and for this act of self-denial he was canonized. If such a pope ever existed, he was a more admirable successor of Saint Peter than we always find occupying the papal see. We are prompted to suggest that Mr. Ballou was somewhat like-minded to this apocryphal pope. Both had a kindly, accommodating disposition toward those who wished to confer on them the honors of martyrdom.

Perhaps as great a trial of his power to control his laughter as ever came to him was at Wrentham, Massachusetts. The few Universalists in the town in 1820, unable to secure a meeting-house or even school-house, were obliged to hold their services in the hall at the Mann Tavern. Rev. Mr. Fisk, the pastor of the Congregationalist church in the town, was greatly disturbed by Mr. Ballou coming into his parish. He consulted a shrewd physician, Dr. Samuel Bugbee, as to the propriety of his meeting the new preacher face to face, and exposing his error. Dr. Bugbee had heard Mr. Ballou preach, and he tried to dissuade his friend from such a venture. But he was not to be dissuaded. He attended Mr. Ballou's services; and when, after the sermon, liberty was given to any one to offer remarks, Mr. Fisk was immediately on his feet. "In the first place," he said, "the speaker of this evening is to be blamed for leaving his own church and coming into this town and preaching his pernicious doctrine." "Would you," interposed Mr. Ballou, "decline a respectable invitation to preach in Boston?" "Oh," exclaimed Mr. Fisk, "if the sainted Messenger and Mann and Bean, former pastors of this parish, should look down from the blissful abodes and see what is going on here to-night, it would fill their souls with sorrow." "Do you," interjected Mr. Ballou, "think there is sorrow in heaven?" Mr. Fisk was perplexed. He was more than perplexed, he was nauseated. The scent of heresy may have had a tendency to turn his stomach. Some surmised, however, a less æsthetic cause of his sudden illness. He was what some Americans would call a "powerful" tobacco-chewer. He had masticated in unconscious vigor during Mr. Ballou's sermon. Cuspadores were not then in fashion,—at least there was none within convenient reach of this valiant soldier of the cross. As a natural if not logical result, when he attempted to answer Mr. Ballou's question he was overpowered by his emotions. He was observed by the sympathetic crowd to look longingly toward an open window. A way was cleared for him, which he traversed in haste. While his head was protruded from the window the congregation waited. It would be inexact to say a breathless silence was meanwhile maintained. In due time the distressed minister was relieved, and went back to his place and resumed his speech. He proceeded to quote the stock passages of Scripture in an attempt to prove the doctrine of endless punishment. He felt evident exhilaration in his own speech; perhaps also his sudden recovery from sickness was pleasing to him. At the imagined success of his argument, he very perceptibly smiled his satisfaction. Mr. Ballou, in reply, gave rapid explanations of the Scriptural citations which were as familiar to him as the alphabet, and in conclusion mentioned the strangeness of his friend showing gratification in trying to prove the dreadful doctrine of endless woe for his fellow-men. "When our Lord," said he, "anticipated even temporal sufferings for the inhabitants of Jerusalem, he wept over the city; what should we think of him if we had seen him, because he thought a far greater punishment was certain for his people, laugh with satisfaction?" Mr. Fisk came once more to his feet; but before he could fairly begin his remarks he again had recourse to the window. He had enjoyed his own turn at laughing; the audience was now privileged once more with its turn. Poor man! A modern Orthodox lecturer declares if he had a dog that chewed tobacco he would shoot the dog. It is evident his brother-clergyman did not need to be shot in order to feel, to say the least, the inconvenience of his habit. When he finally got himself in speaking order, he made a humble and ample apology, not for his habit which a dog would spurn, but for not maintaining due solemnity when speaking on the awful subject of endless misery. There is no record of Mr. Ballou's indulging even in a smile during this protracted appeal to his sense of the ludicrous. One practical result of this discussion was the conversion of Dr. Bugbee to the Universalist cause; of which he remained during his life an earnest and effective advocate.

Mr. Ballou's whole ministry, especially in its itinerant department, was filled with trials. Whenever he preached in a new locality he expected spiteful opposition. To defame him was a religious fashion. Jacob Knapp, the gross revivalist, told in dramatic form the preposterous story that Mr. Ballou publicly confessed guilt of drunkenness, profanity, and Sabbath desecration. Such false evil-speaking against the champion of the gospel of hope naturally caused those who knew him to gather more closely and affectionately about him. He was under necessity of keeping his armor whole and his sword of the spirit ready for use. At Mattapoisett, the resident pastor, Rev. Lemuel

Le Baron, at the church door forbade his entering the church. "You have," he said, "the legal right to do so, by human law; but you have no moral right to preach a doctrine subversive of Christianity." Nevertheless, Mr. Ballou entered the church and preached. In Canton, Massachusetts, after he had discoursed on the Scriptural declaration, "God will have all men to be saved, and to come unto a knowledge of the truth," Rev. Mr. Tinkham, a Methodist clergyman, at the close of the sermon requested permission to say that while God originally willed to save all, man by his transgression had defeated God's will; it was now God's will that the impenitent should suffer forever. "Our brother," replied Mr. Ballou, "thinks the will of God has been defeated; if God's will to save his children cannot be done, how can we say his will to damn his children can be done?" The turn was so adroitly made, that the audience rose as one person and burst into cheers.

Mr. Ballou was not, as far as we have learned, in a single instance placed in discomfiture. When, through temporary failures, like the eaglet practising its wings, he had once gained self-mastery in speech, he was in every known instance master of the situation. Not only could he commend his faith in sustained reasoning; he could, when need was, flash light on an intricate point in an unpremeditated sentence.

We are constrained to say, however, that these trials, born of expected external opposition, were not his hardest trials. Paul's severest experiences were not perils of land or sea, nor opposition of Gentiles and Jews; but those which were brought upon him by his false brethren. Mr. Ballou's hardest

12

trials came to him not from Calvinistic hatred, but from the injustice and unfraternity of those he loved as brothers. He knew the backbiter's sting. During his lifetime he bore his hurts in silence. We believe we fulfil his wish in not definitely recalling these things from fast-coming oblivion. He bequeathed to his family a package of papers, sealed by his own hand, bearing an inscription of this purport: "Never to be opened unless my character needs vindication." We have been kindly asked if in our search for facts from which to evolve his life-story we have come to any question to justify the opening of that package. But of his integrity there never could have been a reasonable question. Of his magnanimity even when he was touched to the quick there remains no tenable suspicion. While we have our human curiosity in regard to every fact pertaining to his life, we deem it best that the package remain unopened. We respect his wish. Its unbroken seal means merciful forgetfulness of the human failings of some of his contemporary brethren. Their wrongs brought to themselves the inevitable fruitage. We know enough confidently to affirm it to be honorable alike to Hosea Ballou's memory and to human nature, that more than an average generation has passed away since his hands fixed the seal on that package, and no occasion has arisen to break the seal to this day.

Not all real martyrdoms are visible. There are heroes without worldly triumphs, and victors without laurel crowns. The spirit knoweth its own bitterness, and the Eternal knows what may be gained in silent endurance and quiet self-abnegation.

XVI.

MOTHER-WIT.

THE aggregate of Mr. Ballou's lightsome qualities — his quiet humor, susceptibility to the comical, his power of repartee, and abounding common-sense — we label his mother-wit.

The phrase itself, however, suggests a pathetic protest. He was not what is ordinarily called a mother's boy. His mother was drooping when he was born, and died when he was but two years old. In her final years she was overburdened and sad of heart. According to the commonly-accepted surmises as to heredity, we can scarcely believe that she dowered her last-born with his buoyant nature. We must believe that he received from her his transparent sincerity, and his quick and fathomless human sympathy; for we behold him in his profounder traits both womanly and manly.

He was, we are wont to think, peculiarly his father's boy. We remember of his father that he religiously endeavored to be sad. He believed this deity-shadowed world no place for laughter. Yet he could not, we remember, altogether repress the true divine tendency in his own nature toward good-humor and gladness. When he by a sudden natural impulse told his boys an amusing anecdote, the laughter was followed by a deep sigh; for his theology taught him that a single moment of merriment in this lost world is sinful. Is it not a justifiable surmise that the father's repressed nature asserted its inalienable rights in his youngest son? We must regret that the father shut out of his own heart the light of his own natural wit and humor; but what he would not concede to himself he could not, under the laws of heredity, withhold from his youngest son, who emerged from the darkness of religious dread into the light of a great hope.

The saying is therefore less Hibernian than it seems, — Hosea Ballou inherited his mother-wit from his father.

However it may be explained, the fact will not be disputed that Mr. Ballou was a very humorous man. He was also witty. Humor is a sustained sentiment; wit is a momentary inspiration. Wit scintillates; humor glows. Chapin was the prince of wits. His wit at times, to recall Beecher's apt simile, glistened like the spokes of a revolving carriage-wheel in the sun. Yet Chapin had but little humor; his prevailing mood was intensely serious. In Mr. Ballou, humor abounded. He had prolonged enjoyment of the comical aspect of things. Laughter, after it left his lips, lingered in his eyes.

Mr. Ballou would not, in our view, be properly called a brilliant wit. "I lived long," said Dr. Porson, "before I discovered that wit is truth." Mr. Ballou's wit was better than brilliant; it was natural. His statement of simplest facts was often strangely enjoyable.

When in the humorous mood his manner, ingenuous, childlike, very quiet, was itself amusing. His peculiar manner is the proper setting of his peculiar wit. We cannot recall any one reporting a humorous saying from his lips, who did not endeavor to imitate his quaint, appealing tone.

Without attempt at arrangement or analysis, we open our budget and offer its miscellaneous contents in testimony of his lightsome traits.

In his old age he was one day starting in good season for a journey. "Do not be in a hurry," was persuasively said to him. "I do not want to be in a hurry," he said, "so I will start now." The remark was treasured for the wisdom of its wit.

In a company of ministers he was studying a passage of very florid rhetoric. "What can the man mean?" he asked, with a puzzled expression on his face. A fluent brother volunteered a lengthy exposition, which was quite as obscure as the redundant passage itself. With a look of great simplicity Mr. Ballou said, "Like as not, that is what he says." How could it be more exquisitely suggested that the ambiguity of the passage still remained?

Dr. Paige remembered a remark he made when commenting on the doctrine prevalent among some religious people of his day; namely, that no one can be sure of his own salvation, and every one should live in fear of being lost. The logic of the doctrine was of course anxiety. "Yes," said Mr. Ballou, "they would be scared to death if they were not afraid."

"In my boyhood," said an aged clergyman to us, "I heard Mr. Ballou preach, and one remark he made I have not forgotten. He had been advertised to answer the attack of an opponent. He began the service before a crowded audience in the School Street Church, by reading the tenth chapter of Romans. When he had read the second verse, — 'For I bear them record that they have a zeal of God, but not according to knowledge,' — he paused, and said: 'Paul must have included my opponent in this very just observation; I bear him record that he is very zealous, but, as we shall see, he does n't know much.'"

Mr. Ballou was extremely considerate of others, and did not, save a good purpose was to be served, wound by his words; but at one time he felt justified in giving a proper rebuke to a country-woman with whom he was tarrying as a guest. "Mr. Ballou," she said at the dinner-table, where there were also two other clergymen, "will you take a piece of this apple-pie? It is really so poor, — I had such miserable luck at my last baking, — I am sure it is not fit to eat; I am ashamed to ask you to taste it." Mr. Ballou knew she was inwardly priding herself on her superior cooking. He said: "You must excuse me, madam. I am, I will acknowledge, particularly fond of apple-pies; but to attempt to eat of such a pie as this would, I fear, prejudice me against all apple-pies hereafter." Her chagrin at being taken at her word can be easily imagined, and was morally medicinal.

In the constant opposition he encountered, his readiness of reply often served him a good turn. When about to begin a service at Reading, Vermont, a Baptist deacon approached him, declaring he wished to ask him one question. "Are you the Mr. Ballou who is to preach here this afternoon?" he asked. "I am." "Well, although I understand you are in a great hurry, I wish to ask what you think of the case of a man who goes out of this world cursing and swearing, and calling on God to damn his soul."

"Why deacon," said Mr. Ballou, "a profane swearer is no doubt a very wicked man; do you think God will answer the prayer of so wicked a man as that?" "No, I am sure he will not." "Well, deacon," he said, "you have answered your own question;" and he passed in to begin the service for which the people were waiting.

"What would you do with a man who died reeking in sin and crime?" was asked of him. "I think," he said, "it would be a good plan to bury him."

It was a theory of Rev. John Murray that the goats and the sheep spoken of in the twenty-fifth chapter of Matthew symbolically represent the human race and the devils. The sheep, that is, mankind, through their union with Christ, he contended, are to be saved in the judgment day; the goats, or devils, or fallen angels, having no part in Christ's sacrifice, are to go into remediless fire. When he proposed this interpretation to Mr. Ballou, the latter said: "Father Murray, those on the left hand, the goats, you will observe, are accused of not having visited the sick. Do you think it so desirable to have the devils visit the sick, that they will be condemned to everlasting fire for having neglected that duty?" Mr. Murray, it is said, walked hastily across the room and deeply sighed, and the conversation closed.

Mr. Ballou at one time received a letter from an anxious inquirer, who was troubled by a then current report that Mr. Ballou, having been called to attend a dying young man, went home and dreamed three times in succession of seeing the young man in hell; which, as the rumor ran, so impressed him, that the next Sunday he publicly renounced his universal hope.

The anxious inquirer, with palpitating heart, wrote to learn if this story was correct. Mr. Ballou, as editor of the "Magazine," replied in his own behalf. "As Mr. Ballou," he said, "did not dream himself into the doctrine of God's universal goodness and impartial salvation of the human race, it is not at all likely he will ever dream himself out of it!"

While editor of the "Magazine" he received a letter from a Presbyterian postmaster at Bradleysville, South Carolina, in which an attempt was made to be satirical. The letter was dated "Infernal Pit;" it proceeded: "My Good Friend,—Continue as you have done to disseminate your princely magazine, and be assured you shall have one of the most exalted thrones amongst us. Yours, with all the love of a fiend, Nick Lucifer." Mr. Ballou printed this delectable composition, and made this characteristic comment: "We have long been of opinion that it is not necessary to go into the future world to find the infernal pit so much talked of, and we are now furnished with a demonstration of the correctness of our opinion. The above letter came directly from that pit, where, it appears, there is a post-office and a postmaster. We have the satisfaction also to learn that the 'Universalist Magazine' does not please those who are in this infernal pit, for the number we sent there was sent back with the above letter; but it was not scorched, nor was the smell of fire or brimstone on it."

"There was one good thing in your sermon," said Mr. Ballou, after he had for the first time heard Thomas Whittemore preach, and was walking homeward from Roxbury with the young man. "What was that?" asked the young preacher, very eager for any word of praise. "The text: that was excellent." Mr. Whittemore afterward acknowledged that the implied severe criticism was just; it was uttered in good will, and its effect on the forward young man was salutary.

Mr. Ballou was once more severe in needed criticism. He had in early life a conceited neighbor who occasionally preached among the Baptists. This neighbor said one day, "Mr. Ballou, I am awfully tried with myself." "What is the trouble with you now?" "To think I should ever try to preach and know so little; what do you think?" "Well, I think if you knew a little more, you'd never try again."

When riding in Troy, New York, he passed a house shut away from every agreeable outlook, and itself seemingly built as a model of ungainliness and discomfort. "The people who live there," he said, "ought to enjoy life." "How can they," it was asked, "in that place?" "They ought to enjoy life," he said, "because they have nothing else to enjoy."

When the question was asked of him by a special acquaintance, "How is your health?" he was accustomed to reply, "What health I have is very good."

When he was preaching before the Southern Association at Milford one afternoon, the sun shone through an unblinded window directly in his face. His hearers being slow to take a hint through their eyes, he by a little detour in his sermon referred to God's impartial love as like the glorious sun, "which," he said, "now nearly blinds me with its superabundant light." There was on the part of several hearers an instantaneous movement toward the window, and a coat was made to serve the purpose of a screen.

He once approached a company of ministers, when one of them pleasantly said, "Father Ballou, we are telling stories about you; but they are all true ones." "When I had ugly stories told about me," he said, "I used to say to my wife that we need not care, because they were not true; but now it is time for me to look out, if you are beginning to tell true stories about me."

At the Eastern railway-station in Boston he bought a horn comb of a woman of poverty-stricken appearance. After paying the price, he said, "Madam, perhaps you have some use for this comb; if you will accept of it you are welcome." "May all the saints bless you," said the grateful woman; "may the Holy Mary, the mother of God, bless you." "Has God a mother?" he asked. "Sure he has; are ye such a heretic as not to know that?" "Is she a good woman?" "A good woman, is it? Hear the man! The Holy Mother of God a good woman! There is none the likes of her, you poor heretic; she is the best of all the women, bless her holy name." "I am very glad to hear it," he said; "I am very glad to know God came of a good family."

He was capable of enjoying the discomfiture which over-zealous people sometimes unwittingly brought on themselves. From Nantucket, where he had preached, he was, having been ferried across Vineyard Sound, returning home in a stage-coach. A stranger said to him, "Are you from Nantucket, sir?" "I am." "They say old Ballou is down there preaching; did you hear anything of him?" "He has been preaching there." "Did you hear him, sir?" "I did, several times." "Well," said the stranger, "I do not like him; he preaches that all men will go to heaven when they die, just as they leave this world." "Did you ever hear Mr. Ballou preach?" "No, I never did; and I have no desire to hear him preach." "How do you know, then, he preaches in that manner?" "I have heard so a thousand times." "But you may be misinformed; I am quite confident he would tell you, if you should ask him, that he preaches that men are not to go to heaven in their sins, but that they are to be saved from their sins." "No such thing; but how is it you know so much about him?" "I live in Boston, sir." "What church do you attend?" "Mr. Ballou's." "Are you personally acquainted with him?" "My name is Hosea Ballou, my friend." It is probable that the over-confident stranger felt after this a touch of embarrassment.

On another occasion, when riding from Roxbury to Boston in an omnibus, he was accosted by a very zealous Orthodox lady: "I want to know, Mr. Ballou, if you preach as Jesus Christ preached when on the earth?" "Well, I don't know, madam," said he, slowly and mildly; "I believe I intend to do so." "Ah, but are you faithful, sir? Do you set forth the punishment of sin as faithfully as Jesus Christ and his apostles did?" "I would not be self-confident in such a matter; but I try to preach the doctrine of my Master." "Do you," said she, growing excited, "preach to your people every Sabbath, 'Ye serpents, ye generation of vipers, ye hypocrites, how can ye escape the damnation of hell?'" "No, madam, I do not." "Why do you not? Jesus preached in that way; why don't you preach the same?" "That class of people don't come to my meeting."

These instances sample his mother-wit. Some one defines wit as "an unexpected combination of distant resemblances." By this standard Mr. Ballou cannot be called a witty man. He was not given to play upon words. Save in the one instance, at the Reform Festival, there is no record of his ever making a pun. His wit did not consist in any degree in a combination of distant resemblances. It was precisely the sort of wit Dr. Porson was so long in discovering. It was the pleasing grace of simple truth. He had the direct vision of the single mind. He saw in plain truth its amusing aspect.

We note that all these samples of his wit bear the stamp of his own personality. No one else could have spoken them; and it is difficult for us to see how he could have repressed their utterance. His humor, we also observe, was always of excellent quality. He had no aptitude whatever for mere drollery. Some people, from reports of his preaching, imagined him boorish and pert in the pulpit; but his witticisms never lowered the high themes upon which he uniformly discoursed. "It was no uncommon thing for him," said Rev. O. A. Skinner, speaking of his preaching, "to excite a smile; but usually it was done by some ingenious argument that would electrify every one present." It is not known that any person ever listened to one of his sermons who was not so impressed with his sincerity, dignity, and earnestness, that the recollection of his occasional humorous sayings was held subsidiary and helpful to his main serious purpose.

His mother-wit was sanctified. It served a divine mission in diffusing cheerfulness and health.

XVII.

SPIRITUAL SONS.

LEADERSHIP is self-multiplication. A photographer brings forth many pictures from one; a master-spirit multiplies himself in his disciples. Alfred the Great, Charlemagne, Washington, Garibaldi, all renowned swordsmen, indeed; had conspicuous genius for transforming other men into their own likeness. The fact holds as to religious epoch-makers. Followers of Augustine, Loyola, Luther, Calvin, Fox, Edwards, Wesley, were severally like their leaders. The true disciple yields to his chieftain a glad self-abnegation; his yoke is easy; his bondage is liberty. His master magnetizes him into the semblance if not into the reality of a new person.

Did Hosea Ballou possess this power of self-multiplication? Is he to be classed among the religious leaders?

Prophecy is history in the future tense. We are studying Mr. Ballou as he was in his own age.

It is significant that, from middle life, he was among Universalists popularly designated as "Father Ballou." In domestic life he had, indeed, some claim to the title; he was the happy father of three sons and six daughters, and these all yielded him rare filial devotion. But in the spiritual life he was much more extensively a father. Innumerable souls gladly acknowledged indebtedness to him for birth into a diviner range of being. "I question," said Rev. O. A. Skinner, "whether there was ever a preacher who made so many converts by his pulpit labors as Father Ballou. Thousands on thousands were convinced by him; and his converts were always remarkable for ability to reason and for hearts of benevolence." Mr. Ballou himself at one time spoke of those who had confessedly received through his words a new impulse of the better life, as "ten thousand friends and more." It was not mere sacerdotal courtesy, therefore, that conferred on him the honorary title of "Father."

This chapter is designed to be a free word-picturing of a few of his more notable spiritual sons.

If Mr. Ballou, during his first Sundays in School Street Church, happened to cast an especially observing eye on his voluntary choir, he must have marked among its members the face of a certain young man. Thomas Whittemore had uncontested ownership of the face. He had at this time barely turned eighteen, having been born on the first day of the century. We do not mean to insinuate that he was himself ashamed of his countenance, or had reason to be greatly chagrined at this item of his very meagre ancestral inheritance. The features were heavily encased in flesh; earthliness was prominent, but not dominant; intelligence, humor, good-will, honesty, self-assurance, blended in the expression; the eyes were full, gray in color, penetrating, and facetious; his lips were unusually prominent. The countenance was in all its traits strong. It was tense with a seemingly inexhaustible vital force, and mobile with a restless temperament. The owner was at this time a boot-maker's apprentice. He was fatherless, and virtually motherless. He was hilarious and exuberant, with abundance of green material in him of that burlesque of manhood, a Boston rough. He was crudely and boisterously sceptical. He had, however, an intense passion for music. When, therefore, the new preacher who had been so thoroughly shaking up the religious dry bones was to come to Boston, he, having nothing more amusing on hand, volunteered to assist with his bass-viol in giving him a suitable choir-accompaniment.

But he soon became an interested listener to Mr. Ballou's novel preaching. It had to him a peculiarly personal appeal. Might it not be worth one's while to believe such a gospel of hope and charity? At a distance he respected the earnest preacher. He felt a better spirit taking possession of him. He had so far been neglectful of even his slight school privileges. Now, on the opening of the evening school in the autumn, he became a constant attendant.

When the school closed in the spring, and he had completed his nineteenth and begun his twentieth year, he ventured to call on Mr. Ballou, toward whom his heart had more and more yearned. Arrayed in his modest best, and feeling some assurance in the fact that Mr. Ballou rented his house on Blossom Street of his employer, Abel Baker, he knocked at the door of the manse. Would Mr. Ballou kindly assist him a little in the study of English grammar, now the evening school was closed? The busy preacher was gracious, and his wife was unaffectedly maternal. They kept the homeless young boot-maker through the evening, and he left under promise to come again soon with a composition for his new teacher to criticise. A few evenings later he brought, as fruit of his midnight oil, some rude rhythmic "Reflections over the Grave of an Infant." Did he instinctively know that rhyming was Mr. Ballou's foible? The critic was pleased, and greatly pleased; the young man had done surprisingly well. The adolescent effusion was kept, and in a few days appeared in the "Universalist Magazine." In print! The young boot-maker was in a state of exaltation. A new life-purpose was formed within him.

To further tell how, on reaching his majority on the 1st of January, 1821, he entered Mr. Ballou's house as a student; how, after his first sermon before his teacher, he was complimented on having selected a good text; how he, after a year as pastor at Milford, in 1822 settled in Cambridgeport, where he was pastor for nine years and resident during his life; how in 1828 he purchased the "Universalist Magazine" and appropriately changed its name to "The Trumpet;" how he in 1830 published the "Modern History of Universalism;" in 1834, "Notes and Illustrations of the Parables;" in 1837, "Songs of Zion," a conference hymn-book, with some original songs and tunes; in 1840, "A Plain Guide to Universalism;" in 1852, "A Memoir of Rev. Walter Balfour;" in 1854–55, "The Life of Hosea Ballou," in four volumes; in 1859, "The Early Days of Thomas Whittemore, an Autobiography;" in 1860, the first volume of a new edition of his first book, "Modern History of Universalism," and was preparing the second volume at the time of his death, March 31, 1861; how he was a man of

THOMAS WHITTEMORE, D.D.

extraordinary business capabilities, holding for many years the presidency of the Cambridge Bank and the presidency of the Fitchburg Railroad; how he was the representative of his town in the Legislature, and served as an alderman; how it was during all his life his greatest happiness to preach the impartial gospel; how he travelled incessantly as an itinerant; what hold he had on the popular heart by his exuberant wit and his preaching power, — this, while its mention swells a paragraph, could be adequately told only in a volume. Picturesque, unforgetable man, in intensity and activity almost miraculous, he was in a real sense given to the world by Hosea Ballou. He himself ascribed to his "Father Ballou" all that was noble and victorious in his life.

Another spiritual son of Mr. Ballou, extremely unlike in form and texture, shall introduce himself in the letter following: —

HARDWICK, MASS., April 23, 1823.

To Rev. Hosea Ballou.

DEAR SIR, — Although an utter stranger to you, I take the liberty of addressing you, presuming you will be willing to pardon me for obtruding myself on your notice. In early youth I was taught to believe that God had determined to render happy after the slumbers of death a part, and a part only, of his offspring. My parents were both believers and professors of this doctrine; but their hearts were so much better than their doctrine, that they lived such a life as induced me to suppose that their opinions must be right. I placed unlimited confidence in them, and believed their doctrine to be true, because they considered it so. At times, it is true, I was somewhat astonished at some expressions used by ministers of the Calvinistic faith, which appeared to me to implicate the character of God. On inquiry of professors the reasons of such expressions, I was almost invariably informed that such things were spiritually discerned, and that my not discerning them was the effect of my not having been renewed; and as I had never experienced such transports as are by them deemed the only proofs of regeneration, I thought it probable that what they said was correct. At length, however, the inconsistencies of Calvinism appeared so glaring that I set about reading the Scriptures, particularly the New Testament, more carefully than I had before done. The effect you probably anticipate; it pleased God to remove the veil from my heart, and cause me to see that he is a tender parent of all his children, that he consults their best good, and that he will finally make pure, sinless, holy, and consequently happy, all created intelligences. About this time I had an opportunity to peruse your "Treatise on Atonement," and it is a duty which I owe to you and to myself to state that it was a mean in the hand of God of removing from my mind many clouds which had heretofore obscured my vision.

L. R. PAIGE.

Over this characteristic letter we in reminiscent mood linger. It is, at the date we write, more than sixty-five years old. Yet the hand penning these words was but a day or two since in the friendly clasp of the hand which more than threescore and five years ago penned this epistle. The youth of that day, delicate, sensitive, painstaking, is now the veteran Dr. Paige, nearing his eighty-seventh year. He has fulfilled the prophecy of his youth. As we linger over this epistle, at once aged and young, it seems to us that the studied sentences, so exact, conscientious, and graceful, might have been written yesterday by our clear-visioned and buoyant old friend. As he was when he had the crown of life to win, he is now with the crown of life won. He was Thomas

Whittemore's successor in Hosea Ballou's home, beginning his specific preparation for the ministry soon after reaching his majority. The demand for preachers was in those days too urgent to admit of more than a few months devoted to preparation. He was very soon graduated into the school of experience. Two years an evangelist; four years pastor at Springfield, Massachusetts; two years pastor at Rockport, Cape Ann, where, in imitation of Mr. Ballou at Portsmouth, he supplemented his inadequate salary as preacher by school-teaching, — in May, 1832, he began his ministry in Cambridgeport, being, as once before, Thomas Whittemore's successor. Seven years his faithful pastorate continued, and his residence in the city continues to this day. By self-mastery and perseverance he has fulfilled extraordinary tasks. For livelihood, he was town clerk, afterward city clerk, in Cambridge; he was bank treasurer, cashier, and president; such employment, like Paul's tent-making, being, however, incidental to his life mission. In 1833 he published a book revealing the scope of his biblical studies, entitled "Selections from Eminent Commentators." It was to all observant biblical scholars in that day a surprise; to some of the old school it was a shock. In the exact language of eminent Orthodox commentators, every passage of Scripture popularly supposed to teach endless punishment was expounded as harmonious with the universal hope. Scholarly believers in the endlessness of punishment based the doctrine on certain passages, conceding that it was not taught in other passages which had been quoted in its support. A search among all the reputable commentators revealed the astonishing fact that some standard Orthodox authority had conceded to Universalism every passage which could be quoted against it. After the publication of this book the scriptural battle was made easy for Universalists. Not one passage could be quoted against them where they could not confront their assailants with an Orthodox exegesis contrary to Orthodoxy. In 1838 he published a book entitled "Questions on Select Portions of the Gospels, designed for the Use of Sabbath Schools and Bible Classes." In 1844 appeared the first volume of the work on which his fame most securely rests, his "Commentary on the New Testament," the sixth and last volume of which appeared in 1870. The excellency of this Commentary is widely acknowledged. Its correctness in statement and quotation, its candor in reasoning and exegesis, its reverent faith, its direct and limpid style are readily apprehended by its students. Yet the heroism of its preparation but few have known. While itself diffusive of light, it is largely a product of the night. Patient night-study after days of wearying secular toil, — study persevered in through years, under a burden of delicate health, necessitating utmost care and temperance, and through repeated family bereavements such as would have wrecked the energy of many a physically stronger man, — such the roots; the Commentary the flowering and fruitage. Produced under any circumstances, the work would have honored its author; produced under such circumstances, this pioneer Universalist Commentary is both a monument and a crown for its author. Following this protracted labor of love, in 1877 Dr. Paige published a "History of Cambridge," a book involving an amount of research in the early annals of the city

LUCIUS R. PAIGE, D.D.

of his adoption sufficient itself to be for a man a life work. Following this he published, some years later, a history of his native town of Hardwick, — a book, like all his others, of utmost trustworthiness of statement or restatement. And through all the years he has been a preacher of the faith which early awakened him to a cheering hope. When his health has permitted he has been in the pulpit, where his modest demeanor and crystal style have made him the delight of the thoughtful; at all times, by the unmistakable testimony of a heart cheerful in sorrow, a courage valiant in pain, love unfailing, and hope all-conquering, he has been a living example of his faith. He has not been, like Whittemore, a master of emotion; but on one theme he could never speak without a kindling of the eye, and not often without a trembling of the voice. "To that man," he once said to a company of fellow-clergymen, pointing to an engraving of Hosea Ballou on the wall, "I owe my deepest gratitude; he was my father, my guide, my friend." Dr. Paige, tall, slight, with no ambition for scholarship outside divine revelation and American history, and very impatient of all schools of metaphysics, is a distinctive personality; yet in him reappears in likeness his honored master.

In 1814, as we have seen, Mr. Ballou in Portsmouth, New Hampshire, eked out his scanty income by school-teaching. A young man bearing precisely his own name was his assistant. Hosea Ballou 2d he always wrote his name. He has in later years been commonly designated as Dr. Ballou. To this name must be conceded a high place, even if it be not yet widely conspicuous, in the temple of fame. He was a grandson of Mr. Ballou's oldest brother, Benjamin. He was born in Guilford, Vermont, Oct. 18, 1796. His parents were Baptists. Tradition tells of the second Hosea being also a youthful subject of a Baptist revival. At the age of fifteen he was a precocious district school-teacher. At the same age he began, under guidance of Rev. Mr. Wood in Marlborough, Vermont, to make his way through the Latin language into the Latin literature. When he came to Portsmouth to assist his great-uncle, he had been a teacher three winters, his summers having been divided between farm-work and study. He had also, through an experience we cannot now with the means at our command rescue from obscurity, become a Universalist in his faith. He could doubtless, in language, literature, and science have taught his teacher; but in theology and biblical exegesis he was a most reverent student. An apt student, indeed, he must have been. He preached his first sermon at nineteen in Monroe, Massachusetts. An expected preacher not appearing at a school-house, he obeyed the instant summons to the desk, and acquitted himself with credit. His first settlement was at Stafford, Connecticut. In 1821, a large edifice having been erected in Roxbury, a suburb of Boston, where Mr. Ballou had been the missionary, he was called to this important pastorate by the recommendation of his former teacher. Seventeen years were spent at this post; fifteen years as pastor at Medford, another suburban town of Boston, followed. He then left the pastoral ministry to enter, after a year of travel and study at the universities of Europe, on his duties as first President of Tufts College. He held this position till May 27, 1861, when he was summoned to his final rest. He is pre-eminently the Universalist scholar. In 1829 he published the "Ancient History of Universalism." This exhibition of his researches in church history at its sources in the dead languages was the wonder of the learned. Dr. Edward Beecher says of the book, "The work is one of decided ability, and is written with great candor and a careful examination of authorities." Dr. Beecher's own protracted studies in the same unfrequented field, led him, contrary to his expectation in the beginning, to the same conclusions reached by Dr. Ballou; namely, that Universalism was the dominant doctrine in the church in the age immediately succeeding the apostolic. For many years Dr. Ballou was editor of the "Universalist Expositor," and its successor, the "Universalist Quarterly." The heroism of his devotion to scholarly literature in the service of his faith but few in his generation understood. The ardor of his desire that his brethren might lead the church in sound learning, and appreciate the true and good in philosophy, made him a pioneer among Universalists in education, as his great-uncle had been in theology and exegesis. He had very slight oratorical gifts. He had the scholar's shyness; in manner he was usually introversive and dry; yet he was heard with eager interest by those who could appreciate the substance of his utterances. In prayer he always kindled to eloquence; and in conversation with a kindred mind, or with two or three friends, he was unconstrained and charming. Unlike his senior, he shrank from the presence of a multitude; he found no exhilaration in public address; he distrusted and underrated his ability to interest the mass.

But with his pen he had freedom and easy mastership. He could make hidden things visible, and follow a sure clew through the most intricate problems. He was at once a logician and a seer. His studies of will-freedom and necessity, of the testament written in human nature in connection with the testaments of revelation, have never been surpassed for perspicuity and profundity. For spiritual discernment he can be named with Pascal, Channing, and Martineau. More than any other man of his generation he explored the entire system of Universalist doctrines, and apprehended the Christian faith as a philosophy. In his personality, we must confess, he escapes our descriptive words, even as his shy spirit when in the body shrank from recognition. It is easy to say he was single-hearted, in candor transparent, an utter stranger to envy, that he had no small trait; yet such affirmations can only suggest to those who already know them the indescribable attractions of his deep and loving nature. He was the plainest of men in his method of life, yet he has never been explained. No one has attempted to write his too-long-delayed biography. His name among Universalists is like the name of Socrates in the world of letters. There is fascination in the name itself. Chapin and Starr King found enchantment in his companionship. It is to be regretted that neither of these eloquent men revealed in full delineation the charm of this personality, so profound in simplicity, so grand in mental proportions, so sublime in self-abnegation.

It is well known that Dr. Ballou did not follow his elder namesake in the belief that punishment of sin is bounded by mortality. The theology he learned of

HOSEA BALLOU, 2D.

his great-uncle in Portsmouth he did not during his life unlearn or disbelieve. In his later years he was called a new-school man; in reality he was, in this point of opinion, of the original Ballou school. This divergence of conviction, however, did not in the least disturb the mutual friendliness of these kindred spirits. In joint editorship, and in appreciation of each one's peculiar gifts, either was the virtual completion of the other. Dr. Ballou, by counselling unity through forbearance and charity, rendered the Universalist Church a signal service during the Restorationist controversy. He was in doctrinal sympathy with the seceders, yet by his calmness and candor kept many turbulent spirits from excesses of zeal.

The two Ballous blend in spiritual union. To the younger will be conceded the wider range of scholarship; the older excelled as a biblical specialist. The work of the younger supplements that of the older in our denominational history. For the gift of Hosea Ballou 2d to the church we now bespeak gratitude to the senior Hosea Ballou.

Rev. John Boyden, who died Sept. 28, 1868, when nearing the completion of the thirtieth year of his pastorate in Woonsocket, Rhode Island, was also a spiritual son of Hosea Ballou. Not varied and profound in scholarship as Dr. Ballou, not a patient plodder in books like Dr. Paige, not a general genius like Dr. Whittemore, he was, in his own place, no less than either esteemed. He had genius in loving. He diffused about him an atmosphere of love. He was born in Sturbridge, Massachusetts, May 14, 1809, and had early country-school privileges, which he faithfully improved. At fourteen he heard Mr. Ballou preach one sermon in Brookfield. The subject was "The Unsearchable Riches of Christ." With his usual directness of address the preacher at the climax of each division of his discourse asked, "Do YOU see the unsearchable riches of Christ?" The sermon was a revelation to the eager young soul. Three or four years afterward he heard Mr. Ballou preach again, when his subject was, "We preach not ourselves, but Christ Jesus the Lord." "After reading his text," Mr. Boyden long afterward wrote, "he carefully folded his glasses, put them in his pocket, as was his custom, and while the audience was waiting with breathless attention to hear the first word that fell from his lips, he began thus: 'The text *supposes* that there *is* such a thing as a man preaching *himself*.' The audience breathed,—a token that it already possessed the key to the sermon." This discourse carried the young man captive to the hope of the whole world's redemption. On the 14th day of May, 1829,—the day he was twenty years old,—he entered Mr. Ballou's house as a student. He was a shy country-boy, but was soon made to feel at home in the large and affectionate family. Such, in those days, was the urgency of the demand for preachers of hope, that Mr. Ballou sent the young man to preach in Annisquam, Gloucester, in the place of the pastor, Rev. Mr. Leonard, on the first Sunday of the month following. As he was preparing to leave for Gloucester, with trepidation and misgiving in his heart, Mr. Ballou gave him this charge: "Be in earnest. Don't speak one word without making the people understand and feel that you believe it with all your heart."

How the young preacher succeeded in Annisquam on that Sunday he was not inclined to confess; but he left on record the confession that through all the subsequent years of his ministry, whenever he in the pulpit felt the effects of a wearied frame in languor of speech, he could instantly arouse himself by recollecting the words of his spiritual father, "Be in earnest." This was indeed his real life-motto. He was distinctively an earnest man. He was in 1830 ordained in Berlin, Connecticut, where he remained four years; he was in Dudley, Massachusetts, six years, and in 1840 became pastor of the new society in Woonsocket, Rhode Island, where he completed his life-work, and where his memory is still fulfilling a blessed ministry. He resembled his spiritual father in being specifically a Bible student and preacher. He was a resolute preacher of righteousness, an antislavery and temperance reformer; he was as true to the right as the needle to the pole. But the winning love of the good man, the gospel grace, — how can it be portrayed? He was the personification of the loving spirit. He felt divinely beloved; it was his cheerful necessity to humanly love. "Who at once can love and rest?" asks Mrs. Browning. He had the gospel light and heat which illumines and radiates; his ministry was visibly active, and in this sense unrestful, yet his heart was securely anchored and at peace. He was so perfectly a representative of the Lord Jesus, that it seems scarcely improper to say, in behalf of those who through responsive love felt the depth and tenderness of his affection, "He hath borne our griefs and carried our sorrows." We know not who in his generation surpassed him in largeness of love, — the

Christian love which recognizes the Infinite in the finite, the Divine in the human, and feels another's joy and sorrow as its own. No name among those held in honor by the Universalist Church is regarded with more affection than John Boyden, the Christian pastor, who had a genius for loving.

It is our privilege to add that all Mr. Ballou's children, bone of his bone, flesh of his flesh, were his in spiritual likeness. The proverbial erring one, the stray-away, was not known in his household. No pillows were wet because of a recreant or thankless child. It was the father's happiness to see two of his three sons choose his own profession.

Hosea Faxon, in early manhood, preferred a farmer's life, and was settled in Monroe, Massachusetts; but at thirty, as was the case with his grandfather, the call to the ministry became irresistible. He was ordained in Boston, June 30, 1833; he settled in Whitingham, Vermont, where he remained pastor nearly twenty-five years, and then removed to Wilmington, Vermont, where he was pastor fifteen years, when the infirmities of age caused him to retire from the pulpit. He had marked resemblance, both personal and mental, to his father. When he appeared at the centennial celebration in Gloucester, in 1870, many of his brethren wondered why he was not conceded the leadership in the church, of which he was so manifestly capable. The explanation was his entire content in quiet country life. He reared a large family, and had happiness in his home. He was held in high esteem by his fellow-townsmen. He was in Whitingham town clerk; in Wilmington he was twice elected a member of the

REV. JOHN BOYDEN.

Constitutional Convention, and once was elected to the State Legislature, and was president of the local savings-bank. In this thrifty country-life his ambition was satisfied. When he died in Wilmington, May 20, 1881, at almost the precise age at which his father died, it was largely conceded that no man in southern Vermont had been for fifty years held in more reverent esteem than he had been, and none more than he had influenced religious opinion.

Another son of Mr. Ballou, Massena Berthier, quite early entered the Universalist ministry, settling at Stoughton, Massachusetts. After fulfilling an active pastorate of twenty-five years he relinquished the care of the parish, and became one of its members and supporters. He is at this writing still living at Stoughton; he is nearing the completion of his eighty-eighth year, and is, we believe, the oldest living Universalist preacher. The beauty of his spirit, the gentleness of his heart, the uprightness of his life, are affectionately witnessed by his neighbors. "My father named me," he once said to us, "after two of Napoleon's marshals for whom he had great admiration. It was the only mistake I ever knew him to make: I am utterly destitute not only of the love of warfare, but of the desire for controversy; there is no fight at all in me." But in the warfare which the lamb represents, — that of appeal to the better nature of man, — who will say this gentle soldier of the Cross has not fought a good fight of faith?

The youngest son of the subject of our biography, Maturin Murray, in his biography of his father, shows his deep appreciation of his honored parent. He early turned his attention to literature and the publishing business, and won marked success. In later years he has been an extensive traveller in unfrequented portions of the earth; his descriptive books have commanded a very wide reading.

We reluctantly leave this aspect of our theme. The real leadership of Mr. Ballou could be in striking instances much more extensively proved. His followers, as we behold, were all faithful to their own native characteristics. They were by no means servile imitators of their chosen example. Yet in every one the spirit of Mr. Ballou reappears.

Only a real religious leader could be the father of such a company of freeborn spiritual sons.

XVIII.

IN THE PULPIT.

WHOEVER once saw Mr. Ballou in the pulpit was not likely to forget the fact. Yet one needed to see him repeatedly, under widely different circumstances, to appreciate the range of his pulpit gifts. Whether in a country farm-house, or in a city pulpit, or at a convention, he was equally at home. Before the greater multitude he was undoubtedly at his best; yet he needed to be seen on all the lesser occasions, that his best might be rightly measured.

In the early years of his ministry, while itinerating from Dana and Barnard, he frequently preached in an imaginary pulpit in a farm-house.

Let us conjure into visibility one of these specimen experiences. It is brought about somewhat in this way.

Mr. Ballou is a much-talked-of man in the country districts. He is spoken of by the "unco guid" as a very dangerous man. He is, they say, an emissary of Satan with beguiling words, destroying saving faith in many a precious soul. Yet there are some who bravely testify in his behalf. They declare he does not speak like an infidel; that he commends a cheerful faith with great zeal and undeniable sincerity. Some friend of fair play is moved to say to his fellow-citizens of the farming community: "Let us have him preach for us some evening, and learn of this sect everywhere spoken against." The suggestion is received with some favor. An application is accordingly made for the Congregationalist church for a week-day evening service. The refusal is prompt. In another section of the town is a Baptist meeting-house; an application is made for that, on such terms as it is sometimes let to a travelling panorama. The refusal here is both prompt and emphatic. These sects have not yet learned to love each other very fervently, but they agree in the determination that the perdition-filling heresy must be kept out of the town. What now is to be done? A number of people have become eager to hear the new preacher. The conflicting stories they have heard make them curious. At this point a thrifty farmer, having a commodious house, offers it for such an evening service. The offer is cordially accepted. The request is sent to Mr. Ballou that he will favor the inquirers with an evening discourse; he replies with glad consent, and names the first evening at his command.

Notice of the meeting goes abroad. Many tongues advertise the coming event.

The evening, dreaded by some, impatiently waited for by others, at length arrives. The house has two spacious rooms opening from either side of the hall, and in the rear a large kitchen, the "living-room" of the family. The people arrive in groups, many bringing their own chairs; they arrange themselves in rows in the three rooms, until the space is completely occupied.

The assembly is a good representation of New Englanders of the second generation after the Revolution.

One can here see how the doubly-named caricature "Brother Jonathan" and "Uncle Sam" is rooted in actual New England country life. These people, it must be confessed, are guilty of not having been born in Paris; they are, consequently, crude in some of the social graces. Yet a more thrifty, intelligent, incorruptible populace can nowhere be found. "What can be raised here?" was asked of Daniel Webster, as his eye rested on the barren granite hills of New Hampshire. "Men," was his reply. Those eager people now waiting to hear the new preacher are representative New Englanders of the closing years of the homespun age. They have been trained to do their own thinking; they are not laggards in the business. The audience — the faces of the people being dimly visible in the light of tallow dips, while rays from the blazing wood in the open fireplace dance through the rooms and cast fantastic shadows on the walls — is a human picture curious and historic.

The time for the services has arrived. The buzz of whispered conversation ceases. The preacher has taken his place in the kitchen, midway between the doors which open on either side into the crowded front rooms. He rises and announces a hymn, holding a hymn-book in one hand and a tallow dip in the other.

He shows his full six feet of height. His hair, parted in the middle, falls to his neck. Later in life he will wear it more shortly cut; now, he follows the prevalent ministerial fashion. His voice is mild, with an occasional hint in it that under stress it can become sonorous.

He has finished the reading; he invites all to engage with freedom in the singing, remarking that he cannot assist them, yet fully appreciates the ministry of sacred song. It is the era of country singing-schools. Not a few are willing to assist in psalmody on any public occasion. The familiar hymn is vigorously sung; all the parts are properly rendered. A chapter of Scripture is read, and accompanied by explanatory remarks. A prayer is offered, varying from the prayers commonly heard; its simplicity, its absence of stock-phrases, its process of reasoning, under guidance of the Infinite Intelligence, marking this portion of the service as singularly original. At the reading of the second hymn a glistening has come into the preacher's blue eyes, and a persuasiveness appears in his manner. Some of his hearers have already ceased to regard him with dread.

The sermon begins. It is precisely the one inquirers will be glad to hear. The text is a passage often quoted as conveying a threat of endless punishment. He states the case fairly. No Orthodox minister could say more in behalf of the commonly-accepted interpretation than he says. He means at least to be frank. Now comes his own explanation. Very simple and plain he makes everything. He knows all about farming; his illustrations are taken out of our every-day life. And now he is growing eloquent. Part of the time we see only his back, as he talks to those in the other rooms; but we easily hear his words, and we follow, without loss of a link, the chain of his argument. Now he turns toward us. Easy and fluent his speech has become. He looks directly at one of his hearers, whose face seems to make objection, and he at once clothes the objection in words. It really seems the hearer who is speaking. He has begun his answer to his critic, when his hearer appears to make another objection. "Wait a little," he says, "I am now speaking to the remark you just now made; remember this new objection, and we will return to it soon." What interest is seen in the face of every hearer! The preacher is making clear his doctrine that God is the Father of all, and Christ the Savior of all. He is surely a man of good heart and human sympathy. One would think the Scripture must mean what he says; it does not look reasonable that it can mean anything else. What a happiness to believe there is no literal lake of fire into which almost all mankind are to be plunged! And now he is closing. Quickly the time has passed. It was seven o'clock when he began his sermon; now it is fifteen minutes to nine. The hour and three quarters have seemed less than half an hour. Well, we have a great deal to think of when we are at work in the field, and we must read the Bible in this new light. If ever this preacher comes within twenty miles of us we must hear him again.

As seen in the mirror of a hearer's mind, such was Mr. Ballou's preaching on many an evening in a country farm-house.

By aid of the historic imagination we now transport ourselves to School Street Church, Boston.

The period is near the completion of the first quarter of the nineteenth century. This is the church which was built for Mr. Ballou before he came to Boston. We are here before the people have begun to arrive. We look about us. The auditorium is plain, home-like, designed rather for use than to solicit admiration; with galleries extending around three sides, it proffers seats to near a thousand people. Opposite the pulpit are the singing-seats, affording accommodations for a large voluntary choir.

Now the people begin to assemble. They are, forsooth, unregenerates; they dare to discredit Milton's Satan and Dante's Inferno. Christians? Their neighbors class them with Pagans, Infidels, Atheists. Little, however, these people seem to care for their ill names. They have, we note, begun to vary the ancestral Puritan type. The typical long face has shortened, the formal dress has been changed to a more worldly fashion; the heavy heart within, which was in other days esteemed religious according to its heaviness, has been lightened with some strange cheer. These people are happy, cordial, of independent thought, and of generous heart. The regular worshippers nearly fill the seats. To such seats as remain the strangers are welcomed. Before the hour for service has fully come, the congregation has solidified to a dense mass.

Is that man sitting behind the pulpit Mr. Ballou? Yes, it is he.

In one thing, at least, we are disappointed. We have heard of him as a wit and the preacher of cheerfulness, yet his face now looks cheerless, gloomy, almost morose. It is indeed true that his face does at times give strangers the impression of his being in ill-temper. While travelling he has appeared to observers a man in bad humor. When Dr. Lucius R. Paige recalls his first sight of Mr. Ballou, it is in language like this: "On reaching my majority I hastened from Hardwick to Boston. I arrived in time to attend a service at School Street, and without calling on my future teacher, I went to the church. My first impression of Mr. Ballou was that he seemed, as we New Englanders say, cross; for a few moments I thought him the crossest man I had ever seen." And what is the explanation of this most unexpected appearance? It need not be said that as far as it suggests ill-nature it is altogether deceptive. It signifies simply that his mind is severely striving with his theme. He is to preach with no manuscript to guide him; his sermon he carries in his mind in all its logical completeness. His stress and introversion he shows all unconsciously; it is pictured in his countenance, because his face is quick to respond to his passing mood.

After the choir-anthem he rises, and begins the reading of the Bible. Almost immediately we concede that he is a natural elocutionist. A school-taught teacher could, no doubt, instruct him as to the customary pronunciation of certain words; but not every teacher would attempt to improve his method of emphasis and modulation.

His pronunciation is interesting as a remnant of his boyhood. At this time — 1825 — a bright, finely-organized boy, Thomas Baldwin Thayer, is a student in the Boston Latin School; he is Mr. Ballou's sharp yet silent verbal critic. The boy is coming under the preacher's spell, yet he makes note in his memory of the mispronounced words. When he has himself become an eminent advocate of the doctrine he is now learning of Mr. Ballou, he will smile — laughter filling his eyes while barely touching his delicate lips — as he declares to a ministerial brother, "In the first sermon I heard Father Ballou preach he uttered this extraordinary sentence: 'Brethering, I perceed to dev-il-ope and illusterate the follerin p'ints.'" Probably Mr. Ballou will never afterward in mispronunciation match this sentence. This characteristic of Mr. Ballou's speech will pretty much disappear in his maturer years. It is natural that, like a Scotchman or a Yorkshireman, he should speak his native idiom. He has at this day so rarely heard polished public speakers, and has been himself so constantly speaking, that he has had but little opportunity to mend his native style. In the country, his pronunciation is not peculiar; in the city, if it make an occasional critic smile, it has a pleasant home-sound to many of his country-born hearers.

Mr. Ballou, while we delay in these reflections, continues his reading.

We note that the look of ill-nature, introversion, anxiety, whatever it was, has entirely vanished. As he reverently reads the sacred words, his countenance expresses the newly-awakened emotions. In the reading of the hymn he finds evident enjoyment. It is sung by the choir with marked skill and enthusiasm. The prayer, simple, spontaneous, dominated by the reason, is offered, and another hymn brings us to the sermon.

We now see him as the preacher.

His face has become the witness of deep earnestness. By utter absence of self-consciousness he favorably impresses his observers. He is very quiet, but no one can doubt his consciousness of mastery. He announces his text deliberately and distinctly. We now see him in vigorous middle life. The Muse of history prophesies that later he will have a habit of putting on spectacles to read his text; then, before beginning his sermon, taking them off and encasing them; then spreading his handkerchief across the pulpit,— a procedure in his case peculiarly adapted to invite and fix attention. He has not, at our present beholding, attained to the distinction of wearing spectacles. Indeed, spectacles will always be to him more ornamental than essential; at eighty he will not need them in reading fine print. He now, we observe, has no such dramatic introduction. The opening words of his sermon are explanatory of the biblical setting of the text. In a few sentences he shows his text to have bearings on great questions and great principles; in these relations it is soon discerned that its traditional interpretation is not reasonable.

His speech is very simple. It has the ease and the occasional lapse and recovery of familiar conversation. Yet there is in it a singular dignity. He personifies "the objector" and reports "our opponent," making their utterances forcible; he gives them courteous and complete answer. Meanwhile, interest in the congregation is being aroused. He is himself becoming absorbed in his speech. It is no longer possible to be critical of his manner or observant of his quaint pronunciations. His gestures are so entirely the appropriate accompaniment of his emotion, that in themselves they attract no attention; in after years they will be remembered only by some exceptional hearer who has reflected on their remarkable naturalness and grace. In utter self-forgetfulness he declares his vision. We begin to feel that, whatever his topic, he can have but one central subject. God's Fatherhood, God's Love, made manifest in persuasive power in the Lord Jesus

Christ, the Savior of the world, — all his themes are tributary to this at last. Different aspects of his special theme now give him the logical divisions of his discourse. On each he is complete, yet wastes no word. All his positions are indissolubly connected with his established premises. He is surely a master in logic. Scriptural passages from every portion of the sacred writings come to him like his own spontaneous speech. He seems in the very atmosphere in which the Bible was born.

His discourse has now become majestic. A bubbling mountain spring, clear and sweet; a trickling stream; a rivulet with tributaries; now a broad river, swift, irresistible, hurrying to the ocean, — such is the parallel of his discourse. He is speaking as one inspired. He is vehement, yet under full command; as by instinct he summons all his reserve forces to the front. He projects his great truth into the minds and hearts of his hearers. To the whole congregation he has become irresistible. His words are as nails fastened by a master of assemblies. All faces are as one face. When the theme for a moment seems tangled, on the general face is suspense. A few rapid explanatory words make the crooked place straight: a beam of satisfaction passes over the common countenance. An opponent's confident objection is so quickly and entirely dissolved that the process seems like juvenile play: a smile, yes, a laugh, broadens the common face. Soon a picturing of Divine compassion becomes a joy full of pathos: the eyes of the common face swim in tears. The preacher is the embodiment of the Living Oracles. In him the truth is life and light. It suffuses the hearer's heart; it illumines the whole horizon of experience.

The sermon, by orderly approaches, reaches its artistic climax and is finished. The audience, instructed, awakened, exalted, quietly disperses. The spell of cheering hope and worshipful love, nevertheless, will long remain in the hearers' hearts.

Our picture of Mr. Ballou in the School Street pulpit is a composite of many gathered memories, especially of those who were his frequent hearers. Certain recorded idiosyncratic recollections of occasional hearers — among which must be classified some of the graphic reminiscences of Rev. Dr. E. G. Brooks — are not sustained by general testimony, and therefore are not reproduced in this generalized picture.

We have recalled Mr. Ballou when he was at his best; yet the evidence is uniform that he was in the School Street pulpit almost always at his best. Age in due time lessened his extraordinary fertility and oratorical exuberance; but even then the quantity and vehemence more than the quality of his preaching received modification.

At all Universalist Conventions for more than half a century he was the one minister the people could not excuse from preaching. In his maturer years his presence in the pulpit at the general convocations was itself a benediction. He was usually the preacher reserved till the last; he alone could be trusted to bring the series of meetings to a fitting culmination. Rev. Dr. A. A. Miner recalls hearing him at the New Hampshire State Convention in 1838. "Tears of joy," he wrote, "rolled down the cheeks of the gray-haired fathers as the hopes of the gospel burned anew in their hearts." When he had preached at the General Convention in Akron, Ohio, in 1843, an editor of a secular paper said, "No other made the brown faces of the old farmers so fairly shine with admiration as Father Ballou."

The many extant sermons of Mr. Ballou are admirable as specimens of the art of sermon-making. Unmistakable in statement, without verbal waste, pictorial, logical, at every stage intrenched in Scripture, they are in themselves worthy of careful study. Yet the notable charm of his pulpit oratory was in his personal presence. He possessed the manifest attractions of a simple nature. It was impossible for a candid person not to see in him the stamp of sincerity. His voice, his gestures, his speaking eyes, his mobile countenance, conveyed the magnetism of spiritual emotion. These things elude transmission through the inanimate printed page.

XIX.

HOME LIFE.

PARALLEL with the public career of Mr. Ballou was a home life singularly pure and felicitous. We are constrained to believe that his visible life could not have been so heroic, and yielded such beneficent public influence, if his heart had not been constantly nurtured at home.

Only slight glimpses of his domestic experience are possible to us; yet these are, fortunately, sufficient for our understanding of the rare quality of his life at the fireside.

He fulfils the Psalmist's description of the man who walketh not in the counsel of the ungodly, and is like a tree planted by the rivers of water. At the roots of his being he was fed by two rivers. One was the law of the Lord. This was his unfailing delight. Day and night it was his joy to meditate upon the endless theme. The other invisible river was his home. What Prince Rasselas could not find in courts or schools or scenes of revelry, — content, — the poor misanthrope might have found in Mr. Ballou's household. Here was the peaceful realm of a true queen. Children's voices, both in its early and later days, made it musical. Why need Mr. Ballou, indeed, care for the harsh tones without, that condemned and traduced, so long as he had such a fountain of joys at home? Truly, rivers of water fed the sources of his life, and kept him young and strong.

When Ruth Washburn Ballou first claimed our notice, she was, we remember, a bride of seventeen. We take a peculiar pleasure in reviving the memory of her wooing. Before she herself appears to have seriously thought of marriage, she was, we recall, selected by Rev. Caleb Rich as the wife of our hero, then a bashful young preacher. Mr. Rich pleaded with her not to be too coy if the lonely young man should confess his need of her assistance in his rugged pathway of life. She did not, to be sure, commit herself in advance; but we recall her naïve confession that when she, knowing his errand, saw the manly young preacher approaching her home in company with Mr. Rich, she heard an inner voice saying, "There is my future companion." She needed no second glance at the blushing young candidate, nor a second message from her own heart, to convince her that her duty and inclination coincided.

Love at first sight, under such circumstances, is, we venture to affirm, admirable.

Tradition ascribes to Mrs. Ballou in her youth quite unusual personal beauty. She was tall, of graceful form, with light brown hair, blue eyes, and clear complexion. She was in early life an almost ideal New England girl. Abundant health, a buoyant heart, and abounding common sense were her conspicuous traits. She possessed in unusual degree what New Englanders of her day called "faculty." She could easily make a comfortable home on her husband's Hardwick-Dana salary of five dollars a week, and be happy as the queen she was. She did not repine at her husband's necessary absences on his appointments; and she lighted up his home-coming with radiant happiness.

Truly, what joy of love flooded the young husband's life!

To see her bright face in the home-greeting, after a tussle with the winds and drifts on the hills in the wintry weather, left him in no doubt that heaven is a reality. The little piece of it he had in his home showed him the fibre of it all.

Children were born to the young couple with a frequency that might have perplexed less trustful hearts. The gift of children, however, only deepened the content of the home. It has been a query why such romantic names were given to the daughters. We assume it was the result of a foible in the father, kindred to his rhyming. For *such* daughters, common names would be by no means appropriate. Of course not! Cassendana, Mandana, Clementina, Fiducia, — these are the names the delighted father fancied his unequalled daughters deserved. And Mrs. Ballou, the happy mother, consented, we assume, to have her daughters so distinguished, believing the father would be pleased, and her girls receive no irreparable harm! Our smile at the paternal foible, good reader, should be at least respectful; it may well be almost covetous.

The final count of children born was eleven; nine survived infancy and reached maturity.[1]

[1] The children born to Mr. and Mrs. Ballou, surviving infancy, were these: Fanny, Oct. 13, 1797; Hosea Faxon, April 4, 1799; Massena Berthier, Nov. 28, 1800; Cassendana, Jan. 9, 1803, born in Dana, Massachusetts; Mandana, Sept. 17, 1804, born in Barnard, Vermont;

The mother, it will be readily conceived, needed to look well to the ways of her household. She did not, to be sure, literally lay her hands to the spindle and the distaff; by-gone, in her day, in village life, was domestic spinning and weaving. But of making and mending, of sewing much and cutting close, there was no end.

By the time her husband had arrived at Salem, on his predestined way to Boston, she had become inured to rigid economy. When increase of salary and profits from his books made heroic economy no longer a necessity, the simple and prudent life was for its own sake preferred.

Through all the strenuous period of the family experience she was dowered with unfailing health and cheerfulness. The husband at times, under his burden of labors, was distraught; her courage was his tonic. At one period, early in his Boston ministry, he was seriously sick: he was for a season almost disheartened; but she kept courageous, and did more than all the physicians to bring him back to health and hope.

Mrs. Ballou had, meanwhile, her own trials. Two new-born children were afterward missed from the home circle; not, we may be sure, without pangs of grief. But she, with Divine aid, ruled her own spirit, and bravely bore her own burden. Her help to others was the overflow of her own victory of loving faith.

Beautiful is she in her faithful and contented motherhood. "Her children rise up and call her blessed; her husband also, and he praiseth her."

Elmina Ruth, April 30, 1810; Clementina, July 10, 1812; Fiducia, May 1, 1814, born in Portsmouth, New Hampshire; Maturin Murray, April 14, 1820, born in Boston, Massachusetts.

As her life neared its close she became yet more beautiful. The testimony of beholders is uniform as to the rare grace of her declining years. Her memory was burdened with no painful regrets. Charity, good-will, loving-kindness, made her slightly-furrowed face bloom with an ever-deepening happiness. Her childlike mildness was combined with decided mental vigor. "But few such women have ever lived," said Thomas Whittemore. Her motherhood in her later years had become a many-jewelled crown. Two of her sons had become preachers of the faith she loved; the youngest was prospering as an author and publisher. Two of her daughters had married preachers of the great hope. All her sons and daughters were happy in their own home relations. Her grandchildren, numbering in her later days no less than forty, kept her fresh in the human joy of motherhood.

Beautiful indeed was she in old age; her beauty touched holiness.

Even in this Beulah period, however, she still had trials. This world is not heaven, and no heavenly condition can long exist. She lived to take the last farewell of her oldest daughter. Grandchildren were taken, and with them faded so much of her human hope. Not long at any period of her life was she permitted to forget that this is a mortal state.

But her life-joy, while her husband remained by her side, rose high above her heart-sorrow. Her wifely love grew more spiritual, trustful, reverential, as the final home was more nearly approached. Those often in her presence in her peaceful last days, seeing her as she sat in her rocking-chair, spectacled, reading, or in reveries of memory, silently hoping and loving, the picture of an ideal grandmother, sometimes saw her as one who was anticipating by slow transfiguration the heavenly state.

The devotion of her husband corresponded with her own. Benjamin B. Whittemore, Esq., a grandson who spent some years of his youth with his grandparents, said to the writer: "My grandfather could not have been more chivalric toward his wife in their honeymoon than he was in the last years of his life. I remember my grandmother as a delightful woman in my day, companionable, and the confidential friend of the children."

The husband's devotion was expressed not alone in words, but in deeds. Prudence, industry, and simple tastes had, as we have observed, brought the reward of competency to their natural resting-time. With characteristic thoughtfulness he desired her to surrender to competent younger hands the cares of the household. It was therefore arranged that the second daughter, Cassendana, wife of Joseph Wing, Esq., should be the responsible head of the household. For thirty years Mrs. Wing fulfilled the duties of this position, which would have been a hard one in most households, an impossible one in many; and the result was all the patriarchal husband and father anticipated. It was a household absolutely without jealousies. "A more cheerful and happy home," wrote Maturin, "it would be difficult for fancy to paint."

The peaceful happiness of these two intermingled lives in their last days testifies to the sacredness of true marriage. It may be that the best success Mr. Ballou achieved was, after all, in his own home. His life brought to fulfilment the divine promise, "At evening time it shall be light."

His whole home experience was of the same substance as the final evenings his son Maturin so graphically pictures. "How well," he writes, "can we see him at this moment, in the mind's eye, as he used to appear at the centre-table, with his book close to the lamp, and his wife opposite to him, listening to him while he was reading aloud to her. Such is almost the last evening scene we can recall in connection with him; his clear, distinct pronunciation, proper emphasis, and fine voice, even in old age, seeming to portray with singular accuracy the author's ideas, and to add a charm to the subject treated."

We shall not be suspected of having any excess of regard for Mr. Ballou's rhymes. But, as may be remembered, we made some exceptions to our sweeping unappreciation. There is, we must persist in thinking, more poetry in our hero's daily life than in many of his crude lines. We offer an illustrative instance. It is, in our view, a poem to see him, with the gallantry of youth, present to his wife an Autograph Album, after they had passed their golden wedding-day. Still more poetic is it that he should write in the Album some verses to his wife of more than fifty years. And the poem itself, we are free to declare, delights the heart with a grace all its own: —

TO MY WIFE.

Thou dearest of the dear to me,
  Of the beloved the best,
Couldst thou but read this heart, and see
  The treasures of my breast,

Assurance surely would be thine
That undiminished love,
By age grown better, like to wine,
Can never faithless prove.

Not when the virgin rose of youth
Blushed on thy snowy breast;
Not when we pledged ourselves in truth,
And were by Hymen blessed,
Could strong affection boast as now
Of such resistless sway,
When age sits wrinkled on my brow,
And mortal powers decay.

The secret of this happy home was its religion. The religion was not ostentatious; it was not made onerous with forms. "Before the noonday meal on the Sabbath," writes his son, "with his family assembled about the board, he always asked the Divine blessing in an impressive manner; but on no other day was he accustomed to do so aloud." Religion was real in the household; its spirit pervaded all amusements as well as duties. Mr. Ballou was himself, when with children, exceedingly playful. He accorded children their full rights. He governed his household in the spirit of his faith. The rules he wrote for Christian parents, he proved in his own home to be divinely wise.

"When giving your children commands, be careful that you speak with a becoming dignity, as if not only the right but the wisdom also to command was with you. Be cautious never to give your commands in a loud voice or in haste. When you have occasion to rebuke, be careful to do it with manifest kindness. When you are obliged to deny the request that your child may make, do not allow yourself to do this with severity. It is enough for the dear little ones to be denied what they want, without being nearly knocked down with a sharp voice ringing in their tender ears. You will find they will imbibe your spirit and manners. They will treat each other as you treat them. If you speak harshly, they will, when they have formed their habits, treat you with unkind and unbecoming replies. If you treat your little ones with tenderness, you will fix love in their hearts; they will love you and each other; they will imitate the conversation they have heard from the tenderest friends children have on earth."

Mr. Ballou's home life was fashioned after a deeply-meditated plan. His own childhood had been full of austerities; his little heart in those years must often have ached under the government of a religion of hate and fear. But in his maturity and old age he had such sympathy with children, and drank with them so gladly at the same fountain, that he redeemed for himself the natural childhood of which he was in his early years defrauded. He became the leader of children through friendship, as well as their parent exercising authority. And what love he won from his children; what glad obedience they gave him! "The idea is perhaps an extravagant one," wrote Rev. Sebastian Streeter, "but I have often thought that his house was the nearest fac-simile of the great mansion of the Infinite Father on high, of which I could form a conception."

This home is in visible form now no more in the earth. The writer has passed through Blossom Street, peering at all the houses, because he knew that in some one of them Mr. Ballou first made his home in Boston; knowing that in the walk up and down he must pass the door at which Thomas Whittemore, when an unlettered boot-maker's apprentice, stood and knocked. The writer has also, under guidance of Dr. Paige, gazed long at the house at the head of Garden Street, with the external staircase, where the Ballou family was living when Dr. Paige was a student with his spiritual father. The writer has also lingered in front of No. 24 Myrtle Street, where Mr. Ballou established his last home on earth. To revive in imagination the domestic life once lived under that roof, was more than the gratification of an idle whim; it was a heart-offering at a worthy shrine. With such a spell on us as was ours while reading Frederika Bremer's exquisite home-story, "Neighbors," and was again ours when we read Goethe's "Hermann and Dorothea," we stood before the visible remains of this real home which almost transcends the beauty of romance.

The home itself is now a memory; yet its spirit must, while the world endures, be reproduced in every household that truly realizes the Divine Fatherhood in domestic life.

XX.

TOWARD EVENING.

IN due time age proffered to Mr. Ballou its trials and triumphs.

Soon after he was seventy he received an unambiguous hint that he was growing old. Certain members of his parish urged the settling of a colleague. This to another man might in itself have been a grievance. For it was not, be it marked, the offer of an associate to do the pastoral drudgery. It was rather the suggestion that a young man divide with him the honors and emoluments of his office. But Mr. Ballou beheld the situation without grief. Whatever promised to promote the welfare of his loved people could meet no opposition from him. He would not have hesitated himself to retire from the pastorate if he could have seen in the act a prophecy of new prosperity for the parish. Nevertheless, when the subject was brought to a vote, it was made manifest that a decisive majority of the society had undiminished regard for their old pastor, and held to him in his maturity as vines to a supporting oak. He was assured that any wish he would express in regard to the matter should be eagerly granted. He had learned, however, the important life-lesson of coming down without giving up. The cordiality with which he joined the minority in asking for a colleague makes it doubtful whether the act cost him even a struggle.

Rev. T. C. Adam became temporary junior pastor, May 1, 1841; but the experiment of a substitute for Mr. Ballou was not in the first instance successful. Mr. Adam remained only a few months. For three years more Mr. Ballou, with occasional aid of various ministerial brethren, fulfilled the duties of the pastorate.

April 8, 1844, Rev. H. B. Soule became experimental junior pastor of the society, and held the position nearly two years. Mr. Soule was devoted and gifted; he regarded Mr. Ballou with reverence, and appreciated the greatness of his genius; and Mr. Ballou was as helpful as possible to him in his trying position. Yet it was plainly discovered that it was Mr. Ballou the people wished to hear preach. He was still the magnet at School Street.

When Mr. Soule had gone, the question was asked if any man could maintain himself as junior pastor under Mr. Ballou. It was then that shrewd eyes were turned across Charles River; in Charlestown they saw a young man who was stirring the elements. It was assumed that Rev. E. H. Chapin, if he would accept the position of junior preacher, would not be overshadowed by his veteran associate. But this meteor-star, this poet-preacher, was known to be expensive. He lived a rapt life, in utter disregard of the common economics. Mr. Ballou, the frugal, thrifty man, could hardly be expected to favor such a privilege of genius. That the young man disagreed with him on the question of future punishment, and was outspoken in his convictions, did not appear to lessen the veteran's regard. But he was frank to say the young man should not be pecuniarily so extravagant. Nevertheless, he so esteemed the young spendthrift that he made the

E. H. CHAPIN, D.D.

AT THE AGE OF 30.

extraordinary proffer of the relinquishment of his own entire salary, while still retaining the office of senior pastor; he was to this extent desirous that his people should profit by the rare gifts of the unequalled preacher.

Accordingly Mr. Chapin was duly chosen and installed his associate, Jan. 28, 1846. He was, correctly speaking, Mr. Ballou's first colleague. For two years he made the School Street pulpit the most famous in New England. Mr. Ballou had been a magnet; the new preacher was an electric battery. His oratory was the incarnation of emotional energy. He was in sympathy with the rising reforms of antislavery and temperance; his intense preaching constantly touched the great practical living issues. He was not specifically a Bible preacher; he never attempted exegesis; he preached Universalism inferentially and in broad generalizations, rather than in direct statements. In these things he was at the extreme of unlikeness to the senior pastor. But he was faithful to his own vision. In fervid eloquence he had in his generation no peer. He was at times tumultuous, again rapid as the lightning's flash; his voice, musical and sonorous at all times, became a thrilling trumpet in his impetuous climaxes. No man could more completely magnetize an audience. In each sermon in those days his hearers had an experience like the prophet Elijah's in Horeb, with this difference,—the irresistible modern prophet combined whirlwind, earthquake, flame, and the still small voice in almost simultaneous presentation. That the church was at every service thronged, that even the aisles and pulpit steps were appropriated by the fascinated visitors, and that Mr. Ballou was eclipsed in the popular interest, is all matter of course. For the first time in his ministry Mr. Ballou was retired to a second place in the popular estimation; but it does not appear that his equanimity was in the least disturbed. When at home on Sunday he was always among the most appreciative of the junior pastor's hearers. Perhaps he was never in spirit so great as during this period, when he exhibited such cheerful contentment under another's shadow.

After two years Mr. Chapin accepted a call to New York, and began the long ministry which was in its day renowned throughout the nation, and remains to this day a wonderful tradition.

May 31, 1848, Rev. A. A. Miner was installed in School Street as Mr. Chapin's successor. A man more after Mr. Ballou's heart could not have been found. He was scarcely less a master in the pulpit than his predecessor; yet he was of different quality. An exact logician, a thoroughly furnished expounder of Scripture, a fluent rhetorician of grace and lucidity, a prophet of righteousness, earnest and fearless, in the full measure a man in the pulpit and in daily life, on coming to Boston he instantly commanded general esteem. At this writing his ministry has been continued more than forty years over the same parish (now Columbus Avenue Church); in its usefulness and renown it has fulfilled its early prophecy. Rev. A. A. Miner, D.D., LL.D., is at this writing the recognized leader of the Universalist Church. He is famed for practical sagacity; for pioneership and kindling zeal in the establishment of Universalist educational institutions; for heroic exaltation of intelligence; for uncompromising devotion to temperance as an element

A. A. MINER, D.D., LL.D.

AT THE AGE OF 33.

of the gospel; for the popularity and scholarly finish of his easy extemporaneous utterances. Few men living are more enriched by unfeigned human esteem. We here add a laurel-leaf to his crown in reviving remembrance of his affectionate and faithful regard for Mr. Ballou during the four final years of the veteran's life. By thoughtful attentions and becoming deference he cheered the old preacher's heart under its increasing burdens, and made more peaceful his confident journey toward the shadows. These two servants of the Lord — one with the light of the setting and the other with the light of the rising sun in his heart — were remarkably adapted to be helpers of each other. The younger has essentially prolonged the mission of the older, and still wears the mantle of the translated prophet.

Had Mr. Ballou been another man, or like some men, he would in his old age have saddened his own heart and those nearest him with complaints. Instead, his old age was triumphant. He gratefully accepted freedom from the former exactions of his profession. He was now enabled freely to answer calls for his coveted Sunday services. He travelled extensively, visiting every New England State, and New York and Pennsylvania, renewing old friendships and learning by experience how generally and profoundly he was loved. In his last years he more completely than ever before fulfilled the duties of his natural bishopric of the entire Universalist Church. It was the greatest pleasure of his life to preach to those eager for instruction and open to reasonable conviction. In his old age his preaching lost none of its logical force or persuasive quality. In his latter years he became more subdued in manner; yet there was no falling off in the popular interest. In convincing power through sound reasoning and candid appeal he was without a peer among his younger brethren. He was everywhere treated with tender consideration, and honored as a patriarch. He was to the very last a great master of assemblies.

He also had leisure carefully to set his own house in order. He had, as we have said, accumulated a property that relieved him of all sense of dependency in his old age. He now conceived the project of being the opposite of a dependent, — a benefactor. Why should his children wait till after his death for their patrimony? Why should he be burdened with the care of property no longer needed by him and his companion? Some who had beheld his rigid practice of economy had feared that, as his riches increased, he had set his heart on them. But he valued money only for its uses. His self-denying habits, early formed, had never been inspired by selfishness. He now performed an act as rare as it was wise. While in the full possession and calm exercise of his faculties, he divided his substance with his children, reserving for his own use the portion he regarded as requisite for his need. The prosperity of his children was more dear to him than his own. He invested all his fortune in their happiness and gratitude. This is one of the marvels of his life, — that he executed, probated, and administered his own will.

He also had leisure to prepare some thoughtful final words as a legacy to his church. He was near eighty when, at the solicitation of a publisher, he sent forth the volume entitled "A Voice to Universalists." The first edition of the book was needlessly enlarged by a collection of his rhymes made from newspapers and magazines by a hand other than his own. This collection was very properly omitted in the second edition. We claim the right to see Mr. Ballou at his best. He was a voluminous writer; he almost always wrote well in prose, and almost always wrote ill in rhyme. His rhymes would have fulfilled their proper mission if they had not been raised from their graves in the old newspapers and magazines. It was a resurrection to condemnation. The book comprehended "A General Epistle to Universalists," full of excellent exhortation; "Advice to Young Men who design to enter the Ministry," embracing paternal advice based on his own long experience. In one article he attempts to unravel the problem of problems. His theory is stated in the title, "The Utility of Evil." In this essay he maintains that evil is a resultant of prior good; "if we say that the cause which produced evil was evil, we thereby say that evil existed before it existed;" and again, that good will continue after evil is no more. He gives many scriptural exemplifications of evil becoming useful. He does not commit the error of maintaining that evil is good, or good evil, but declares the permanence of good and the evanescence of evil. The logic exhibited in this production of his pen is worthy an Edwards. The remarkable title of the article seems fully justified. It is noteworthy that the veteran, under the weight of almost eighty years, should begin such a profound speculative study; it is not less noteworthy that he treats it with a perspicuity and vigor he could not have surpassed in mid-life.

When he drew near the completion of his eightieth year, Nov. 10, 1850, he preached a valedictory sermon. It was not his last sermon, nor designed to be; but the last which he committed to writing, and the one he purposed to preach under such responsibility as he would feel if it were known to him to be his final utterance. His appropriate text was 2 Peter i. 15: "I will endeavor that ye may be able, after my decease, to have these things constantly in remembrance." It is a review of his ministry, and of the doctrines he had rejected and the doctrines he had preached. He strenuously maintains the Divine Sovereignty as the solvent of all theoretic problems.

In treating of one point, however, he seems to us to lapse a little from his usual high courtesy and candor. "Of late, the writer of this," he says, "has seen an inclination in some of the professed teachers of Universalism to adopt some of the peculiar opinions of our Unitarian fraternity. . . . Among other things is the opinion that men carry into the next world the imperfections of this; so that their moral condition hereafter will depend on the characters they form while here in the flesh; while it is affirmed that they may, and will, improve and progress in virtue and holiness in the spirit world." We think Mr. Ballou is here a little unlike himself. It was no doubt natural for him to regret the admitted tendency of the denomination away from the doctrine of exclusive earthly penalties, of which doctrine he had been the champion for thirty years; but it was not like him to even suspect that this tendency was for strategic reasons designedly toward Unitarianism. It was in fact toward a doctrine he had himself believed during half his ministry. We observe that when Mr. Ballou comes to this point in his valedictory sermon, he for the first time in the discourse becomes tangled in his language. He says of the doctrine that there will be penal effects of sin beyond death: "This opinion being rather newly adopted, and as it seems to ingratiate them in the favor of Unitarians, it is quite natural for such preachers to devote not a small share of public labor to lead the minds of their hearers to the adoption of such views of the future state." We do not remember another instance where he tries so hard to say so simple a thing. He apparently means to say that some of his brethren, merely to please Unitarians, preach too often immature opinions as to the future life. With this exception the valedictory sermon is worthy its author.

We would be glad to think that this exceptional passage, in which is seeming want of courtesy, was intended as a facetious reference to Dr. Ballou. This careful scholar, in the "Quarterly" of the preceding January, had published an article in which he had stated that the great change of the denomination under Hosea Ballou was to Unitarianism. He maintained that there had been three marked changes in the doctrinal tendencies of the Universalist denomination. "The first," he says, "occurred about the commencement of the present century, when the former doctrines of the Trinity, of the vicarious or penal character of Christ's death, of Antinomianism, began to give way to Unitarian views on these points." This was of course a virtual statement that Hosea Ballou had led the denomination into Unitarianism. "The second took place between the years 1817 and 1824, when the tendency, which had been long increasing, to confine sin and its evil consequences to this life, assumed a more determinate character, and became predominant. The third change, if it prove to be general, may be said to have begun within a few of the last years, when the current of opinion has run more strongly in favor of a moral connection of the present life with the future, and when the sharp outlines of doctrine in general have been softened down, if not sometimes obliterated, to say nothing of certain movements occasioned by the rationalistic and transcendental tendencies without." Of the existence of this last-named tendency, Mr. Ballou, senior, had previously expressed doubts; now, in his valedictory sermon he admits its existence, but makes the apparently serious objection that it is toward Unitarianism. The pioneer of Unitarianism in America ought to have been in a facetious mood when he thus implied horror of a tendency toward Unitarianism.

If, however, the denomination in his last days was departing from his doctrinal standard, it surely was not in any degree losing its reverential love for its great pioneer preacher.

"I had hoped," said Hon. Israel Washburn, Jr., while presiding at the Universalist Reform Festival in 1851, "to see here that good old soldier, Father Ballou, who has done more for the cause of Christian truth than any other man living. We may not all agree with all his distinctiveness, but we can all honor, respect, and esteem him." The statesman voiced the sentiment which pervaded the entire Universalist Church.

Near this time Mr. Ballou preached one Sunday in

Charlestown. "To look upon that venerable form," wrote one describing the occasion, "which, like some aged tree having stood the blasts for many years begins to yield and bow its head, and upon those snowy locks whitened with the frosts of eighty winters, and then to reflect that for so long a period all his time, talents, energy, his very heart and soul, have been devoted to the glorious cause in which he is still engaged, conveyed a silent lesson to the heart, as impressive as it was beautiful." In every Universalist congregation he was in like manner revered.

The Universalist Reform Festival of 1851, of which mention has been made, was one of a series famous in the history of New England Universalism. An intense spirit of humanitarian reform, especially as regards slavery, intemperance, war, and capital punishment, was kindled in the Universalist Church. The people who exalted the Fatherhood of God and the Brotherhood of Man as cardinal doctrines of Christianity were naturally susceptible to human appeals. On Anniversary Week — the last week in May — various reform associations held meetings, and in 1847 the meetings culminated in a Reform Festival. It was a breakfast in a small hall, about two hundred being present. No extended report of this first festival was preserved. The presiding officer was Hon. Richard Frothingham; with him appears one other layman in the list of speakers. The clerical speakers were Revs. C. H. Fay, A. A. Miner, J. G. Adams, Sylvanus Cobb, Henry Bacon, E. H. Chapin, S. Streeter, J. S. Dennis, J. M. Spear. Last on the list was Hosea Ballou. Mr. Chapin, at this time his colleague, then as ever the peerless after-dinner orator, in an apostrophe to the Universalist pioneers thrilled and enraptured all present. Mr. Ballou was in feeble health, and spoke briefly, yet appropriately brought all previous speeches to a practical application. He was in sympathy with every reform which promised progress. In closing, he expressed the hope that the Reform Festival, then inaugurated, would become an institution among Universalists, and that a larger hall would in future be secured to accommodate the hundreds who would be present. The desire he expressed was, while he lived, yearly fulfilled.

In 1848 the Festival took the form of a dinner in the spacious Boylston Hall. Mr. Ballou had an engagement in the country which necessitated his leaving while the intellectual festivities were in progress. He remained, however, to speak some wise words on reform, as having its basis in true religion and to be effected under Divine guidance. He exhorted his young brethren, some of whom had advocated iconoclastic sentiments, not to undervalue good things because they are old. "We use the same numerals now," he said, "that were used of old, and the first principles of numeration and multiplication still hold good. We find use for the same sun, moon, and stars now which people used to see thousands of years ago. Do not cast everything behind you. Do not suppose that you are going to *surprise your Maker* by any operation you can perform." This sentence, pronounced with an inimitable mingling of simplicity and drollery, convulsed the audience; again and again, as the venerable speaker attempted to proceed, the applause and merriment were renewed. He concluded by reminding the audience of their all-inclusive hope, and remarking that he must not miss the cars, he expressed in parting his desire that if he should never be permitted to meet with them again on the earth, they might all see God's glory together in eternity. As he left the hall, a solemn hush was on the assembly. Mr. Chapin, the peerless, was the one remaining speaker. He spoke in reverential terms of the veteran, from whom he was then separating as a co-laborer; of the kindness and consideration the father in Israel had uniformly shown to him; of the conservatism of the old warrior, which was not inconsistent with any reasonable promise of progress. "He is conservative," he said, "*but he will never be too late for the cars!*" The pat allusion was of course irresistible.

The Festival of 1849 was also held in Boylston Hall, and was so like that of the preceding year as to need no separate description. That of 1850 was again a repetition of its predecessors, with some distinguishing characteristics. The name of Rev. Thomas Starr King appears among the speakers. The sensation of the day was the speech of Rev. T. B. Thayer, touching the work accomplished by Universalists. "Behold," he said, "what has already been done by Universalists! See that old patriarch out there!" pointing to Mr. Ballou, who sat at the head of the hall. Great cheering followed this allusion to the venerable presence. "What a noble work has he done! We are all heartily glad to see him here to-day. Let us follow his example. His place at these festivals will by and by be vacant, for he must depart; and when he goes it will be like the falling of a mighty oak in the midst of the forest, when, from the echoes, it would seem as if every tree far and near had taken up a wailing for its fall. But we hope he will be with us many years yet." Then, directly addressing the aged patriarch, he said: "And when at last thou shalt depart, return to us; come again, after thou art gone, in the influence of thy gentle spirit, in the power of thy undauntable resolution, in thine example, and in the energy of that good old heart of oak." Indescribable the emotion of the audience on the utterance of these words of prophecy. When, a few moments afterward, Mr. Ballou was called up, and in the midst of repeated cheers began to speak, he said: "It is the privilege of old age to be garrulous and egotistical. I will endeavor to guard against this habit of the aged; but I will say a little about myself, — I cannot leave myself out altogether." This clause, pronounced in his peculiar style, caused great merriment. "I have been compared to the old oak that is just ready to fall in the forest; but perhaps that old oak, if you get it ignited, will make as much fire as even *green wood.*" This may have been a pun, — his only known offence of this sort, — as Rev. Thomas J. Greenwood sat close to him, among the veterans. There was prolonged hilarity in the audience, ending in cheers. "Looking backward sixty years," he said, on resuming his speech, "I can see how much the cause of true reform has progressed. It has gone on so effectually that even the old partial God in whom the theologians believed has got reformed. He is so changed that the old clergy, if they were to hear him described now, would not know him. Our heavenly Father has become a real Father. The Bible has felt the reform. What was thought to be hostile to Universalism is now seen to be favorable to that doctrine. All sects seem coming to harmonize on the great truths of the paternity of God and the brotherhood of man." In this strain he made a quite lengthy address.

As implied in the words quoted from Hon. Israel Washburn, Jr., he was not present at the Festival in 1851. It is probable he was then absent in the country.

At the time of the Festival of 1852 his wife was prostrated with a serious sickness. He was reluctant to leave her bedside; but in response to an urgent appeal from his brethren, seconded by members of his own family, he was prevailed upon to leave his wife in the care of those whose solicitude was like his own, that he might add to the pleasure of those who were scarcely less dear than his nearest kindred. That day Boylston Hall was splendidly decorated with flags, pennons, and festoons. Benjamin F. Tweed, Esq., was the presiding officer. At the pronouncing of the words "Father Ballou," as sponsor for the sentiment, "Our denominational fathers, we honor them for what they were and are, and for what their glorious life-power shall be in the strife and progress of the future," there was long-continued cheering, which was immediately hushed to perfect silence when the patriarch began to speak. "I am an old man," he said; "I avail myself of the privilege of an old man, — to be a child. 'Once a man, twice a child.' I remember the child of long ago. That child was fond of praise, and loved to be petted and called a good boy. Now I am an old man, yet find myself the same boy, and of course I love to be praised now. Well, I have said enough about myself, and will turn to something of more importance. I am to speak about reformation, or [turning to the president] is the word 'progress'? [The president stated that the word was progress.] Ah, I like that better; it does not imply that I have been wrong. Progress! I am well posted on that. Certain Scriptures relating to progress come to my mind. I recall the 'handful of corn upon the top of the mountain; the fruit thereof shall shake like Lebanon.' This was progress. The same law of progress is seen in the Savior's metaphors of the leaven hidden in the meal, and of the mustard-seed. I saw the Universalist denomination when it was like that handful of corn upon the top of a sterile mountain; I saw it when it was a grain of mustard-seed; and I have seen it as I see it this day. Does not the increase shake like Lebanon? I have lived to realize, and be confident, that there is not an opposer of Universalism in the world who is not at heart a Universalist. And how long do you suppose they can keep out of their heads that which is in their hearts?" As he sat down, the whole assembly rose as by one impulse, and gave three cheers. And afterward, when Rev. B. M. Tillotson, in response to a sentiment complimentary of New Hampshire, said of Mr. Ballou, "That brave old oak," — modulating his voice to tenderness and repeating, — "that brave old oak was transplanted to Massachusetts from the New Hampshire fields," there was a spontaneous rising all over the hall, with cheers, and waving of scarfs and handkerchiefs.

Such unfeigned gratitude and devotion helped to make light the even-time of the honored prophet of hope. The deeper night-shadows, nevertheless, were coming on apace. "The night cometh; also the morning."

XXI.

VISIT TO THE OLD HOME.

PERIOD, 1851. AGE, 80.

FRIDAY, Oct. 10, 1851, Mr. Ballou was on the Cheshire rail-train journeying toward Richmond. He had left his wife with a married daughter at Lancaster, Massachusetts; invisible company attended him on this pilgrimage to his heart's early shrine.

The rail-track on which he was travelling had been but recently laid. The little box-car in which he was seated was no doubt a great improvement on the stage-coach it had superseded; but as compared with the luxurious rail-carriages of the trunk-lines of later years, it was as a dump-wagon to a liveried Central Park turnout. This plain railroading was to our traveller entirely satisfactory. He did not feel as vigorous as in the days fifty, even sixty years before, when he had driven his own horse over the same journey. He could then enjoy a chaise-ride through this rugged hill-country. Now, he was whitened with age. He was still reputed to be hale. It was often said of him, as of Moses, "his eye was not dim, nor his natural force abated;" but he unmistakably bore in his frame the weight of more than eighty years. When he was in the glow of preaching, it is true, he seemed almost youthful in his enthusiasm. But in repose, especially when in deep meditation, the wrinkles on his face were deep; there was visible shrinkage of his form, prefiguring the great transformation. He was more easily wearied than in other years. In his early life, in an exigency, he had driven in his chaise from Boston to Richmond in one day. He must now be more moderate in his endeavors. Railroads at this time were comparatively new. He was quite sixty years old before the first tramway was constructed for a steam-locomotive. Pleasant now to go over the old route in such comfort! He had always had a kindly thought for the horse that had drawn him up the steep hills. He need waste no sympathy on the unwearying iron horse now drawing his carriage. On the whole, this modern wonder, the railroad, added vastly to the aged man's comfort.

And he was going back to his childhood's home! In former years it was for him a heart-necessity to frequently visit the old place; but in more recent years the old home had become but little better than a memorial of bereavements. It had now been some years since he had made a pilgrimage to the scenes of his childhood.

At the little village of Fitzwilliam he left the railroad. His cousin, Luke Harris, a kindred spirit, was waiting to take him to his hospitable home. Of the old stock, Mr. Harris was his nearest living relative. All the brothers and sisters of Mr. Ballou had followed their parents to the "silent land." It was indeed natural it should be so. Hosea was the youngest of the old family; he was himself now past eighty years of age. It is remarkable that not a relative of the name of Ballou was left in the old town.

In our narrative we are held rigidly to the proved

facts; nevertheless, with our mind's eye we see the greeting, not effusive but sincere, between these aged remnants of a generation gone. Mr. Harris regarded his famous relative with fervid affection. To grasp his hand was an epoch in his life.

The ride to Richmond was through a country since but little changed. The time, we must not forget, was early October. The atmosphere was crisp, clear, and invigorating. The hills, in autumnal gold and scarlet and crimson, were like dream-pictures. The golden-rod and wild aster bloomed by the roadside. In the woods, the beeches, maples, ashes, and birches mingled their brilliant hues with the many-shaded green of pines, hemlocks, balsams, and spruces. From each hill-brow was a scene to make heart-revelling for an artist. Some years before, when riding one October day with his son Maturin on a hill overlooking the Connecticut valley, he asked his son, who was holding the reins, to draw up the horse. Among the words he then uttered, his son recorded these: "What a mild and holy religion is breathed by Nature in such a scene as this! It teaches no terror, no gloom; it rouses no fierce passions in the heart; it is calm, it is forgiving." Nature's benediction and Divine forgiveness are indeed of nearer kindred than our unpoetic theology has always admitted. Mr. Ballou had a rare love for the beautiful in Nature. He was appreciative of the strikingly brilliant in colors, and had pleasure in all the finer tints. At Niagara, when he beheld the rainbow over the cataract, and through a prism saw the strange combination of the flashing iris-hues, his delight was that of a rapt spirit. "My soul! my soul!" he exclaimed, as Thomas Whittemore reminded him that they must linger no longer, "how can I leave this place?"

But now, we suspect, he saw all the autumnal coloring on his journey to his old home with scarcely more than a passing remark. Poor and constrained is speech to one under the spell of teeming memories.

The journey lay through the village of Richmond. The town had changed since his boyhood, but mainly in ceasing to be a new settlement and maturing to an old New England village. In population and thrift there had been no progress. The streams had not attracted manufacturing enterprise from abroad, nor awakened it among the citizens. Hillside farms which were once cultivated, and sustained homesteads, had been abandoned, and were returning to their original pine-forest state.

On entering the village, at his right he saw the Universalist church, which he afterward described as "respectable for size, conveniently constructed, neat in appearance;" while of the society worshipping therein he said, "It is not very numerous, but more so than any other denomination in town; and better-disposed disciples of the Divine Master are seldom found." Farther on, at his left, he saw the old Baptist church in which his father preached. Thirty-one years afterward, Aug. 20, 1882, Rev. Dr. G. H. Emerson saw this building. "It is," wrote Dr. Emerson, "black with age. It seems hardly strong enough to keep timber and board and shingle together. The very sight of it takes us back to a former and very primitive age. The glass is held to the sash by bits of tin; the putty long since got tired and 'let go.' We cannot enter, but we can look through the windows. On the north side is the great square pine pulpit, possibly one that never knew the smell of paint. The square pews have high seats, from which only tolerably long limbs can touch the knotty floor. There is no grace of form, no cunning device of architect, nothing to woo a trained fancy. In and of itself, it is a hulk that only cumbers the ground." Yet Dr. Emerson confesses that "because nearly a century before, Rev. Maturin Ballou preached in the pine pulpit, and among his regular auditors, possibly the most thoughtful of all, his little legs dangling from the rough benches, sat his youngest son Hosea," he was moved to "look often, long, and spellbound upon the wretched old rookery." As Mr. Ballou in 1852 saw this meeting-house, it had much of the same decrepit appearance.

But what a memorial was this uncouth building to him! Are we unfaithful to probability when we say that the strange light his acquaintances sometimes saw in his glance — he at such times seeming to live apart from his bodily presence — now came into his eyes as he while passing looked upon his first church home?

The journey led a mile and a half beyond the village, through the farm on which he was born. With eager eyes he looked at his old home. His precise birthplace was marked only by a mass of rocks and a ruined cellar; the renovated house near by was the same as his birthplace, yet not the same. In external form it was as in his boyhood, a goodly-sized one-story cottage. The original frame-timbers were in the new structure. The immense central chimney, at the base of which the log-fire blazed, in the light of which he had in the far-away winter evenings learned to read, had furnished the material for the three small chimneys of the remodelled house. New windows of modern style added some briskness of appearance to the substantial farm-house. The barn and the corn-house, however, at the rear, had been spared any modernizing touch. Mr. Ballou, we may be sure, at a glance noted all these things.

Then he saw Grassy Hill at the east, at the foot of which his old home nestled, up the side of which the Ballou farm reached. He looked at the other hills, which make his birthplace a natural amphitheatre; he noted the fields of the plain, and Ashuelot's and Miller's gleaming waters. What was his emotion? His pen recorded: "All around lay the hills and mountains, the valleys and streams, which I always carry with me on the map of fond memory. But where were the father, the mother, the brothers and sisters, who watched over my infancy and guided my youth?" His reply to this question, which was born of his sense of human loneliness, was the brief, triumphant Christian answer, "In heaven." He had a joy in his confident faith deeper than the profound sorrow of his human solitariness.

He arrived at the house of his host, not far from the Ballou farm. Here he received such cordial greeting and kindly attentions as brought back to him a little of the home feeling. It was an event for Luke Harris's sons and daughters to have "Uncle Hosea" with them once more. They were in the vigor of manhood and womanhood; some of them had homes of their own near by; they were such estimable relatives as the simple-hearted old man regarded with affectionate pride, and he was held by them in loving reverence. It was now more than pleasure to have him in their midst: it was comfort. Two daughters of the family had one after the other been recently consigned to the grave. The home circle was yet under the dread shadow. Who like "Uncle Hosea" could speak the word of divine cheer, and bring peace to the troubled hearts? By ministering to their grief he lessened his own.

In the evening, Rev. Joshua Britton came to offer his greeting to his parishioner's distinguished guest. Mr. Britton was the Universalist pastor at Richmond. In early life he had been a teacher, and had made an extensive acquaintance with books; he had been brought from Presbyterianism to acceptance of the world-wide hope, and had obeyed the inner call to testify to the light that was in him; he was now in mid-life fulfilling a pastorate divided between Richmond and Winchester. He was a mild and loving man, of marked spirituality. When he died, at Fort Atkinson, Wisconsin, Oct. 30, 1878, in his seventy-sixth year, he left an untarnished name as a legacy to the church. By his assiduous attentions he contributed greatly to Mr. Ballou's satisfaction during this visit to his old home. He had given notice in his pulpit, on the preceding Sunday, of the probability of Father Ballou's preaching in that church the Sunday following. Would Father Ballou fulfil the expectation which had been raised? Yes, gladly would he do so. To fulfil this purpose he had refused all other proffered engagements.

He inquired of the local pastor for one after another of his old friends. "How is Brother Luther

Cook ?" he asked, referring to one of the veterans of the faith he held in special regard. "Did you not know Father Cook has passed on ?" Other sorrowful surprises came to him as he was told of companions of his boyhood having finished the earthly journey. He expressed a wish to go the next day to such of the bereaved homes as he could visit; and with Mr. Britton he spent Saturday in the ministry of sympathy and divine comfort.

Going with Mr. Britton to the church on Sunday, he found the edifice filled with expectant people to the last inch of its space. Such an audience had rarely before been seen in the little country town. Accustomed as Mr. Ballou was to crowds, this was to him a surprise. He looked over his congregation. So much had he travelled through the country, preaching the Word, that in almost every town he had esteemed acquaintances. He afterward recalled people in this congregation from Swansea, a company from Fitzwilliam, representatives from Troy, Warwick, Royalston, Orange, and Winchester. It was a testimony of the extent to which his fame had gone abroad. He was one of the exceptional prophets who live to be honored in their own country. "I beheld this large assembly," he afterward wrote, "all of whom seemed moved with one spirit, every countenance presenting the same expression of desire and expectation."

How inspiring the sight of such a congregation! But while the preacher looked at this throng of eager faces, it all, by a process not strange, vanished from his vision. He saw instead a little evening assembly in a private dwelling; he saw a boy essaying to preach — and failing! He himself tells his story: "I could not avoid a comparison between what I then saw, with the condition of the cause of divine truth sixty years ago, when I first attempted to speak in its defence in a private dwelling in this Richmond. Then, but few could be collected to hear the impartial and sufficient grace of the Redeemer proclaimed and defended."

Of his last sermons in Richmond no report has been preserved. He brought from his treasury, it is safe to infer, things both old and new. His reminiscences were not gloomy; his hope made all hearts buoyant. To behold the old victor in the pulpit, so simple, so paternal, so cheerful, peacefully awaiting his crown of life, was itself a sermon; it was the Word made manifest. There can be no doubt of the truth of Mr. Britton's testimony, — "It was a happy day for us all."

On Monday morning, in company with Mr. Britton, he resumed his calls upon his former townspeople. He was solicitous that none, however distant, who he believed would receive profit or pleasure in his presence should be neglected. Where need of comfort was manifest, he fulfilled the holy offices of his loved profession. To those who told him of their faith-problems or religious hindrances he gave wise counsel. He showed a friendly interest in the welfare of all. "Those not acquainted with Father Ballou," wrote Mr. Britton, "can hardly conceive of the ease and success with which he familiarly approached all, the young, the middle-aged, and the aged."

It was the time of apple-gathering. When he found farmers at work in their orchards, he would go among them, seeming to take peculiar interest in their employment. When the best specimens of the orchard-fruitage were offered to him, he courteously declined to taste them. He had regular and temperate habits in eating; but there was one notable exception to this rule of the day. Mr. Britton accompanied him to the old Ballou homestead; the owner, like his neighbors, was at work in his orchard. Mr. Ballou, on seeking him there, was greeted with the same heartiness with which he was everywhere received. An invitation was given to the two clergymen to remain and dine, and was accepted. Before dinner Mr. Ballou, with his companion, wandered about the orchard. Some of the oldest of the trees were unforgotten friends of his boyhood. He needed no invitation to eat of their golden offerings. "We walked about and found apples," says Mr. Britton, "of which my companion ate." What other orchard-fruitage, or apples of Hesperides, could compare with the juicy yield of these well-remembered trees?

"We visited the old burying-ground, and stood by the graves of the parents of my aged companion," Mr. Britton writes. While standing by these grass-grown graves in the burial-plot on the hillside, it is not unlikely his memory was too busy for speech. Here was the dust of the mother who had been an ideal blending into a heavenly hope through all his remembered years. Here also was the dust of the tender-hearted father, who under hard necessities had striven to fulfil both a father's and a mother's duty to the motherless boy. Sacred their ashes! On a previous visit, in 1843, in company with his son, Rev. Massena B. Ballou, when standing by the moss-grown slabs in the rank grass, he had said: "I believe I could sleep more sweetly here, among the hills of Cheshire, by the side of my early home and kindred, than in the grounds of Mt.

Auburn." Yet he thought not of his dearly-loved parents as tenants of these graves. With full assurance his heart recalled them as living and united in heaven.

Three busy days he happily spent visiting the companions and scenes of his youth.

Before one farm-house door a group of friends was gathered. The spot commanded a full view of Ballou Dell and Grassy Hill, mellow yet radiant with autumnal tints. Could Father Ballou recall some verses he had once written, entitled "My Native Richmond?" Yes, easily; they were favorite verses of his, and had often been sung in his home by his children, with an instrumental accompaniment, to the tune of Dumbarton's "Bonny Belle." Could Father Ballou repeat the verses from memory? It was a severe test for an old man, but he would try. Without hesitancy, his countenance expressing intense poetic delight, with a graceful waving of the hand toward the Dell and Grassy Hill at the appropriate places, he recited these lyrical words: —

MY NATIVE RICHMOND.

There are no hills in Hampshire New,
  Nor valleys half so fair,
As those outspread before our view
  In happy Richmond, where
I first my mortal race began,
  And spent my youthful days;
Where first I saw the golden sun,
  And felt his cheering rays.

There is no spot in Richmond where
  Fond memory loves to dwell,
As on the glebe outspreading there,
  The home-place at the Dell.

There are no birds which sing so sweet
As those upon the spray,
Where from the brow of Grassy Hill
Comes forth the morning ray.

Unnumbered flowers, the pride of spring,
Are born to flourish there,
And round their mellow odors fling
On all the ambient air;
There purling streams have charms for me
Which vulgar brooks ne'er give;
And winds breathe sweeter down the lea
Than where magnolias live.

So passed the happy week till Friday, when he was conveyed to Winchester, to renew acquaintance with old friends there, and on the following Sunday preach in the church where the Confession was adopted forty-eight years before. A cold, stormy, dreary Sunday was in strong contrast with the beautiful Sunday preceding. He came back on Tuesday to Richmond, seemingly loath to take what he felt would be his last parting with his native town. On Tuesday, with Mr. Britton, he visited some friends he had not before seen in their homes.

When asked if he should visit Richmond again he uniformly replied: "Should life be spared, and my health continue as good as at present, I think I may." There was, however, doubt implied in his tone. Still, he was cheerful. He had no aptitude for scenes or final farewells. His last evening in Richmond was spent in the company of happy young people at a singing-school in the Universalist Church. He had, as we have noted, never been himself a singer, yet he had pleasure in simple melodies. The old man was as young in his heart as the youngest.

He spent the night with Mr. Britton; the next day he was conveyed to Fitzwilliam, rejoined his wife at Lancaster, and came back to his home in Boston; having in his pilgrimage to Richmond enacted a poem of the heart inferior to none ever clothed in the rhythmic words of the poets.

XXII.

THROUGH DARKNESS TO LIGHT.

ON Wednesday, June 2, 1852, the Massachusetts Convention of Universalists is in session in Plymouth.

Meetings of this body at this period are gala seasons. The anti-inferno controversy is general and hot. From all sides come reports of polemical triumphs and numerical increase. How slight is the regret, among these cheerful believers in the great salvation, that they are regarded with high-headed disdain by the older sects! They have, it is plain to see, abounding and all-sufficient joy in their own household of faith.

This Convention especially is a feast of happy fellowship. Various incidents contribute to its exceptional excellence. The time is June. The place is by the sea, in historic Plymouth; the new Pilgrims in the realm of ideas will enter into the labors of the older Pilgrims who ventured for religious liberty. And not least among the favorable incidents of the Convention is the fact that to-day the patriarch, Hosea Ballou, is expected to be present, to make the convocation a Thanksgiving festival of home-coming for his reverent and grateful spiritual family.

During the morning Rev. Massena B. Ballou receives a telegram summoning him to Boston on account of the sickness of his father.

The news almost instantly fills the church. The veteran is expected to arrive in the first train from Boston. A hopeful suspense till then is reasonable. The train arrives, but Mr. Ballou does not appear. Yet many brethren have come from Boston, — some who are known to be often in the house of the old preacher. What report do they bring? They had not, before leaving, heard of Mr. Ballou's sickness. He was yesterday nearly as usual; a slight cold, some hoarseness, a little cough, this was all; the variation from his usual health seemed scarcely noticeable. Yes, there must be some mistake in the sending of the telegram. Mrs. Ballou, it is recalled, has been seriously sick with a fever for three weeks. Her husband has been anxious on her account. It was only when her symptoms became favorable that he could be persuaded to leave her bedside. May she not have had a relapse? It is altogether probable. This would account for the failure of Mr. Ballou to start for the Convention, and for the summoning of the son to the paternal roof.

The work of the Convention proceeds; yet there is a spirit of suspense in the air. In mingled hope and fear is the premonition of an approaching shadow.

Meanwhile, what has transpired in Boston?

Those who were watching by the bedside of Mrs. Ballou had heard Mr. Ballou coughing at intervals through the night. But he rose betimes, and made his usual preparations for a journey. No slight illness could keep him from fulfilling his ardent wish to be with his brethren at Plymouth. He came from the chamber which he had occupied during Mrs. Ballou's sickness, and entered his wife's room. With a graceful hand he smoothed her pillow. He lingered, and with tender solicitude looked upon her. "When I return, dear," he said, "I hope to find you still further improved." The worn sufferer could speak only with difficulty. With brightened eyes and a smile she made her affectionate response. He gave her his accustomed kiss, and left the room.

That was the parting! Could leave-taking for the final farewell of earth be more appropriate?

It was noticed that Mr. Ballou at the breakfast-table was disinclined to eat; and on his return to the sitting-room he cast himself on the sofa. A fever-flush on his face suggested to Mrs. Wing, his daughter, the question whether it would be prudent for him to attempt that day to go to Plymouth. His ready consent to remain at home — so unlike his usual persistency in fulfilling his purposes — occasioned instant alarm. Such easy yielding to bodily weakness it was not remembered he had ever shown before.

Immediately all was done for the sick man that anxious affection could suggest. Within a few moments from the discovery of his father's sickness, Rev. Massena B. Ballou was summoned home from the Convention.

The alarm at the Convention was natural, yet slight as compared to that which had now encompassed the home. That strange thing called a chill — diffusing pain through all the nerves, and causing a visible withering and sinking of the vital forces — had been experienced by the sick man. When the physician arrived, there was no need of his pronouncing that word — not so familiar then as when afterward it became an omen of dread in New England — *pneumonia*, to convince the distressed beholders that the suffering one was in a severe struggle for the continuance of his hold on mortality.

A bed was made for him in the room where he was lying. All members of the family living near were in immediate attendance. The sufferer had passed into a dazed state, between sleeping and waking, his face seeming as if thinly veiled; he was beheld as one on whom the shadow was deepening.

Anxiety had by this time become widespread. At the assembling of the Convention in Plymouth on Thursday the dangerous sickness of the honored father in Israel was known. An undertone of solemnity pervaded the proceedings. Earnest prayers for the doubly-shadowed home-circle were offered.

It was nevertheless recalled that the "old man eloquent" had with his wonted vigor addressed his brethren at the Reform Festival only seven days before; it was reported that only on the Sunday preceding he had preached two sermons at Woonsocket, Rhode Island, with an ease and power he had but seldom surpassed. Not without apparent reason was it therefore hoped that his remarkable physical resources might withstand the severe trial, and his sanctified presence still longer bless his brethren.

A similar spirit pervaded the Universalist believers in Boston. When brethren met on the street, the first inquiry was for the sick ones. The reports continued of the same tenor: "Mrs. Ballou is convalescent; Mr. Ballou shows no signs of improvement." The thought of the possible loss of the old standard-bearer, the spiritual "father," saddened many a heart. It was becoming manifest to all how deeply and truly the good man was loved.

Again we stand by the bedside of the sufferer. Days pass; no material change is to be noted, save that the disease is increasing in intensity. The strong mind of the sufferer appears at times struggling to clear away the gathering mists of the fever. On Saturday, consciousness is regained sufficiently to answer the question how he felt, with the clear reply, "I am very sick." On Sunday, in a restless sleep, he imagines himself at a Convention, with a pressure of perplexing committee-work on his hands, and great duties to urge on his brethren. He is raised in his bed, but immediately he faints. When on reviving he sees his children whispering, and says, "You did not understand what each other said," it is evident he means he did not himself understand their whispered communication.

Alas! alas! it is too evident to be doubted, that he has entered that lonely path where all the footprints point onward,—the path where is no turning.

The long hours pass; still the fever burns.

At the dawn of Monday, June 7, it is apparent that the end draws near. An old friend, a noted physician and brother in the faith, Dr. A. R. Thompson, of Charlestown, calls; he sees that the patient is beyond medical aid; he speaks some heartfelt words of spiritual reassurance, and reverently retires. Mr. Ballou rouses a little to say, "I do not think I understood what the doctor said." These were his last words. Ever was he trying to understand. Rev. Thomas Whittemore calls; he is permitted the exceptional privilege of going to the bedside. The sufferer, too weak to speak, recognizes his spiritual son with a smile. Mr. Whittemore takes the proffered hand within both his own, and covers it with hot tears and kisses. He retires. The family is now all present, including Dr. Hosea Ballou 2d, the grand-nephew, who has just entered. The crisis has come. All eyes behold him passing into the valley of shadows. Not one present can doubt that the Shepherd leads him, and with his rod protects and with his crook comforts him. No human aid can reach him now; but the Divine One is present whither he is going, no less than on the hither side the veil.

And now his breath has ceased. His features relax from their stress. Behold, there comes into his face an unwonted look. It is loving and peaceful. Some query whether this is not evidence of the passing spirit's first response, before it has quite left its house of clay, to a radiance not of earth.

Through darkness to light! Whither he has gone our human eyes may not yet discern; but our inner eyes behold him in ravishing light on the other side the valley of shadows.

Many are the hearts now to be saddened. The new-made widow is informed of the calamity which has befallen her. She hears the words from the hesitating lips of a sobbing daughter: "Mother, he is at rest; he will suffer no more!" She understands it all; yet she is strangely calm. Her one duty in life will now be to wait in the patience of hope till her own change shall come. Before a year has passed she too will go; till the welcome hour arrives she will live in peaceful memories and heavenly anticipations.

Brethren meet, and tell of the heavy sorrow that has

befallen the whole church, and with tearful eyes many a spontaneous eulogy is pronounced on the revered servant of God. Thomas Whittemore, on hearing of the bereavement which touches him so nearly, retires from the large Monday gathering of his ministerial brethren at 37 Cornhill, to his private room, and for relief to his full heart writes these words of unmetred poetry, appropriately voicing the spirit now in the air: "Father Ballou is dead! What an event! How it will touch the hearts of the thousands of his brethren throughout the land! The dear, venerable man is gone. That voice which we have heard so often in prayer, which has thrilled us so deeply when expatiating on the themes of the gospel, we shall hear no more on earth. That example of humility, justice, faithfulness, and charity, which I have had before my eyes for more than thirty years, I shall see no more, except as I shall see it in that indelible image of his life which a long acquaintance with him has impressed upon my memory. The last struggle is past. He cannot return to us, but we shall go to him."

On Wednesday, June 9, the funeral was held in School Street Church. Preliminary private services were held at the house by the family pastor, Rev. A. A. Miner, in the hearing of the bereaved widow, still prostrated with her sickness. At the church, every seat and every inch of room in the windows and aisles, excepting the seats reserved for the family, was occupied by the sorrowful people a full half-hour before the services. The church was heavily draped.

At three o'clock in the afternoon of the June day the services began. Rev. O. A. Skinner read the

Scriptures, prayer was offered by Rev. Thomas Whittemore, the sermon was preached by Rev. A. A. Miner, and the concluding prayer was offered by Rev. Sebastian Streeter. The sermon was a masterly presentation of the gospel hope as exemplified in the life and teachings of the departed father; the text was 2 Cor. v. 1: "For we know that if our earthly house of this tabernacle were dissolved, we have a building of God, a house not made with hands, eternal in the heavens." The sermon by the bereaved preacher was a rare filial tribute; it was entirely worthy the occasion; yet no sermon of words could equal in eloquence that of the sight of the hushed and reverent multitude. The body was placed in the vestibule. The assembly, on passing out, briefly viewed the mortal remains of the risen soul.

The funeral procession was one of the most memorable ever seen in the streets of Boston. The body was temporarily deposited in the burial-plot on the Common. The procession was formed in the following order: The body, with the bearers; the standing committee of School Street Church; the clergy of the Universalist denomination; the members of the School Street Society; friends from neighboring towns; the family in carriages. When the formation of the procession was completed, its head was at the turn of Boylston Street, while the rear was at School Street Church; it extended up School Street to Tremont, on Tremont to Boylston, — the distance being scarcely less than half a mile. There is no record of the number forming the procession; it is known that there were a hundred clergymen walking in the clerical section; and throughout, the procession was dense.

At the tomb, the remains were again uncovered for the farewell gaze of the many who were unable to gain admission to the church. The June sun was near the western horizon when the grand solemn pageant was brought to a close.

And this remarkable scene but expressed the general mourning. All the Universalist newspapers, some with blackened borders, published elaborate eulogies of the honored dead. Probably not a Universalist pulpit but inculcated some moral lesson of his noble life. Bereaved School Street Church moved to erect a monument to his memory; a general request came from Universalists of the whole country that they might have part in the grateful tribute. The statue now standing in the cemetery on Mt. Auburn is the denomination's unsolicited offering to the precious memory of the great pioneer champion of all-embracing hope.

So in triumph he left the world. The earth has been the better for his having lived in it. The common heart has wider hope and larger charity since he has fulfilled among men his Heaven-appointed mission.

Through darkness to light! We have seen how the deprivations and gloom of his childhood were turned to human benefit in his later years. So, under the same Providence, out of the mists and shadows of earth must be an issue into the enduring light.

STATUE OF HOSEA BALLOU IN MOUNT AUBURN CEMETERY.

XXIII.

TRAITS AND HABITS.

THRIFT, a necessity in Mr. Ballou's early life, remained a favored companion of his later years. He had an especial aversion to incurring any pecuniary debt whatever. His purchases, large and small alike, were always paid for on the spot. Rev. Thomas Whittemore once said to him, "Suppose, Father Ballou, you hurriedly start for Cambridge to see me on a matter of importance; on the bridge you find you have not with you the one cent for toll. Suppose you meet a friend willing to loan you the one cent; would you then break your habit and borrow?" Mr. Ballou, after due meditation, replied, "It is not a conceivable case; if I had my senses I would n't start for Cambridge without one cent in my pocket." No one can at least recall that he was, for any similar reason, ever forced to borrow even the smallest amount. Any debt unpaid over Sunday would, he maintained, detract from the sacredness of the holy day.

He was also — it was a part of his life-plan — insistent on being promptly paid. No urging would cause him to take more than his due; but that he desired in good season. When he left Portsmouth, having alienated some of his hearers, there was a nominal arrearage of salary due him; this he remitted. On leaving Salem, after a lax method of parish business common in those days, by no means peculiar to that city, he likewise had a claim on his parish for unpaid salary. The fair-minded business men of the society thought none the less of him when they found he was himself a man of business. An interest-bearing note became to the practical preacher thereafter available capital. This, however, was made a matter of complaint by some parishioners, who thought the going away of a minister was itself the cancelling of all parish delinquencies. His salary of two thousand dollars in Boston was paid with promptness, and it more than sufficed for his home needs. His publications were profitable; his investments were prudent, without hazard of speculation; he was in constant demand as an evening preacher, and believed the laborer worthy his hire; economy, not rigid but constant, prevailed in his household; so it transpired that his store grew to an ample competency. The altogether remarkable thing is that he himself knew the fact. There were some, as we have said, who thought he loved money and set his heart on riches. This is the exact opposite of the fact. He had no love for Mammon other than as a servant. What mercenary man could have done as he did in relinquishing his entire salary as pastor, when silence would have brought him statedly the lion's share? What money-loving man would have refused compensation for constant newspaper contributions during his mature years? Thomas Whittemore testifies that he repeatedly urged a just remuneration upon him, which was uniformly declined. Mr. Ballou had, indeed, a friendly regard for Franklin's "Poor Richard;" but he did not live by Poor Richard's monetary standard.

When he once saw his large family established in a prospect of worldly comfort, his care for money lessened. He at no time begrudged any outlay requisite to a substantial and pleasant home; and we remember that, while living, he made a free division of his surplus gains with his children, that they might be happier in their own homes. A better example of the self-denial requisite to accumulation, and of self-mastery in applying gains to unselfish ends, it would be difficult to find. The peaceful independence of his age was in some part the natural fruitage of his early and persistent habits of thrift.

When Thomas Whittemore's apprenticeship as a boot-maker expired, he was possessed of only such rudiments of education as he had, after neglecting his early school privileges, been able to secure by attendance on the public evening schools during two seasons. He was moneyless, and in knowledge of books not properly qualified for public gospel service. He ardently coveted an education; he purposed to work at his trade until he could secure means for the prosecution of his studies. Mr. Ballou, seeing his zeal, and knowing his impatience to enter the ministry, offered to assist him in Bible study. At the close of a Sunday morning service he called a few of his members together, and stated to them the practical problem in hand. A few moments afterward Mr. Ballou had one hundred and fifty dollars in his possession for the education of his protégé. This would give him board and clothes for a year in Mr. Ballou's home. The young man entered this first modern Universalist theological school with alacrity and gratitude, and pursued his studies with an enthusiasm that made long days and short nights. A few months afterward — in response to an urgent call for some preacher of the great salvation — he began his public ministry. He was called to Milford as soon as he was heard; and leaving an unexpended balance of the first Universalist educational endowment fund in the hands of Mr. Ballou, accepted the call.

This work of ministerial education, thus begun, was continued by Mr. Ballou for a score of years. We cannot give a complete list, and will attempt none, of those who studied theology with him. Members of Mr. Ballou's family recall not less than twenty of these students as living in their household, who afterward became heralds of universal hope. So quietly, in such business-like manner, was this important educational work done, that it at no time attracted general attention. While some remember that Mr. Ballou was doubtful in regard to the utility of established theological schools, he is but seldom spoken of as in his example one of the practical champions of education in the Universalist Church.

His method of study was emphatically his own. His range of daily reading might be superficially called narrow; it was really very wide. Some rapid glances at a newspaper, to see how the world was moving; occasionally a brief study given to some standard book of history or general knowledge; then he gave himself to the Book whose study was the master-passion of his life. The Bible was always the freshest of books to him. Dr. Paige, on recalling his experience in the home of his teacher, could not remember once seeing in his hand any volume but the Bible. When Dr. Paige published his "Selections from Eminent Commentators," Mr. Ballou on meeting him spoke of the volume with high commendation. "You do not mean to say that you have read it?" said the pleased young author. "Yes, I have read every word in it." "That you should leave the Bible long enough to do that," said Dr. Paige, "is the most flattering compliment I have ever in my life received." Dr. Paige's book, however, was scarcely a variation in the study of his life-theme; for it was itself a contribution to the solution of his great problem. To find more of the true meaning of the Bible; to discern its own side-light contributions to its central facts; to drink of its life-giving springs in unexpected places; to become more and more assured that God's Fatherhood is the revealed truth around which all other truths revolve, — this was his daily happy experience. From cheerful necessity he was a Bible specialist. Three hundred carefully-selected volumes marked the extent of his book-ownership; but in his well-worn Bible was a limitless library.

When, while bending over the sacred pages, his lips began to move in partial enunciation, the members of his family were careful to offer no disturbance. It was probably his early experience in the fields which fixed on him the habit of giving form to his thoughts in unconscious soliloquy. If his theme became plain to him, his face would soon clear. If it was an editorial he had been studying, he would take his pen and rapidly write his well-meditated thought; if a sermon, he reserved his final expression for the pulpit. If the way through a theme did not soon appear, he had a habit of expressing the fact in groans. Whatever puzzled him made him groan. When he heard Thomas Whittemore preach his first sermon, he responded to the crude utterances with groans to such an extent that the young pulpiteer thought the veteran was attacked with sudden sickness. The groans and the moving lips, in the Ballou household, were treated with delicate consideration. They are interesting as items in a peculiar personality.

In traditions of Mr. Ballou's boyhood in Richmond we find beginnings of one of his lifelong habits. As a boy he won in an unusual degree the confidence of the farm animals. Kindness to animals was to the last a marked trait in his character. For nearly sixty years he kept a horse,—the phrase, of course, meaning a succession of horses. He had a distinct friendship for each one. When one of his sons rode with him a long journey, and at nightfall arrived dusty and weary at an inn, he would observe his father not only give explicit directions for the horse's care, but wait to see that the instructions were all obeyed, before he would seem to remember his own need. He could not be greatly disturbed by human ill-will; but the good-will of his horse he took great pains to merit. And the grateful whinny of his beast, which he could so readily interpret, was often seen to bring a gleam of lively pleasure to his eyes.

He had also something of Dr. John Brown's appreciation of dogs. He would very speedily cultivate a dog's acquaintance, and for the whole canine species had a respectful sympathy. "He was accustomed," writes his son, "daily after dinner to prepare from his own plate food for a large domestic dog that belonged to a member of the family." Again the same eye-witness says: "Even the family cat purred more cheerfully when resting by his feet, while he often gave it a kind caress." He instinctively recognized the truth to which John Ruskin gives expression: "There is in every animal's eye a dim image and gleam of humanity, a flash of strange light through which its life looks out and up to our great mystery of command over it, and claims the fellowship of the creature, if not of the soul."

Some excellent people will regret to be told that Mr. Ballou was a smoker. "Paint me with my wart," said Cromwell. It is true, — we must describe our subject as we find him, — he was at one time a smoker. During a period of his life he might have been seen after each meal burning the malodorous narcotic incense. The old story: Slightly dyspeptic; physician said smoke; habit formed; hard to break; pleasant to continue, — especially to himself. We on the whole, however, commend his example with regard to tobacco; but only in two points: first, he began to smoke after he was past seventy; and second, he promptly left it off when he found the habit was medically a deceit. He gave it a test of three years, and then declined to acknowledge it his master. He had a similar experience with snuff. It was a largely-followed fashion in his day to snuff up pulverized tobacco. He formed the habit; but on suspecting that it interfered with his distinctness of articulation, he at once cast out the little idol. In these respects, as in all others, he was in his final and best years complete master of his inclinations. He was unreservedly swayed by the Spirit of Righteousness to which he professed allegiance.

Mr. Ballou was a total abstainer from alcoholic drinks from before the time when the temperance reform began. He was also abstemious in his food; preferring a simple, healthful diet, that he might have mental clearness and freedom. He was temperate in all things. Through simple living he maintained high thinking.

He was not above indulgence in pleasing stratagems in his household. When, before the era of railroads, he was to visit New York,—the journey then, we must remember, was a stage-ride of three hundred miles,—one of his parishioners wished to place in his care for the journey a daughter just arriving at early womanhood. He readily accepted the charge. The young lady was a very intimate friend of his daughter Elmina; and when his daughter heard of the projected journey, she naturally expressed regret that she was not to be of the company. Mr. Ballou, seeing how much satisfaction might be conferred, consented that his daughter should be included among the travellers. "But," he said, "say nothing to your friend; we will provide a little surprise for her." The stage called for Mr. Ballou at early daybreak. He took his place, after handing his closely-wrapped daughter to the rear seat. The stage then proceeded to the house of the young lady. She, with a salutation to her protector, took her place by the side of her companion. Silence for a season prevailed; few are talkative at such an hour. The young lady, trying to scatter a little of the dreariness, said to Mr. Ballou: "How pleasant it would have been if Elmina could have come with us!" "It would have been pleasant, very," said Mr. Ballou; and lapsed into silence. The daylight increased; the city was left behind; the journey was fairly begun. Mr. Ballou at last said to his young charge, "You seem scarcely to notice the lady who sits by your side." There was instantaneous recognition, and of course much maidenly hilarity. The happy journey was completed in accordance with this promising beginning.

Paul had perils because of false brethren; Mr. Ballou at one time had some peril because of a lazy brother.

Near the end of his eightieth year he had an appointment to preach in Middleborough. He had been instructed to leave the rail-train at a station four miles from the section of the town where he was to preach; he was assured that a man would meet him, and convey him to his tarrying-place. He alighted from the train on Saturday evening. A storm of driving rain was raging. No peering into the darkness could discover the man with the carriage. The station-master assured him that no one would come for him on such a night. "I will wait awhile longer," he said. When the waiting had become a trial of patience to the station-master, who had before him a long foot-journey to his own home, Mr. Ballou asked how far it was to the nearest house. "Not more than a mile." "Can you lend me a lantern ?" The station-master, looking him over, consented to make the loan. With umbrella, carpet-bag, and lantern, Mr. Ballou went out into the wild night, and down the muddy road. The rain fell in torrents; the wind was so fierce that he could scarcely make his way against it. On arriving at a solitary house and knocking at the door, he was cordially invited in. He stated his name and the object of his journey. The family was not of his faith, he was told, they were all Baptists; but they had heard of Hosea Ballou, and were glad to welcome him, — and, indeed, would turn no one away on such a night. He soon felt himself entirely at home; there was kindly ministry to all his wants, and in the morning, the storm having cleared, he was by his host driven to the church where he was to preach, and where he was greeted by an expectant congregation. Among the listening brethren was one who afterward offered a shamefaced apology for not being at the station; assuring Mr. Ballou that he would have gone for him in the morning if he had known where to find him.

Mr. Ballou, in recounting this adventure, expressed no regret at the peril imposed upon him by a lazy brother. He could not regret that he had been himself faithful to his life-long habit of keeping with exactness every engagement, while the fellowship he had found in the hospitable Christian family had enriched his heart. To sleep under a rain-pattered Baptist roof must have been like a return to his own Baptist boyhood in "Happy Richmond."

XXIV.

CHARACTER; FAITH; INFLUENCE.

"PUT it on the titlepage," said an interested friend to us, before we had touched pen to paper on the inviting task which now nears its completion. We had been speaking to him of Hosea Ballou's mission. We had said, "The story, simply in its human aspect, is marvellous." Our friend's advice was unpremeditated. It may have since entirely passed from his remembrance. But it has survived in our recollection, and its justness, tested by patient consideration, has compelled its fulfilment. Not unadvisedly nor hastily have we made for the subject of our biography the claim implied in our titlepage.

Hosea Ballou was not, as the reader scarcely need be told, in any sense a prodigy appealing to a credulous curiosity. He was not an exceptional genius approaching the miraculous. No such claim is made for him. The story of his career will not captivate a crude imagination. His adventures were not visible; his striving was not for fame. For such a hero we can covet no shallow triumph or belated laurels.

Yet Hosea Ballou's life-story is marvellous.

Wonderful in contrast with his hindrances is the work he wrought. Motherless from infancy; the poverty of his early home so pitiable that no shoes could be bought for him through the long winters; precocious in nothing save in the share he took in the hard toil which won the family's scanty bread from the reluctant soil; without books save a Babel-tower pamphlet, an antiquated almanac, an antique dictionary, and the ever-fresh Bible; learning to read by the light of pine-knots on winter evenings, and to write on the birch-bark he had gathered in scrolls from the forest; with no lesson at school till after he was nineteen, and his entire school-advantages compassed by a few weeks, — such was his burdened and circumscribed early life.

We see him again in his maturity.

Paradoxical, yet true: the unschooled boy has become the founder of a school. Marshalled in opposition to him we see all the reputable learning of his generation. In lonely study he has become a master in the aggregate of all sciences, Theology; he is now a scholar and a leader of scholars.

But can he, we ask, as we see him in his conflict, prevail against a foe that surrounds him like the atmosphere?

We hopefully note that he is no wild enthusiast deprecating intelligence. He is no fanatic, under control of a familiar; he assumes no private right of interpretation. He boldly affirms simply that he has discovered a forgotten sense in God's Word. He appeals for the decision of his cause not to hot hearts but cool heads.

He wins his cause. He did not, it is true, immediately capture literary Boston; but he won rural New England, and literary Boston soon afterward unconsciously espoused his cause. He did not, it is again true, drive Calvinism completely out of the field;

but he fatally wounded it, and no one fears it now as it limps toward its own place.

We note that in a hundred controversies the boy whose library was an almanac, a dictionary, a Babel-tower pamphlet, and an English Bible, has been crowned victor against the most throughly-schooled opponents. In no single controversy against Calvinism has his jury, the discerning common people, voted against him.

The marvel of this victory of faith will increase by contemplation. Where, since apostolic days, can we find a religious leader who, against such limitations and hindrances, has waged a warfare of faith to such success? An impartial Orthodox writer has said of him, "He broke the backbone of Calvinism in New England."

The personal aspect of his career is no less marvellous.

Because he could not hide his light he entered the Universalist ministry. At first, his expectation was by daily manual labor to maintain his privilege of speaking on Sunday of his precious faith. He was the champion of an unpopular cause, yet he became a popular preacher. His fame was pleasant to his human heart. The homage rendered him would have made a shallow man vain; it followed him through his happy old age, and became at his death an ovation. He was also prospered in earthly riches. Rare and wonderful, he had enough! He was more favored than many a renowned millionnaire: he knew when he had enough. If he had lived for the world alone, could he have gained more than was "added unto" his consecrated seeking of the kingdom of heaven?

Marvellous also was his home life. Here, indeed, was his dearest and noblest earthly triumph. In his home he lived the poem he did not learn how to write.

In its human aspect, therefore, and not simply because we receive a heritage of faith from Mr. Ballou, we contemplate his life-story as marvellous.

We covet attention while we endeavor briefly to summarize Hosea Ballou's faith.

The distinguishing negative characteristic of his faith is its disregard of the scholastic "scheme" of salvation. He felt no call to deliver the Infinite One from any dilemma into which theologians had in their imaginations thrust him. He believed the creation is proceeding according to the original plan of its Creator. A created Satan defeating the purpose of the Creator; an angry God demanding pacification; an infinite law, with an infinite break, demanding an infinite penalty, yet regardless on whom it is inflicted; an extensive prison-house as the intended dwelling-place of vast numbers of God's children, prepared for them before the first man was born, — these were to Mr. Ballou chimeras, mere human traditions, not teachings of the Bible.

Mr. Ballou was in some points at disadvantage as compared with the trained linguists. But whether it would have been for his advantage, as a leader of common people, to be versed in the historic philosophies and theologies is more than doubtful. He was singularly adapted to the work of popular Bible interpretation. He had by nature the "single eye" whose direct vision fills one's whole body with light. He lived in close relationship with Nature. He was of near kindred to the simple Bible-writers. He was in himself responsive to their deep and harmonious messages. He was thus able to rescue doctrinal Christianity from its grave under the artificial "scheme," and become a school in himself, and the founder of a school.

A fundamental positive doctrine in Mr. Ballou's faith is the sovereignty of God. The phrase has in his thought a distinctive meaning. Calvinism professedly starts with the sovereignty of God; yet the proper meaning of the phrase, as employed by Calvinists, is the supremacy of the Satanic in the Divine nature, and an added subdivision of power with an objective personal Satan. In Mr. Ballou's system of doctrines the word *God* is always to be understood in its strict Anglo-Saxon sense, namely, GOOD. He believed in the sovereignty of good in the universe. He believed that good existed before evil began, and will exist after evil is finished. He could admit of no human freedom not foreknown by the One who saw the end from the beginning. Whatever evil choices are permitted by the Father, he taught are for some final purpose of beneficence. He believed that there can be no evil God cannot overrule, and in his own time consign to oblivion.

The moral of this doctrine of Divine sovereignty was not, "Let us do evil that good may come;" for in his view evil is sure of its appointed penalties, which are pictorially described as wrath and tribulation. It is integral in his system that a man must reap whatsoever he sows. To be in league with evil is to make failure certain; for it is the destiny of evil to be destroyed. Evil, in Mr. Ballou's thought, is absolutely evil. It is not in any real sense good. It is to be overcome in the personal experience because of its own inherent badness; because, also, it usurps the place of the good; because, again, of its inevitable punishment co-existent with itself. The moral of the doctrine, in working form, is this: "If God be for us, who can be against us?"

We must further crave attention while we attempt to unravel one of the more intricate points of his faith.

When he in his scriptural study arrived at one conclusion, he appears to have been long bewildered as to its exact logical outcome. He became early convinced that "the punishment of sin inheres in the sin itself;" that is, he ceased to believe the common doctrine of his day, that the Divine punishments are sporadic or arbitrary. He believed every act carries in itself seeds of judgment. He did not believe the Divine penalty could be separated from any evil act; he did not see in the discovered thief going to jail, and the undiscovered thief escaping the jail, a likeness of the Divine method; he did not see reality in the dogma which affirms the existence of a deserved inferno which may nevertheless be escaped. He believed the Divine penalty to be solely the natural, inevitable accompaniment and sequence of every evil deed.

He furthermore held that punishment is exclusively the sense of self-condemnation in the soul. This, he believed, will not follow one in the forgiven state. Certain effects of sinful deeds will be, he thought, carried into the new life and into the future life, — such, for instance, as regrets and griefs; but these, he held, will not be specifically punishment, and will issue in final good. The Father, having forgiven his child, will no longer punish him.

We doubt whether Mr. Ballou ever arrived at complete opinions on this complex subject. There is no question that during the latter half of his life he emphasized the fact of Divine punishment in the earth, and disbelieved in its continuance beyond death. So much of his extant writing on this point, however, is merely denial of contrary opinions, and so much of the remainder is tentative, that it is impossible to find in his own words a statement that fairly covers his positive doctrine. Apparently, his position is very simple; namely, "The Scriptures teach only of punishment in the earth; show me a single passage that clearly teaches that the glorious immortal state is one of punishment." He had equal assurance of his ability to prove the first member of his proposition, and of the inability of any opponent to answer the demand of the second. But as to the process of the resurrection, save that it must be moral and spiritual, he seems not to have arrived at a definite and final view.

Dr. Miner has told us that the veteran several times sat in the pulpit of the School Street Church and listened to a presentation of his colleague's views of the immortal life, and in subsequent conversations offered no word of disapproval. We find a succinct expression of Dr. Miner's views in the sermon he preached at Mr. Ballou's funeral: —

"Can there be any doubt that the event of death removes one from all those temptations which originate in the flesh, or which necessarily stand connected with the body? . . . May not the wonderful experience it brings to every soul, unprecedented and unrepeated, be an occasion of unsurpassed good? Must we consider it, unlike every other experience of God, without moral utility and without significance? Does it rend asunder no veils of prejudice and passion, and shall it not bring the soul into closer proximity to truth? . . . To the soul unredeemed, death may be an occasion of great good; not itself the source of that good, but the instrumentality by which the soul is mellowed to receive the good, and by which it is brought into more immediate contact with such truth as is the source of it. . . . To the man of God it is entrance upon those immortal joys which have been the theme of his meditations by night and day."

That Mr. Ballou held to this positive view "in substance of doctrine" will not, we assume, be questioned. He often in discussion generalized on this point of faith; yet for a definite statement of the process of the fulfilment of his immortal hope we are inclined to choose the words of his scholarly and clear-visioned youngest colleague.

With exactness and fairness we believe we state this often-caricatured and much-controverted opinion held by Mr. Ballou.

But we wish emphatically to affirm that this doctrine was not insisted on by Mr. Ballou as essential to the universal hope. He rarely, indeed almost never, made it the subject of even mention in the pulpit. Among his ministerial brethren and in the religious newspaper it was a subject of inquiry and discussion; but it was not regarded by him a theme appropriate for pulpit treatment.

His theme — his theme of themes — was God's love in Christ. This subject, with scriptural proof and logical outcome, the people always expected to hear him elucidate. On God's Fatherhood he based his world-wide hope. The grace of the Father, testified in Christ, was to him "the power of God unto salvation." The attractions of the Father as set forth in the Bible; the goodness of God which leadeth to repentance; faith in the all-conquering power of love,—a faith which, by its own elevation, overcomes inordinate regard for the world; the unscripturalness and irreverence of unworthy thoughts of God; the fire of the Spirit in the believing heart, consuming lusts and filling the soul with warmth and light,—these are the things he habitually set forth in his preaching.

After a careful reading of nearly all his published words, we confidently declare that, in a summary of the Ballou Theology, his opinion in regard to exclusively earthly punishments deserves only the merest mention. It should not be exaggerated out of its subordinate relations. His strong and constant affirmation of faith, his comprehensive proposition in regard to penalty, is that every sin will be justly and adequately punished.

This is distinctively the Ballou Theology: *The sovereignty of good in the universe; the paternity of God; the universality of God's providence; the certain penalty and destruction of evil; the universe to be finally harmonized to its Author; the moral appeal of the Father's love to sinful men expressed in the gospel, and especially in the cross of the Son, whose mission is the salvation of the world from sin and from the consequent fear of death, and the modelling of human society into the likeness of heaven.*

Mr. Ballou was one of the most radical of reformers. While other reformers assaulted depravity in human nature, he aimed his blows against the imagined depravity men ascribed to the Divine Nature. He was in fellowship with all true endeavors at reformation. He was all his life a total abstainer from intoxicants, yet not often a zealous anti-alcohol exhorter; he was committed to the anti-slavery cause, yet not one of those who in his later days raised the providential war-storm. He was in the main, however, a fundamental reformer. He saw his people almost wholly given to idolatry; this stirred his spirit within him. He knew the tendency of sincere worship is to transform the devotee into the likeness of the object worshipped. He saw how dreadful must be any human imitation of the Calvinistic idol. He believed that for men to know God as he is, the universal and all-loving Father, and the human race as one family, must promote all just causes and foster all sweet ministries. He felt his high mission to be the reinforcement of human well-being at its sources. He was a true peacemaker. He wrought for peace by wielding the sword of the Spirit, which is the word of God, against the haughtiest and deadliest foe of human happiness.

When the procession of true reformers passes before the Muse of history, not last nor unlaurelled will be Hosea Ballou, the witness of God's Fatherhood, and the apostle of immortal hope.

He was necessarily in some degree a specialist in his work of reform. He was, we must remember, born in a community where there was no outcast perishing class, the barrenness of the common lot making luxurious vices impossible. Conversion in that community essentially meant acceptance of a scheme of doctrines; and salvation meant escape from a conjectured far-off doom. When Hosea Ballou became a Universalist, against this scheme of doctrines his zeal burned. By the Scriptures he proved that fear of a far-away doom is groundless. The people who in the country towns came to hear him were almost invariably righteous truth-seekers, who had been made wretched by their belief in the religion of hatred and fear. It is also undeniable that in the larger towns, the persistently ill-meaning, the irreligious drift and slag had only a momentary interest — indeed, scarcely that — in the preaching of unescapable justice and impartial love. However this may be construed, it certainly is a fact. With due deference to those who have honestly believed Universalists generally irreligious, we testify that the Universalists of Hosea Ballou's day were men exceptionally upright and reverent. It was the injustice of ignorance that classed them with infidels and atheists. They were no doubt influenced by the fact that they had themselves sincerely believed in Calvinism, and had afterward been delivered into spiritual light and joy. They were compelled to battle for their faith against innumerable assailants. That they were not, for instance, like John Wesley and his co-laborers, organized seekers of the lost, — that they did not, by united and sustained endeavor, call sinners to repentance in face-to-face encounters, — is to be predicated of the situation. Their mission primarily was to do a different work.

The theological revolution inaugurated by Hosea Ballou has at this writing been, in New England at least, carried a long way toward completion. Preachers do not, as was the fashion before his day, now picture inferno-horrors without delicacy or reserve. Those who still hold the letter of the old doctrines are now compelled to respect the human sense of right. As a consequence, the inter-denominational dogmatic warfare wanes. To assail the dying dogmas of Calvinism is like warring against belated ghosts. They flit at the approach of dawn; or, better, they are dissolved in the light.

What remains, then, to be accomplished by the followers of Hosea Ballou?

It is a manifest fact that the battle which is older than that against the partial creeds — the battle, namely, against irreligion, against materialism, against besetting sins, against the idol every man carries in his own breast — has not yet been waged to victory for Christ. Every Universalist who lives his faith must be a conscript if not a volunteer in this battle. He believes — it is cardinal in his faith — that Christ is to save the world from its sins. His faith compels him to be a soldier of Jesus Christ. The Universalist Church has no occasion for repentance that it gave its early zeal to a brave fight against superstition. It but followed its genius also when it established schools and exalted intelligence. But now it finds its most dangerous foes in new forms and changed positions. The Universalist Church is a division of the army seeking, under the great Captain, to free the world from sin. While the battle for righteousness continues, the Universalist Church cannot accept a place among the lookers-on or among the reluctant reserves: it must, as the condition of keeping its faith, be in the van of the fight against religious indifference, shallow scepticisim, idolatry of the beast, and professed and unprofessed atheism.

In his day Hosea Ballou was heroically faithful to

his own gospel summons. No Christian warrior in any age has fought for faith with more sincerity or genius of common sense, or with braver heart, or achieved a more manifest success. If he were still bodily among men he would be resolute and uncompromising against the new foes. To attempt to fight his battles over again would be on many a field — yet not on every field — simply to beat the air. Calvinism, with its broken backbone, invites no conflict. As regards that complex atheism, the believer in God's sovereignty can confidently wait for time's revenges; he may stand still and see the salvation of the Lord.

In the duties of a new epoch Universalists need to keep and invoke the spirit of their great pioneer. At the shrine of his memory the musing heart kindles with a devotion like his own.

The gospel of good cheer and universal hope he preached, is the gospel the despairing common heart must always need. Many souls wait, as Thomas Whittemore in his irreligious youth unconsciously waited, for the personal message of a religion it is reasonable to believe and happiness to experience. Fraternity incarnated, the Divine Fatherhood made manifest, — this is the gospel the multitude heard with rapture from the lips of Hosea Ballou. Believers have exemplified its fruits. The same everlasting gospel which the apostle describes as the faith which works by love, and which makes its supreme appeal from the cross, must live in the world till it draws all men to Christ.

A true reformer; a pioneer in paths since by increasing multitudes traversed; a faithful man of God, and every whit a man among men, in very truth one of Nature's noblemen; an apostle of universal hope and religious good cheer, who left the world better and happier for having wrought in it his heroic work; and who will be more esteemed for his genius as he is seen in truer perspective and his prophetic mission comes nearer to fulfilment, — such is Hosea Ballou, whose marvellous life-story, in this most inadequate telling, has now reached its close.

University Press: John Wilson & Son, Cambridge.